*Absent Without Leave* follows three ⟨⟩ lian men from their enlistment at ⟨⟩ in 1940 to the war in the Middle Ea⟨⟩ the Asia-Pacific. Private Stanley Livingston and his two best mates, Roy Lonsdale and Gordon Oxman, would be brothers-in-law as well as brothers in arms by the end of the war, as Stanley would marry Roy's sister Evelyn, while Gordon would marry Lilly Livingston, Stanley's younger sister.

In this case the term absent without leave has no negative connotation. Between their Middle East and Pacific campaigns Privates Livingston and Oxman, and many of their fellow soldiers, abandoned their units to be with their loved ones. These men were not running from battle or responsibility, but to the service of their families who desperately needed them.

This is also an account of the civilian men and women back home, and of Stanley's future wife, Evelyn. Evelyn's war is a story in itself, by day riveting bombers at Kingsford Smith Airport, by night enjoying the spoils of war courtesy of the ever-present and exotic American servicemen.

*Absent Without Leave* gives a deeply human face to the circumstances of war. Like many veterans, Stanley Livingston spoke little about the war, and this book is an attempt by his son to discover the man he had never really known. The result is an extraordinary story about an ordinary man: illuminating, deeply moving and told with no shortage of humour. *Absent Without Leave* unearths a part of Australian history that has largely been forgotten, because no-one ever really talked about it. Until now.

# *Absent Without Leave*

## The private war of
## Private Stanley Livingston

# PAUL LIVINGSTON

ALLEN&UNWIN
SYDNEY · MELBOURNE · AUCKLAND · LONDON

**Australian Government**

This project has been asssisted by the
Australian Government through the
Australia Council for the Arts, its
arts funding and advisory body.

Allen & Unwin
83 Alexander Street
Crows Nest NSW 2065
Australia
Phone:  (61 2) 8425 0100
Email:  info@allenandunwin.com
Web:  www.allenandunwin.com

Cataloguing-in-Publication details are available
from the National Library of Australia
www.trove.nla.gov.au

ISBN 978 1 74331 582 8

Cover design by Lisa White
Set in 12.5/17 pt Minion by Midland Typesetters, Australia
Printed in Australia by McPherson's Printing Group

10 9 8 7 6 5 4 3 2 1

MIX
Paper from
responsible sources
FSC
www.fsc.org   FSC® C001695

The paper in this book is FSC® certified.
FSC® promotes environmentally responsible,
socially beneficial and economically viable
management of the world's forests.

*For Dottie*

# Contents

. . . and how was your war, Dad? 1

Introduction: Two of the boys, a wog, a donkey
and myself 3

1   Three men walk into a bar 7

2   One small step for a Zetland boy 19

3   Hole sweet hole 39

4   Mayhem was only a part of it 58

5   Three men and a barber shop 76

6   A nip in the air 94

7   The home-front line 110

8   Evelyn's war 127

9   Run for your death 138

10   Gaps in the ranks 146

11   Absent friends 160

12   From the Pimple to Scarlet Beach via
     Dead Man's Gully 181

13   Destroy all monsters 200

14   Present and accounted for                    216

15   The ordinary trenches                        232

16   Memoirs of a pacifist smoker                 246

17   Don't give an old digger the gripes          262

Epilogue                                          271

Acknowledgements                                  275

Notes                                             279

Bibliography                                      303

# . . . and how was your war, Dad?

Ever heard the one about the old digger who never talked about the war? So have I—I grew up with one. As a child it never occurred to me to ask, 'And how was your war, Dad?' I took my father's war for granted. His years as a front-line soldier didn't seem to have left any obvious scars. Curiosity came only after I vacated the nest. On my irregular sorties to the suburbs I'd sit in the backyard with the old man, an Onkaparinga blanket covering the Hills Hoist to keep the sun off. To keep the sun off the beer, that is. We talked, one on one; I was eager for anecdotes. I was twenty-nine and in my first year of what some might laughingly describe as a 'career' in stand-up comedy. War is no laughing matter. But then again, you had to be there. Stanley J. Livingston had been there.

I only managed to glean the barest hints of my father's experiences in World War II (I've always found the habit of numbering wars unnerving: it implies a certain inevitability, and there are still a lot of numbers out there to get through). Stanley didn't live to tell the full tale. By wandering through my own memories, as well as those of people who knew him and many more who didn't, I wondered if I might catch a glimpse of the man I never knew.

# Introduction

## *Two of the boys, a wog, a donkey and myself*

One of the most enduring images from Australia's ill-fated campaign in Gallipoli is that of John Simpson Kirkpatrick, 'the man with the donkey'. Legend has it that after working as a merchant seaman for four years, Simpson enlisted in the Australian Imperial Force in September 1914. He was assigned to serve with the 3rd Field Ambulance as a stretcher-bearer, but Simpson shunned the stretchers in favour of a donkey called Murphy, the animal he employed to transport wounded men to the beach at Anzac Cove. In what is claimed were 'lightning dashes' into 'no-man's-land', he is rumoured to have saved the lives of over three hundred men before being killed in action on 19 May 1915. A hush fell over the Gallipoli Peninsula on the day the man with the donkey was slain.

Or so the story goes.

Almost a century after the events of Gallipoli, the mythos of Simpson continues. The tale has crossed continents as accounts of Simpson's feats have been told again and again. Some have Simpson as something of a saintly figure, others a bacchanalian brawler; there are even claims that Simpson was shot by an Australian. What does all this really have to do with young Jack Simpson? Does the elevation of a good man into a superhero enhance or offend his memory? Does it matter? One thing is certain—the legend wasn't Simpson's doing. It was born after his death, the yarn spun and woven through the decades. There can be no denying the appeal of such a myth. The Simpson legend has all the necessary ingredients: heroism, anti-authoritarianism, selflessness, larrikinism and mateship. Throw in a faithful little donkey named Murphy (or Abdul or Duffy, depending on the source), and a legend is born.

The lowly donkey, along with its companions the ass and the mule, has been exploited in more than one famous myth. The Bible is full of donkeys, from the one who spoke to Balaam—'Am I not your donkey on which you have ridden, ever since I became yours, to this day?' (Numbers 22:30)—to the animal's more significant role in the New Testament: Mary, pregnant with Jesus, is said to have travelled to Bethlehem on a small donkey, and just before his own death, Mary's firstborn himself rode one into Jerusalem. The donkey has since been dubbed 'the Christ-bearer'. The story of stretcher-bearer Simpson trading his stretcher for a donkey has some resonance with the Jesus myth: the humble Christ, renowned for helping the sick and broken with no shortage of courage or humility, before entering the arena of his own death. A single image can wield enormous power. After decades or even centuries, a myth may bear little witness to the actualities of its origin. Perhaps this is of small consequence, especially if the myth promotes qualities beneficial to its devotees.

Whether Stanley James Livingston, a private in the 2/17th Australian Infantry Battalion, was mocking Simpson when he climbed aboard a donkey somewhere in the Middle East is not clear. World War I was coming to a close when Stanley was un-immaculately conceived in the year of our donkey-straddling Lord one thousand nine hundred and eighteen, and by the time the photo was snapped the myth was already well and truly ingrained. Perhaps it was the biblical myth that Pte Livingston had in mind? There is every chance he was in the vicinity of Jerusalem at the time. But precisely where and when the photo was taken is not so clear. Does this look like the fresh face of a young man enjoying his first overseas trip, a battle virgin? Or are we looking at a war-weary veteran of one of the most intense and bloody campaigns in military history? What had he got himself into, this kid from suburban Zetland, in the middle of no-man's-land, with, as he put it, 'two of the boys, a wog, a donkey and myself'?

●

Pte Livingston scribbled those few words in elegant cursive on the back of the photo. For an ordinary soldier—and there were few more ordinary than Stanley—taking even an innocent holiday snap was subject to heavy regulation: 'Photographs of a purely personal nature may be included in correspondence, but attention must be paid to the background, which must not include anything the photography of which is prohibited.' This included military vehicles, tanks, signal equipment, artillery, aircraft, ships, fortifications, camps and weapons. There was equally heavy censorship on any message attached. It would seem Pte Livingston was just following orders by maintaining a sparse background and simply noting the subjects in the shot (unless of course a donkey might be construed as a military vehicle), but perhaps he had nothing to hide. Was it merely a photo opportunity with reference to nothing and no-one? Sorting fact from fiction is a perilous pursuit. Myths grow and facts are their casualties. In what follows I have done my best to avoid the pitfalls of myth-making and to instead present an honest account of what it might have been like to follow in the bootsteps of an ordinary soldier. In this case that ordinary soldier was my father. And just to set the record straight, one thing is for sure: Pte Stanley Livingston was no messiah, but he was, from all reports, a very naughty boy.

# 1

## *Three men walk into a bar*

'We were both in before the bugler's lips were moist.'
*Colonel D. Goslett (on enlisting in World War II)*

In May 1942, Pte Stanley Livingston was midway through a seventeen-month 'stunt' in the Middle East. Military campaigns were often referred to as 'stunts' or 'shows', laconic understatement being the diggers' trademark. Intensive training was up and running. Just what they were training for was a mystery to the infantrymen. Those first across the line were generally the last to know what line they were to be first across. But something was up. After marching from Latakia in Syria to Tripoli in Lebanon, the 2/17th Battalion of the 9th Division of the Australian Imperial Force arrived in Jabal Tourbol, a mountainous region in northern Lebanon.

Before long the troops commenced mule training. 'Mule School' was compulsory for all companies, who were put through the handling and loading of mule teams before embarking on a two-day bivouac, complete with mules, a few of the boys no doubt, and perhaps even the odd wog. Twenty-seven mules were attached to the unit, and the official war diaries confirm that all personnel had become thoroughly proficient in leading and handling the animals. Perhaps it was here that Stanley was snapped mounted on a mule? When I showed the photograph to William Joseph Pye, known as Bill, a 95-year-old veteran of the Middle East and Pacific campaigns (who'd been at times within spitting distance of Stanley Livingston, although their paths weren't to cross), he told me he would have sworn it was taken in Palestine. A clue.

Armies tend to recruit individuals to be trained in flying, sailing or, in my father's case, walking. The infantry is the perfect place for the walking man. Military nomenclature can be confusing, so here are some basics. A division is a grouping of brigades commanded by a major general. A brigade is a grouping of battalions commanded by a brigadier. A battalion is a grouping of companies commanded by a lieutenant colonel. Each company contains around a hundred and twenty men commanded by a major or a captain. Companies contain platoons of thirty or so men commanded by a lieutenant. These men are collectively called the infantry.

Individually, infantrymen are described as 'foot soldiers who engage the enemy in close quarter fighting with the aim of destroying their capacity to wage war'. I doubt this was how they advertised the job in 1939. I imagine the 'Call to Adventure' would hold more allure for a working-class boy from the inner-Sydney industrial suburb of Zetland. The sound of adventure calling gets a lot of attention in the history books. Legendary tales of soldiers born for battle and chomping at the bit in World War I had already taken a firm hold at the start of the second stunt. Bit-chomping may have been true for some young adventurers enlisting in that first Great War, but many more were acting on a sense of duty, to empire, to country and to community. It wasn't so much that young people in 1914 listened more to their elders as that their elders didn't much listen to them. The 'me' generation was decades away; this was the 'us' generation. Individuality was not the norm. Sticking to the norm was the norm. Dr John Connor puts it succinctly: 'Family responsibilities generally loomed much larger in a young man's life in Australia in 1914 than it does today. In a time before pensions, superannuation, retirement villages and nursing homes, parents required their children to keep and care for them in old age.'

At the beginning of World War II, the norm still stood, unchallenged. In his memoir of that war, *The Reluctant Volunteer*, veteran Peter J. Jones admits to having been morbidly fascinated as a child by the events of World War I. It was this fascination mixed with horror that struck the boy when his father took him to see the original film version of Erich Maria Remarque's *All Quiet on the Western Front* in 1930. He also shared every little boy's fascination with the maimed, and was deeply curious about the men with empty sleeves and trouser legs who limped through the streets in the 1930s. 'Shell shock' was the term his father used to describe these destitute veterans of the Great War, and these strange creatures induced in the boy no immediate desire to go to war himself. With the onset of World War II, Jones recalls it was a sense of duty, and the example of his friends, that prompted his reluctant enlistment. Jones also had the example of his father, who had enlisted without question and was one of those who landed at Gallipoli on 25 April 1915. Jones sums up his philosophy: 'Like the bulk of humanity, I was and am a peacelover—but never a pacifist imagining, in spite of promptings of commonsense, that non-resistance is suitable in all circumstances. Practicalities have a way of overawing wishful thinking.'

While the cause was common, and the call to duty shared, nevertheless the ranks of the newly enlisted consisted of a diverse range of characters from all walks of life who were not shy in exhibiting their own peculiarities. G.H. Fearnside, former sergeant with the 2/13th Battalion, remembers this diversity. There was 'Harry the Knife' from the Redfern slums, a Rhodes scholar, a pimp, ministers of religion, barristers, clerks and drovers. Fearnside notes that the army 'accepted anyone who had two arms and two legs, and the requisite number of heads'. From the relative safety of his St Kilda apartment in 2012, former Rat of Tobruk Eddie Emmerson recalled, 'We had one bloke, Bobby Fink—he was a bloke who worked the boats between London and

New York playing poker. You . . . had criminals and you had blokes dodging wives, dodging the law, but they were a good mob, you know.'

William Pye was in 1941 a 24-year-old evening student in the faculty of economics at Sydney University. His father had fallen upon hard times and gone AWL from the family, leaving Bill to support his mother and his sister, who was still in school. Bill had intended to enlist, but the pressures of family kept him occupied until an opportunity arose when an employee the university wanted to retain was in danger of being recruited. Someone was required to take his place in the army. Bill Pye was their chosen man. Bill joined a good mob too, the 4th Anti-Tank Regiment, and he was in charge of many of them, having attained the rank of lieutenant by June 1941.

●

On 4 June 1940, Stanley Livingston walked through the gates of the Sydney Showground to join a stream of men duty-bound for enlistment. What prompted his decision? Rumours of a war in Europe had been building for some years. In January 1939, the world-renowned science-fiction writer H.G. Wells was visiting a complacent Australia, and his predictions for the country's future did not go down well. Wells had a predilection for prediction. Some of his hits were lasers, nuclear weaponry, wireless com-munications, answering machines and, in his 1933 novel *The Shape of Things to Come*, World War II. Wells didn't hold back. From the safe distance of Australia he slammed Hitler, calling him a certifiable lunatic and putting the boot into Mussolini at the same time. No-one took much notice of Wells' comments, and the prime minister at the time, Joseph Lyons, publicly rebuked Wells for rocking the boat. Australia had no reason to make waves. H.G. Wells would not be silenced, ominously warning that the absence of the British Fleet would leave Australia isolated in the Pacific and that 'the so-called Japanese menace to Australia is no bogey'. After Wells' departure, Australia maintained its 'no worries' policy until a couple of months later when Adolf Hitler invited himself unannounced into Poland.

Another Wells, a local with the initials H.D., walked into a milk bar near Waverley Oval in Sydney at around 9.30 p.m. on 3 September 1939. Harry David Wells stopped and listened as the voice of a new Australian prime minister, Robert Menzies, crackled over a radio: 'It is my melancholy duty to inform you that, in consequence of a persistence by Germany in her invasion of Poland, Great Britain has declared war upon her, and that, as a result, Australia is also at war.' Those with memories of the previous stunt felt dread, while the youngsters felt a nervous rush of excitement, but on the whole, the opening act of World War II failed to impress. Many dubbed it a phoney war and thought it would be all over soon enough without too much fuss. But by 3 June 1940 it was clear to Harry D. Wells that this war was not going to disappear overnight, and so he headed to the Sydney Showground to enlist, where he was promptly photographed, X-rayed, vaccinated and given a number, NX27792. He then joined another group of fresh diggers, all bearing their issue of the only belongings they would be needing for the journey ahead: a knife, a spoon, a dixie (cup), a palliasse and two blankets.

It was the very next day that Stanley Livingston ambled through those same gates. He was not alone; Stanley had recruited two of his best mates, Roy Lonsdale and Gordon Oxman, to enlist with him. It is not too far a stretch to imagine that the decision to join up would have been conceived over a few beers in the pub where they had all first met as thirsty young men in the year leading up to World War II, the Tennyson Hotel on Botany Road, Mascot. It had been love at first sight. Gordon had his eye on Stanley's younger sister Lilly; Stanley had his eye on Roy's younger sister Evelyn; and Roy had his eye on a schooner of Reschs Pilsener. Roy's was the greatest love, and one that all three shared. Roy lived directly across the road from the pub at the back of a barber shop run by his father, Ernest Arthur Lonsdale. Stanley lived up the road in Tramway Street, while Gordon had to stumble back to Wollongong. It would become a familiar regime: with Gordon claiming he had no money to get home, Stanley had no choice but to let him camp at 77 Tramway Street, within close proximity of Lilly Livingston.

On 2 June 1940, the trio had been celebrating Stanley's twenty-second birthday at the bar of the Tennyson Hotel. They had something else to drink to that night: all three had committed to enlisting in the AIF. On this their second-last night as civilians, the boys ingested as much false courage as possible. They had to be quick—like all pubs at the time, the Tennyson closed at six o'clock. The idea was to get the men out of the pubs and back to their families; in reality, the measure created a culture of binge known as 'the six o'clock swill', which had men knocking off work and heading straight for the bar, where they drowned as many sorrows as was humanly possible before six. Alcohol was possibly a major contributing factor in much of the volunteering for the military, and not just in Australia. One American volunteer recalls acting on an alcohol-induced impulse only to suffer an overwhelming sense of imprison- ment once he sobered up. Alcohol remained this soldier's main means of coping with the next four or five years of service. Alcohol would also become Stanley Livingston's main weapon of choice, not only in his army years but well into civilian life as well.

Two days later, while the rest of Australia were going about their business, life was set to radically change for the three men. There's no way of knowing if they had time to grab a newspaper on the way to the showground, but had they picked up a copy of *The Sydney Morning Herald* they would have been met with a half-page advertisement boasting, 'Fitness Wins! Drink a daily glass of Tooths Sheaf Stout.' That's the kind of order these boys were happy to obey. On the fashion page, the English correspondent reports that 'Stalin and Hitler at their worst never did a more thorough job of purging than the war has done to fashion', and if you looked hard enough, one tiny paragraph states that the new recruit reception depot at the Sydney Showground received its first drafts of men the previous day. One thousand men were drafted.

•

On 4 June 1940, Roy, Gordon and Stanley joined a further thousand men as they endured a seven-hour process of poking, probing, doctoring and dentistry, until eventually, around 9 p.m., they were marched to the Anthony Hordern Pavilion where they were to make themselves at home along with hundreds of other new recruits, including H.D. Wells, Peter J. Jones, Harry the Knife, a Rhodes scholar, a pimp, ministers of religion, barristers, clerks and drovers. These men would eventually find each other in another hemisphere, in the same brigade of the same division, the 20th Brigade of the 9th Australian Infantry Division. For the moment, the call to adventure would be limited to the inner walls of the showground, where they bunked down on straw-stuffed palliasses in haylofts, pigsties and horse stalls.

The army officially recognised Stanley Livingston as NX20181, a native-born 22-year-old Australian factory worker, five feet nine inches tall, with brown eyes and fair hair, Roman Catholic and single. Roy 'NX20180' Lonsdale was a five-feet six-inch machine-fitter residing at 1187 Botany Road, Mascot, single, Church of England, aged twenty-two and five-twelfths. Gordon Grant 'NX20277'

Oxman was the youngster at only twenty-one and three-twelfths, a single Roman Catholic labourer from Wollongong. At six feet and more with blue eyes and fair hair, he towered over the other boys, garnering him the nickname 'Storky'. Those first weeks in the showground proved far from adventurous, and the monotony led Pte Oxman to absent himself without leave on 5 August at 1330 hours. He was back by 2330 the same day. Gordon hadn't been able to resist the temptation to pay a visit to Lilly Livingston in Tramway Street, a short march from the showground. For this he was confined to barracks for three days—a punishment most felt they had already been suffering for months.

In September, the three privates were moved to a training camp in Tamworth. Gordon wasn't too pleased with this arrangement and embarked on his second AWL, this one lasting five days. He was fined five pounds. Not to be outdone, Pte Livingston took a break from training in Tamworth and went AWL the day Gordon returned to camp: he lasted a week. After being admonished for the offence, he decided that this AWL lurk was worth the effort. He was reported missing again on 27 December: having spent his first Christmas away from his family, Stanley had decided to bring in the New Year in Sydney. He reported back to camp on 7 January 1941. This time he was fined five pounds and confined to barracks for fourteen days. Pte Lonsdale, meanwhile, had been behaving himself. It had been a shaky start to army life for Roy: he'd been ill for the first two months as a result of a bad reaction to the vaccines he'd been given on enlistment day. This did not bode well, but little did he know that his battles had barely begun.

On 27 June 1941, the three men departed Sydney for a destination unknown, but it didn't take too much reflection to hazard a guess at where that might be. The situation for the Allies had deteriorated. The Germans had attacked through Crete and Greece, sending thousands of Allied troops into retreat. Over six thousand Australians would not be coming home. The troops were also feeling the heat in North Africa, especially in Tobruk. Reinforcements were obviously required. Apart from recent excursions to training camps in Tamworth and Dubbo, Stanley's travels had thus far extended from Zetland to Mascot, a distance of 3.3 kilometres, and to my knowledge Roy's travels were mainly to and from the Tennyson Hotel. Gordon was by far the most seasoned traveller, hailing from Wollongong.

A convoy of six ships left Sydney Harbour on the twenty-seventh. Pte Stanley Livingston was on board the converted passenger liner *Queen Elizabeth*; not far away was another converted luxury liner, *Aquitania*. These former floating palaces delivered thousands of men to and from the various theatres of war. When Stanley sailed out, Eddie Emmerson was keeping his head down in Tobruk, having earlier embarked on *Queen Mary*. He had fond memories of his first voyage out of Australia, lazing on the deck drinking beer out of six-pound prune tins. He said, 'The thing that impressed me the most was these little green and red arrows wherever you walked, and underneath it were three words—To The Sea. That's how bloody big it was.' Bill Pye, on the other hand, assured me his journey to the Middle East had not been spent in luxury's lap. Lieutenant Pye would later board the British navigation ship *Aronda*. There were twelve cabins on it—just enough for the officers. The troops were stored like cargo below water level with the light on twenty-four hours a day. Hammocks were strung up on hooks above mess tables, with the men's gear stowed under the tables. Lt Pye was disgusted:

> The men who were seasick were vomiting onto the mess tables . . . there were no lavatories . . . they had taken the ship's railing down and put planks out, and you sat there with your arse out over the sea, and that was it . . . I was really very upset for my men . . . it took us seven weeks and five days to get to the Suez Canal. They were appalling conditions, absolutely appalling . . . It was a dreadful bloody trip.

As the convoy steamed out past the heads into open ocean on a journey formerly reserved for the wealthy, Stanley Livingston, on his maiden voyage, may have felt that he was travelling to another planet. Or perhaps it was the other way around. Australia was the distant alien land, and the liners steaming towards Europe were carrying reinforcements from Mars.

# 2

## One small step for a Zetland boy

'I have a feeling we're not in Kansas anymore . . .'

*Dorothy*, The Wizard of Oz

After over a month at sea, the convoy and its human cargo docked in the Suez Canal. There was no time for sight-seeing as troops lined up for a 250-kilometre rail journey to training camps in Palestine, just north of Gaza. For Stanley, the contrast between the dilapidated railway carriages and the spacious liners was not welcome, the seats being so uncomfortable that many men chose to sleep in the luggage racks. For Bill Pye and his men, it was to be a case of out of the frying pan.

> When we got to Suez, they took the ship in close to the side of the canal and we had to climb down ropes, with all our gear on. They took us to the shore and there was bugger-all there, just sand . . . The officers who'd

been sent down from Palestine said, 'Look, you see that hillock there, you go over there.' There were no toilets, no running water, nothing there and we stayed there that night . . . They took us and we got on a train, and the trains were absolutely filthy, the lavatories were full of excreta, there was no water, they took us to Gaza and we went into camp there. It was bad enough on the seven weeks over, but arriving there, it was even worse, and we all wondered what we'd got into.

On arrival in Palestine the three as-yet-unbattalioned privates were sorted for duty. The 9th Division had been under siege in Tobruk since April. Pte Roy Lonsdale drew the shortest straw and was marched out to the 2/13th Battalion. He was soon on his way to Tobruk. Pte Oxman's straw was not much longer: he was marched into the 2/17th Battalion and followed Roy just in time to catch the last two and a half months of the siege. For the moment, Pte Livingston was marching nowhere.

As the boys were arriving in the Middle East, Australian commanders were pushing for the 9th Division to be withdrawn from Tobruk. The troops were exhausted. The British Prime Minister, Winston Churchill, did not share this opinion and instead shared his own on the matter with a succession of prime ministers who were falling like dominoes back in Australia. Three Australian prime ministers, Menzies, Fadden and Curtin, lobbied for troop withdrawal. Menzies was forced to resign in August, making way for the hapless Arthur Fadden to reign, as he put it, 'for forty days and forty nights', before John Curtin settled into the job. Churchill reluctantly backed off and the withdrawal began in September. While Stanley remained in Palestine, the intensity of the siege began to decline. Gordon and Roy soon discovered that declining intensity still required them to take their turn on the front line as enemy aircraft relentlessly bombed those in the rear. Being bombed in the rear was something Roy would become familiar with in the not-too-distant future. By late October the 2/17th were preparing to move out of Tobruk, one of the last to leave. Gordon's harrowing initiation into front-line warfare was over. Pte Roy Lonsdale's battalion, the 2/13th, ran out of luck: the final convoy making its way to relieve the troops was attacked and forced back, so the 2/13th were left behind. It had been a brutal six months for the battalion and now they were worse off than ever. G.H. Fearnside, now a sergeant in the 2/13th, said of the moment they were returned to Tobruk, 'the battalion was re-equipped and re-armed by British quartermasters and packed off to the front before it committed the unsoldierly—and psychologically unsound—error of feeling sorry for itself'. The 2/13th became embroiled in tank and infantry battles during three days of hell from 29 November to 1 December. A couple of weeks later they were out of the stunt, the first in and the last out. Seven hundred and eighty-eight men of the 9th Division didn't make it out of Tobruk at all.

In late October, Pte Stanley Livingston was marched in to join the weary ranks of the 2/17th just as the battle-scarred

9th moved out of harm's way. Or, to be more precise, the 2/17th marched in to Stanley, who had not left camp in Palestine. Roy, Stanley and Gordon were reunited just in time to enjoy their first Christmas overseas, at Hill 69, a camp maintained exclusively for Australian troops 50 kilometres south-west of Jerusalem. Their quarters consisted of row upon row of eleven-man tents, spread widely and surrounded by slit trenches, safer havens than tents in the event of an air raid. Pte H.D. Wells described the trenches as 'a perfect trap for AWL drunks on moonless nights'. The narrow roads and lush green fields surrounding the camp reminded Pte Peter J. Jones of children's book illustrations of biblical scenes. The 'occasional sight of a small donkey carrying a large Arab' only heightened this. A photo opportunity perhaps? Had veteran Bill Pye guessed correctly?

I could find no mention of any mule-training in Palestine around Christmas. The official war diaries suggest that the main concern was to rest the men as much as possible. Large numbers were sent on leave. After eight months of desert warfare, the boys of the 9th deserved some down time. A concert party was held and nominations were called for participants, including first and second comics, a tenor vocalist and a female impersonator. (The Stanley Livingston I knew could have auditioned for three out of four of the above—on second thoughts, make that all four.) The only other demands for the holiday season were orders that all blankets were to be aired, that ablution sheds not be used for purposes other than those for which they were intended, that latrine seats be kept closed at all times when not in use, and a footnote stating that the latrines marked 'Natives Only' were being used by troops and the practice must cease immediately. Cross-cultural abluting was obviously frowned upon in this man's army.

The only real action of the month was a series of security patrols in the local villages. Visits to these villages were to be as short as possible and it was made perfectly clear to those on patrol duties that 'To the Arab, women-folk are invisible. One thing which he will never overlook is interference with his women and this includes attention be it ever so polite. If possible avoid even looking at them.' These patrols were performed by companies B and D; being a member of C Company, Stanley Livingston didn't get the chance to treat the local women as if they were invisible.

Stanley Livingston had a strict Roman Catholic upbringing, and his first Christmas away from Australia probably included celebrating mass in the YMCA hut reading room. He may or may not have attended the confessions that were heard beforehand. Perhaps he had no reason to—after all, he kept his latrine seat down, aired his blanket and hadn't so much as glanced at an Arab woman. Or perhaps, as Pte Peter J. Jones and many other Catholic boys did, he upped the antichrist and committed the mortal sin of AWL in exchange for the once-in-a-lifetime temptation to attend the high mass at midnight in Bethlehem's Church of the Nativity. The *Palestine Post* reported on 26 December

1941 that thousands of serving men and women of all ranks, many of them fresh from the battlefields, had crowded into the church on Christmas Day.

Jones and fellow Catholics Jack 'Griffo' Griffin, Harold 'Wart' Waterhouse and Danny 'Haddock' McLaughlin hired a taxi to Bethlehem after stowing away in a unit truck en route to Tel Aviv. They arrived at the Church of the Nativity in good spirits—spirits no doubt purchased in Tel Aviv while lying low in the Australian Soldiers Club before hailing the taxi. The four penniless men passed through the low entrance to the church, known as 'the eye of the needle'. It was standing room only as they settled in with senior officers of the army, navy and air force. Peter and Haddock remained standing for the duration of the one-and-a-half-hour mass while Griffo and Wart lost the spirit and wandered off to nap in the empty confessionals. All four managed to get back to Hill 69 an hour before morning roll call the next day.

Sgt G.H. Fearnside, weary from the gruelling siege at Tobruk, found Christmas in the Holy Land a more sombre experience. He expected much from his well-earned leave: 'I had wanted to hear the chanting of psalms, prayers and holy study coming from the synagogues, prayer houses and yeshivot throughout the city. What was the reality?' For Sgt Fearnside the reality was the pervasive smell of donkey dung together with a poverty and squalor that deadened the senses. Hoping to lift his spirits he visited the great Western Wall, its cracks filled with letters from all over the world, but these were troubled days in the Promised Land. There were rumours of Arabs in the courtyard of the mosque pouring boiling water down upon the devout Jews. 'One could never call back the past,' he said. 'It had been a mistake to have attempted to recapture it.' Fearnside had felt no sense of rapture here. His mate Jack Halcroft was by his side at the Wailing Wall. 'Let's go and get drunk,' he said.

•

Meanwhile, back on Mars, Japan dramatically entered the war with its attack on Pearl Harbor on 7 December 1941. As a result, the 6th and 7th divisions were brought back from the Middle East to defend Australia, leaving the 9th to be part of a force defending the Turko–Syrian frontier. By early January 1942, the 2/17th Battalion were on the move. To where and for what was not the business of an infantry-man. They left Hill 69 and caught the train to Haifa, where trucks were waiting to take them further north across the coastal road through jagged hills on one side and dark rocky beaches on the other. When Stanley described these perilous road trips to me, I got the impression they filled him with as much terror as any battle.

The battalion arrived at Tripoli and encamped at the place where Turkish generals had planned to quash the advance of T.E. Lawrence and his Arabs in World War I. The next morning the road convoy moved higher into the mountains of Syria, to a camp north of Aleppo in the Turkish border area. This was wild country—a lawless land inhabited mainly by Kurdish tribesmen—and murder was common. This was to be their home until March. Special mention was made in the official war diaries in regard to the ploughing abilities of the local people using donkeys and cows. As far as I can make out, there are no mountains in the background of Stanley's photo, and the 'wog' in the foreground doesn't quite embody the demeanour of your average murderous Kurdish tribesman, although he is wielding that dagger with some menace. Stanley spent most of this period billeted in a tin hut that offered little protection from frequent snowstorms. Leave parties to Aleppo eased the tedium of training under wet and muddy conditions. The history of the ancient city was not appreciated by most of the troops, with reports of frequent rowdiness and drunkenness. Presumably, Pte Livingston wasted no time sightseeing around this 5000-year-old city, or its great Citadel, inside where it is said the patriarch Abraham used to milk his cow. Milk was the furthest thing from Stanley's lips.

In mid March the battalion left the Turkish border for Latakia on the coast of Syria. Latakia had been around for some time too, and one piece of history that would have interested Stan was that this city had in the seventeenth century become a major centre for cultivating and trading tobacco and remained that way into the twentieth. On arrival the unit began intensive training in harsh conditions. The casualty count by month's end included seven cases of tonsillitis, two peritonsillar abscesses, one case of venereal disease and two cases of pedicular pubis, or crabs, the latter being dealt with in no uncertain manner by the might of the Australian Field Ambulance forces attached to the brigades.

In regard to these last two afflictions, the Australian commanders were sharply aware that they were in charge of a multitude of young men who had recently been confined to a male-dominated desert for eight months. To relieve the tension, a concerned officer in command of the French forces, General Montclar, suggested that separate regimental bordellos be established for the Australian, French and French Colonial troops in the area. The suggestion drew approval from all sides and, as G.H. Fearnside put it, 'Perhaps for the first and only time in the annals of Australian military history, an infantry battalion came to have its own brothel.'

Liberated from infectious organisms and for the exclusive use of Australian troops, the Maison Dorée was located in a dead-end street on the outskirts of town. Henrietta was the madam, and among her troops were Angel, Baby, Jeanette, Big Tits Betty, Vera the Turk, Linda and Rosie. The result was that in at least one battalion, the 2/13th, not one case of venereal disease was reported in Latakia. I think Eddie Emmerson might have been closer to the truth when he put it to me like this: 'The officers never got venereal disease. The troops got VD, but the officers got urethritis.'

●

Around this time, a letter sent to Brigadier W.J.V. Windeyer of the 20th Infantry Brigade from Lieutenant Colonel M.A. Fergusson, Commander 2/17th Australian Infantry Battalion, contained some straight-shooting advice for the troops under the heading 'Notes on Contra-Propaganda'. Point 8 of the document states: 'Men are accustomed to the belief that the counter to enemy action is to disperse and hide in a hole . . . It is not suggested that this has no value, but it is beyond doubt that a soldier who is more concerned with killing the enemy than with his own protection is the most likely to survive.' In point 11, pontificating on the subject of the morale-diminishing properties of being dive-bombed, the distinguished commander asserts, 'The enemy must be presented with individual targets, each target necessitating a change of direction by the plane.'

Reading this correspondence twigged a memory of the first war story my father ever shared with me. I was no more than ten years old, quietly putting the finishing touches on my scale-model Airfix Messerschmitt Bf 162 bomber. Exactly where the incident he related occurred I cannot recall. It's not that I wasn't listening—as a child I was riveted by the tale—but in retrospect I can see that the 'where' did not matter as much as the 'what'. I can narrow it down to somewhere in the North African desert, for the image burned into my mind is of a soldier wandering across a vast open plain with an enemy fighter bearing down on him; and given that I was at the time gluing the wings onto a Messerschmitt bomber, the desert location seems plausible.

The gist of the story was this. Somewhere in that Western Desert, while strolling across an isolated airstrip, Pte Stanley Livingston, alone and unarmed, came under fire from an enemy bomber strafing the airfield. Stanley found himself in a fair bit of strafe and the only thing he had on him was a blanket, and a well-aired one at that. As the bomber swooped, Pte Livingston lay prostrate on the airstrip, huddling under the blanket as machine-gun bullets sprayed all around him, the futility of his actions only occurring to him later. A drowning man will clutch at a straw; a 23-year-old private being dive-bombed by a German fighter aircraft will clutch at anything, and with no hole in sight to leap into, a blanket would have to do. Surviving the attack unscathed, the shaken private picked himself up and continued on to do whatever it is a private does when he heads out alone into the desert with only a blanket for company.

He was a lucky man. The Luftwaffe put a lot of stead in its dive-bombing proclivities. The aircraft that inter-dicted on the lonely figure of Pte Stanley Livingston as he took his late-afternoon stroll was most probably one of the Luftwaffe's Stukas. The psychological effect of these attacks cannot be overestimated. The Stukas were equipped with dive sirens, or, as the Germans dubbed them, *Jericho-Trompeten*—'trumpets of Jericho', used essentially to unnerve those under attack. Eddie Emmerson will never forget the sound of the bombs. 'What they used to do,' he told me, 'was they'd alter the fins on the bloody bombs, and put an organ tube in it and it would scream.' I can just imagine Stanley under his blanket being strafed to the glorious strains of Wagner's 'Treulich Geführt'.

Eddie Emmerson found himself a target on another occasion.

> I remember once in Tobruk, we got a heavy raid. We seen 'em coming in, a flock of them, and I was with a bloke called Slugger Wright, big bugger, and I said, 'Come on, Slugger,' and he says, 'We'll be alright, they're going on to the harbour,' and so we thought we'll watch this, and next minute he says, 'No. They're coming our way, come on,' and we laid in a hole, and I was laying next to him on me belly, and a bomb came down and it made a different noise, and I said to him, 'So long, Slugger, this is the one you don't talk about.' It exploded a hundred yards away. What had happened, its pins had fallen off and it was tumbling, so it made a different noise. You get used to the scream of them but this one was the one I thought you didn't talk about.

Which brings us to point 15 from 'Notes on Contra-Propaganda': 'In the past the Australian soldier has not had occasion to hate his enemies ... The advantages of destroying the impersonal attitude of the Australian towards his enemies are apparent ... Men will not be so ready to surrender either to the enemy or to their own fears.' Stanley Livingston never had a bad word to say about any German to my knowledge, but he had no time for Stukas, isolated airstrips and well-aired blankets, not to mention *Jericho-Trompeten*.

●

While many idle hands were busy in the devil's playground run by Henrietta, during March and April of 1942, discipline was becoming a concern. A sergeant charged with attempting to obtain money by wearing badges of a rank to which he was not entitled was stripped of his rank and given six months' detention with hard labour. Three privates convicted of striking a superior officer were given year-long detentions, and an unlucky private found sleeping at his post was given ninety days. The thumb of command pressed hard on the troops. Routine orders of 10 March warn that the possession of hashish, cocaine, morphine, marijuana and heroin was strictly forbidden. A report warns that large sums of money were being offered to drivers of military vehicles to smuggle hashish. Rewards were offered for information, and severe disciplinary action threatened for offenders. As the month passed, another dozen court martials were reported, including that of a private who, while AWL, struck another private before striking a commanding officer and then resisting an escort after discharging his rifle without sufficient cause. Another failed to appear at a place of parade and had by neglect lost his clothing. No names were attached to these crimes in the war diaries, and I wonder if Stanley Livingston could have been a culprit. He was partial to a drink, but hard drugs and striking officers didn't seem to be his style. As for avoiding parade while prancing about naked, those who knew him wouldn't have put it past him. Despite Henrietta's valiant efforts, morale had reached an all-time low. The news from home was ominous. After the Japanese attack on Darwin in February, the growing threat to Australia hung over the troops.

Towards the end of April the entire 20th Brigade, the 2/17th, 2/13th and 2/15th, embarked on the five-day, 150-kilometre march from Latakia to Tripoli. The average distance travelled was a touch over 30 kilometres a day at a speed of around ten kilometres per hour. Spring was in the air, if not in the step of the men as they passed groves of olives and mulberries. The locals turned out to watch the parade from balconies and pavements just as their ancestors had done for over two thousand years as countless soldiers marched up and down this coast. In the Australian War Memorial reading room I gently thumbed through a delicate pocket-sized volume missing its cover. The item, listed under 'anonymous', houses page after yellowing page of poignant notes and poems on the minutiae of wartime life in the Middle East, penned by unnamed soldiers. Handwritten in black-inked pen, this communal log contains eyewitness observations, some in verse, some merely facts, of the cities visited and the geography of the lands surrounding the coastal route where

Stanley, Roy and Gordon marched. One reads: 'Along the coast have marched the conquerors of history. The Assyrians, Alexander the Great, the pharaohs, Crusaders, the Ottoman sultan down to the British armies of the great war, and their monuments may be seen carved in the rocks above the dog river north of Beirut.'

By the time the troops marched in to Tartus, halfway between Latakia and Tripoli, a reception of another sort was there to greet them. Henrietta, Big Tits Betty and a few of the other girls had hired a taxi, set off, caught up with the marchers and driven between the rows of soldiers before disappearing ahead. The tempo of the march quickened apace after that. The girls took up their forward position on a balcony above a restaurant in Tartus. As the battalion marched by, the girls raised their skirts as one. As Sgt Fearnside far too clearly recalls, 'No general, reviewing his troops, ever got a more efficient "eyes left" than did Henrietta and her girls that afternoon.'

Unfortunately for Henrietta, leave was not given. A health report during the month of April unsurprisingly shows a distinct spike in foot injuries, a severed tendon of the big toe, a scalded foot, one ruptured calf, a ligamentous injury of the knee and a torn fibular collateral ligament. Among these lower limb injuries was a single case of chronic anxiety. We might assume this was Henrietta when informed of the 'no leave' provision. However, there were rumours of AWLs that night and it is possible

Henrietta and her crew may just have recouped the cost of their taxi fare.

Come May, the boys were ensconced in Mule School. Pte Livingston spent his time learning the mule trade and drinking plenty of arak while on leave in the Beirut cafes. Unbeknown to the ORs (or 'other ranks', as the unranked—such as privates—were ranked), those higher rankers were aware of a worrying situation in the Western Desert: the opposing armies had been engaged in static fighting for four months, but of late the British Eighth Army looked to be in danger of losing its ground.

On 21 June, Erwin Rommel and his forces captured Tobruk. The Australians, the British and the Polish forces had kept Rommel and his army at bay for eight months, but it had been surrendered to the Germans the previous day, 20 June 1942. Winston Churchill was not happy. 'Defeat is one thing,' he said, 'disgrace is another.' Hopes within the Australian troops of a return home anytime in the near future were now sunk. Hitler immediately promoted Rommel to Field Marshal. Meanwhile the British Eighth Army retreated as far as El Alamein in northern Egypt. Field Marshal Rommel was soon at their heels. With his army oozing confidence, Rommel's troops came to a halt 95 kilometres from Alexandria with the prize of the Nile delta now within the Field Marshal's reach.

By 30 June, Stanley's battalion was ready to move. Some over-optimistic rumours suggested ships were waiting at Suez to take them home; others laid money on the ships taking them straight to the Pacific theatre. Unknown to the men, Major General Leslie Morshead, commander of the 9th Division, had received orders to move his men to the Egyptian front. The idea was to maintain secrecy during the move, and disguising a thousand men on the march is no easy feat. Firstly they were ordered to remove the rising sun badges from their hats, so as to be unrecognisable as Australians. Captain Alan Wright describes the order as 'one of the best of the World War Two jokes'. Even removing from vehicles the division logo, a platypus over a boomerang, could not hide the soldiers' accent. Pte Peter J. Jones remembers crowds in Egypt lining the streets shouting and mocking, 'Aussie, Aussie, Alamein!' (presumably without the 'Oi Oi Oi'). The Egyptians were feeling insecure. Their 22-year-old King Farouk was sympathetic to the Italians, who were sympathetic to the Germans, yet the Egyptians on the whole thought the Germans the more unwelcome visitors and were quite happy for the Allies and the Germans to fight it out in their desert.

The men of the 2/17th survived the month of July thanks to supplies received from the YMCA, including twelve table-tennis balls, twenty-four sheets of blotting paper, ten thousand sheets of writing paper, six New Testaments, twenty-four gramophone records, six sticks of chalk, a set of quoits and, thanks to the Australian Comforts Fund, 891 tubes of toothpaste, razor blades and packets of tobacco, and 893 packets of cigarette papers.

Eddie Emmerson claims that the Australian Comforts Fund literally taught the men to smoke, which primed them for the harder stuff. 'Sometimes we went onto British rations and were given cigarettes mainly from India. They were the only cigarettes in the world you needed two hands to smoke. One to smoke them and another to hold the top of your head as you lit it. Geez, they were rough.'

The Australian Comforts Fund raised funds for the troops with the help of 'wives, mothers, fiancées, sweethearts, sisters, aunts and friends'. The Sydney Comforts Fund's shop on Rowe Street became something of a refuge for family members eager to share news from desert or jungle. By war's end the women of the Comforts Fund had provided 3,085,776 pairs of socks, 1,139,087 balaclavas, 592,610 woollen gloves, 274,677 jumpers and six million hankies. Women were also active in the Red Cross, where they used up 500,000 kilometres of twine to produce camouflage netting.

Comfort was much needed by many of the unit, as the monthly medical report lists a high incidence of sandfly fever and gastroenteritis. Apart from the usual bouts of dermatitis and scabies, and just the one abscessed buttock, there were two cases of 'Shizophrenia' (sic), one being an attempted suicide, and a case of 'Post Traumatic & CSM Confusional State'. (CSM remains a mystery to me: it could be cerebrospinal meningitis or perhaps just a confused company sergeant major.) Off the record, the ominous move south may have just quietly unnerved many more of the troops as they boarded a train at 0730 hours on 1 July destined for a rumour of war.

When the train arrived in Sidi Bishr station near Alexandria a couple of days later, it was clear their ship hadn't come in. There was now no doubt they were heading to the Western Desert, and on 9 July the battalion arrived at their defensive position about halfway between Alexandria and El Alamein. The night spent here was described in the war diaries as 'uneventful' with only 'slight enemy activity'. Is there even such a thing as a slight enemy? An enemy who slightly intends to annihilate you? To decimate you just a little bit? It might have been uneventful for some, but I have an inkling that at least one non-battle-hardened private gripped his well-aired blanket very tightly that night. For Pte Stanley Livingston, the slight enemy activity was the first and only enemy activity he had experienced in his twenty-four years. He would have encountered plenty of enemies growing up in the backstreets of Zetland, but none even slightly like the slight enemy he experienced that night. The next day, visiting commander Brigadier W.J.V. Windeyer described the men of the battalion as anxious to 'get into it'. Perhaps some were, but I'd wager many more were just plain anxious.

On 15 July the troops were moved by truck into the desert at El Hammam. The next day they were readied for a further move with an order from the commander-in-chief stating that 'no conditions of fatigue or any other disability can permit withdrawal from our new position'. The new position was towards the El Shammama sector of the El Alamein defence line, where all companies commenced digging in. In this particular desert the sand stopped around 30 centimetres below the surface; from there on down it was solid rock. But they needed holes—for sleeping, for abluting, for weapons. This was more than mere digging; this was excavating.

# 3

## *Hole sweet hole*

'Stuck in me dugout 'ere, down a hole, I feel like I've
grown a rabbit's soul.'

*Signalman Bob Anson*

There was considerable air activity in the area surrounding
El Shammama, with light shelling of the company areas
during the afternoon of 16 July. I suspect Pte Livingston
would have preferred to be back in Zetland listening to
the light shelling of prawns. For the next week the battalion were given constant warning orders to move on two
hours' notice. Having dug in, they had nothing to do now
but wait. For a soldier nearing the front lines, waiting is an
ordeal. Civilians get rooms to wait in, soldiers get holes.
Jack Creber, a 2/17th private, recalls having a smoke near
El Alamein station while digging out a two-man doover
(a term used for any improvised shelter, in this case a hole
in the ground). He heard a loud slap, followed by a cry of
abuse. The same thing happened a few times. The sound
was coming from a hole not far from his. It seems this

particular doover was home to two good mates, one over six foot tall, the other well under. The shorter man had drawn a line down the centre of the hole to indicate territory, but when the larger man dozed off, his knees encroached on the smaller, who couldn't get any sleep. The shorter man, Stan, was unrelenting in giving the larger man, 'Storky', a fierce kicking whenever he crossed the line. The 'Storky' in question was Pte Gordon Grant Oxman, the Stan was not of the Livingston variety, but was Pte Stan Newel, known as 'the Count'. Storky, the Count and Stanley Livingston were to remain great friends for the rest of their lives. How long those lifetimes would last was for the moment uncertain.

The waiting was interrupted on 28 July when Messerschmitts strafed the ground area of the battalion. This was repeated shortly after with another strafing by moonlight. Perhaps one private, AWL from his doover and out for an evening stroll, was huddling under a well-aired blanket? By the end of July, the men were still awaiting the forward call. August and September of 1942 was known as the 'static period', with the 9th Division dug in in baked shallow white stone, now occupying front-line positions at Tel el Eisa. The calm before the storm. The only storms for now were the *khamsins*, raging desert dust storms that scoured the skin and stung the eyes. The only protection was their basic accommodation, the doover. One soldier compared the desert to 'a garden where earthworms have been busy, little holes with freshly turned earth all around, that's all we are really, worms, forever digging holes'. Smoke from shellfire, bombings, vehicles and fires made it difficult to get a decent look at the desolate view before them. The view from the other side of the barbed-wire fence was much the same. As one German soldier wrote home, 'Africa is a comfortless place. We are lying in the desert worried by sand and flies . . . Tommy's aircraft are like bees; you get a funny feeling when one of the bombs comes howling down—and you can't find a hole!'

The general area around Tel el Eisa was known as the Hill of Jesus. It was a godforsaken place, littered with many of the dead, as-yet-unburied men cut down in the fierce battles fought in July. The smoke and haze kept the finer details of their past suffering hidden. The war diaries confidently boast that everyone was 'in high spirits at prospect of real action again'. I wonder how high Pte Livingston's spirit soared as he lay in a hole surrounded by decaying corpses, flies and *khamsins*, savouring his first taste of front-line warfare. The enemy were no more than three kilometres ahead, but they were 65 kilometres wide. Along this line it was Rommel versus rest of the world, and for the moment most of the Field Marshal's attention was directed further south, where he was mounting a major attempt to break through the British line. This line included not only the British, but also Australians, New Zealanders, South Africans, Indians, Free French and Greeks.

Winston Churchill was busy reshuffling the upper decks. He appointed two new commanders, General Sir Harold Alexander and Lieutenant General Bernard Montgomery.

Monty, as the latter would become known, acquired a slouch hat, jammed it down on his head and immediately endeared himself to the Australians. He requested a rising sun badge to wear with the hat; he felt he was entitled, his father being the bishop of Tasmania. Churchill also paid a visit to the 9th Division in early August. He received a full Australian welcome from one of the troops, who called out, 'When are you going to send us home, you fat old bastard?' From all reports the British bulldog took it in his stride and even offered a cigar to another cocky other ranker who demanded one of Churchill's trademark La Aroma de Cubas. Churchill didn't linger: he was off to Moscow for a chat with Stalin. With not a scrap of evidence to support my claim, I'm willing to bet the names of those two hecklers were Stanley and Storky. My father loved a bet, no matter what the odds, and there's a two-in-ten-thousand chance that I'm right.

The men returned to their holes and waited. Leave to Alexandria and Cairo was on offer in September, and those remaining on the front line could enjoy concert parties. During one of these an enemy shell screamed overhead. The audience took cover but the young singer, a woman known only as Merrilyn, a real trooper, carried on singing, and continued to do so after a hand reached out from behind the curtain and placed a metal helmet on her head. The show, as they say, must go on.

At first glance, my father and I have little in common. This remains true for all further glances—except if you take a sideways glance at military parlance. Major battles are called 'shows'. There are 'theatres' of war, 'staging' camps, troops always travel as 'companies', and 'dress rehearsals' are frequently mentioned in the war diaries. As a stand-up comedian I've endured countless shows where I've risked dying. In more than a few I have died. But in my case I lived to fight another day. A comedian has more lives than a cat—and a hell of a lot more than a front-line soldier. One other thing my father and I did share was a sense of humour, and more than a few beers.

Now a bigger show was about to commence, and Winston Churchill, the managing director of this particular theatre of war, had some final notes for General Montgomery. He was advised to launch an offensive of unprecedented proportions. Always start with a bang. Monty, slouch hat cocked, wasted no time in building up troops and weapons in preparation for a large-scale offensive against the enemy at El Alamein. He added another change of script that would directly affect the boys in the holes: he intended to employ the infantry rather than tanks to lead the charge.

In preparation for opening night, the props department were busy constructing a battalion of dummy troops to draw enemy fire. Illuminated by searchlights, the dummies' role was to confuse the enemy. It was hoped the Germans would mistake them for troops on the march, but the sight of brown-overalled broomsticks held down by sandbags and fitted with trip wire set to spring the dummies up as one would not in my book (and this is my book) engender in any way a sense of triumphal assault. Although they might strike fear into a passing crow. If all else failed they could still rely on backup from their arsenal of dummy guns, trucks and tanks. The Germans were using more substantial props. Rommel's forces had laid five hundred thousand mines between themselves and the sandbagged dummies. The job of clearing these mines for the infantry troops to move forward put severe demands on the division's engineers. The sappers were the roadies of the battalion, always going on ahead making sure all was in order for the main cast who followed. Eddie Emmerson recalls their efforts just before the battle commenced on 23 October.

> I went down to the starting line and the engineers, I take me hat off to them. The infantry do a great job, but Jesus, no-one ever thinks of the engineers. And they're sitting on top of tanks. The tanks were ticking over, the big diesels, and they were sitting in a little steel box mounted on top of it, quarter-inch plate, which is cardboard, you know, to the heavy stuff [artillery]. They got a V8 motor there, next to them on top of the tank. Out in front of the tank was two arms with a roller and chains, and they had to drive those things into the bloody line to smash the minefields. Geez, what a job.

On closer inspection the static period was in fact far from it. Patrols were continuous, with small teams moving deep into enemy positions by night, collecting information on movements and minefield positions, and engaging the enemy in raids and counter raids. The patrols did give the men battle experience, but sending small groups of men into complete darkness towards well-defended positions was a decision some might disagree with—especially some who worked the patrols. On 23 August the war diaries nonchalantly report that shelling was normal that day: 132 shells in all. For forty-six days during the months of August and September, the unit was exposed to persistent contact with the enemy. Some 8640 shells fell within the battalion area, which is an average of 188 per day. Yet few physical casualties were reported. The medical reports for August include three cases of ruptured eardrums and two buttock wounds (presumably not on the same man).

Eddie Emmerson clearly remembers his first taste of heavy shelling. 'I was with a bloke called Bob Anderson, and he was an old bloke to us, and any rate, anytime one would hit I'd hit the deck and lay down, and next minute this big bastard would pick me up by the scruff of the neck and he'd say, "Get up you red-headed bastard, you got to be unlucky to get hit."' Bob was a veteran from World War I. His second name was actually Williamson, but he changed it to Anderson because he was sick of being on the end of every queue.

Relief and rehearsal were the order of the day come mid September as the men of the 2/17th were moved to a rear position at El Shammama. Rehearsals by all accounts were of the highest standing in this isolated neck of the war. It's what's known in my business as an out-of-town tryout. Meanwhile, Rommel was making an impression on both sides of the wire and even as far away as Australia. Pte Peter J. Jones wrote to his father that some of the Australian newspapers he'd received were investing Rommel with the glamour of a film star. There was no doubt the man oozed confidence and charisma. At the beginning of October he declared, 'We hold the gateway to Egypt with the full intention to act.' Some of Rommel's fascination had even made an impact on the Australian troops. Montgomery was appalled by the admiration his troops held for Rommel. He was determined to destroy 'the myth of the Rommel invincibility'.

October saw the men shivering in their holes, not from fear but from the bitter cold. The season had changed. But things were hotting up in the HQ tent.

Producers never like to let the talent know exactly what is going on. The cast of thousands outside the tent were not yet aware that opening night was set for 23 October. Day rehearsals were held mainly so that commanders could see what was going on, an option that would not be available to the cast when the curtain rose. Commanding officer of the battalion Lt Col Noel W. Simpson stated that 'a full dress rehearsal was done on the night of the 16th/17th with all supporting arms taking part'. Supporting legs and torsos were by all accounts equally involved—except for the arms and legs of Pte Roy Lonsdale. He was evacuated on 4 October with a boil on the wrist and a strained ankle. Earlier in the year he had spent a month in hospital with abdominal colic. Roy was under attack from all sides, including the insides.

Pte Lonsdale returned to his battalion three days before opening night. On 20 October all cast and crew were finally given full details of the upcoming offensive, codenamed 'Operation Lightfoot'—the show had its title. The cast were given a look at the stage plan, a large-scale model of the entire set. They would share the limelight with 500 fighter planes, 200 bombers, 900 field guns, 1200 anti-aircraft guns, 1000 tanks and 220,000 men. Pte Livingston may have felt like an extra in a Cecil B. DeMille epic. The season would open on a Friday night, 23 October, and run for twelve days, although an extension to the season was possible if the enemy showed enough enthusiasm. Not a long run by any means, but the players would be tested to their limits.

Montgomery advised that the offensive would be a killing match and envisioned the attack would play out over three distinct phases: the break-in, the guts-eating and the break-out. If all went to script, the 2/15th and the 2/17th would open the show and capture the enemy's first line of defence. Then the 2/13th would take centre stage to grab the second line. From their entrance to their final marks the distance was 6.4 kilometres. Of these, 5.4 kilometres would be well downstage, in enemy lines. The boards these men were about to tread were of bare stony rock. They were facing a German division consisting of 9000 men, backed up by an Italian division of 4600 men. Or, more precisely, fronted up by the Italians, who were frequently placed in the line of fire to protect the pureblood

German ranks—'bait for the trap', as Sgt Fearnside described them. When I asked Eddie Emmerson about rumours
of the Italians being less than efficient fighting men, he
said, 'Well, they preferred music, which is not so bad.'

At 2300 hours on 22 October, the battalion were moved
out by motor transport to an area known as 'the Pimple'.
Tucked behind this small, slightly raised mound, the troops
received their final calls—not unlike huddling behind a
curtain before it rises, and providing just as much protection, I imagine. On the twenty-third all troops settled into
their company areas in slit trenches. A slit trench was a
long narrow hole reinforced by sandbags with just enough
room to eat, sleep and shit. I've shared dressing rooms
just like that. From all reports it was an uncomfortable
day and the men were restless. At last light a hot meal
arrived and the troops were encouraged to drink copious
amounts of water, the idea being that this practice would
diminish the effects of major injuries.

At 2030 the battalion moved by truck to the FUP
(forming up place). Pte Peter J. Jones was driving one
of the trucks, and he recalls that as it stopped he heard
the odd sound of bagpipes somewhere down the line. The
troops climbed out carrying weapons, ammunition, rations,
empty sandbags, picks, shovels and grenades before disappearing into the night following a path marked by shaded
blue lights. As they walked the short distance to the starting
lines, the entire Eighth Army had edged along with them.
Two hundred and twenty thousand pairs of feet stood on

standby for their final call. So far everything was going just as rehearsed. Pte Jones was feeling pre-show jitters; he felt the night holding its breath. He quotes Shakespeare's *Henry V* to give a fuller picture of the moment.

> Now entertain conjecture of a time,
> When creeping murmur and the pouring dark,
> Fills the wide vessel of the universe.
> From camp to camp, through the foul womb of night,
> The hum of either army stilly sounds,
> That the fixed sentinels almost receive,
> The secret whispers of each other's watch.

Curiously, this is precisely a verse I learned by heart during one of my own stage battles fifty years down the track. I was in Edinburgh impersonating the Bard—tough crowd. I'm pretty sure I died on opening night.

## Act I—The break-in

'the men were fit and keen for their job and knew their parts well.'

*Lieutenant General Bernard Montgomery*

Zero hour was 2200 on 23 October 1942. At zero minus twenty, the curtain rose. Break a leg, as they say. The real performance is never anything like rehearsal, and the soundtrack and light show that announced the opening of Operation Lightfoot were beyond anyone's expectations.

To the left and right of their position as far as the eye could see, a sheet of flame turned night into day. This was followed almost immediately by the sound of the opening barrage, which could be heard over a hundred kilometres away in Alexandria. The opening scene presented a hard act to follow. In civilian ceremonies, generally twenty-one guns will do the trick. Here, over nine hundred guns positioned behind the infantry bombarded enemy positions for fifteen minutes before Allied aircraft joined in. Tens of thousands of shells screamed over the heads of the infantry. The percussion of the guns made the ground vibrate, and fog and dust were raised as the shells found their marks. And this was just the friendly fire.

Eddie Emmerson recalls the opening barrage with typical understatement: 'Yeah, it was a bit noisy. A thousand guns opened up behind us. Geez it was rowdy.' And dangerous. 'You know the name we gave the artillery? They were known as the bloody dropshorts, oh yeah, every now and again they'd drop one bloody short amongst you.' Eddie spoke to a sergeant with the 2/12th Field Regiment who was on the twenty-five pounders that night. 'I said to him, how many shots did you fire, Bob? He says five hundred and eighty. He said the bloody barrel was starting to look like a banana, it was starting to melt.'

It reminded Pte Jones of childhood cracker nights, unnerving and exhilarating at the same moment. Torches attached to stakes facing back towards the troops, Operation

Lightfoot's footlights indicated unit boundaries. Staring into the velvet blackness beyond the footlights is familiar to all performers: you know they're out there, but you can't tell what mood they're in. In my business, you'd never face a reception as hostile as this. (Although there was that one time in the Mongrel Room in Tasmania . . .)

After the preliminary shots, there was a pause for five minutes as a couple of searchlights scanned the skies like the opening logo of the 1942 Twentieth Century–Fox film *Thunder Birds: Soldiers of the air*, but there was no sign of the gorgeous Gene Tierney on this set. At ten o'clock the searchlights swooped inwards to form an arch over the battlefield. This was the cue for the gunners to resume the bombardment with even more intensity and clear a path for the infantry to advance.

C Company, including Pte Stanley Livingston in his first major role, were given their instruction to advance, but first the sappers crawled forward on their stomachs, feeling around with their hands for mines, before marking the forward path. Once given their cue, the men disappeared into the smoke and fog with enemy fire exploding all around them. According to the plan, a rate of advance of 60 metres every minute was required from the FUP to the enemy wire. From there onwards it was 90 metres every three minutes. The 2/17th were to follow the thin white line while Pte Roy Lonsdale in the 2/13th followed a thin green one. Pte Gordon 'Storky' Oxman, however, was going nowhere. The tall private had suffered a bout of malaria before opening night and was lying in a field hospital listening to the soundtrack.

For the enemy, the attack was a complete surprise—especially to Rommel, who wasn't even on stage. He was back in Germany receiving treatment for a stomach complaint. The man who was left in charge, assistant director General Stumme, had a heart attack and died the morning the offensive began. Rommel would miss the first two days of the battle. Dare I say, the Desert Fox was caught with his Panzer down.

The 2/17th had achieved their goal by five minutes past midnight on 24 October. The opening act had lasted two hours and five minutes—and they hadn't lost a player. One blanket per man was to be taken forward. To Stanley, his blanket was his shield. It had saved him once before and now he'd survived his first two hours of battle without a scratch. After advancing metre by metre through minefields and wire, with their objective reached they began to dig holes in the hard rock, camouflage them, then hop in and wait till dawn.

It was time for the 2/13th to take up the advance. Pte Roy Lonsdale, fresh out of hospital and now a picture of health, sprained ankle and wrist boil cured, marched past his friend Stanley on his way to their objective. The 2/13th did not have as smooth a run as the 2/17th. The battalion became bogged down after encountering mines, wires and small arms fire. Adding further to their woes, the supporting tanks were struggling to keep up the pace and the battalion had to begin their attack without them. Sgt Fearnside of the 2/13th later quipped, 'Tanks are not creatures of the night: like rhinoceros, they do not see well.' Sometime between 2 a.m. and dawn, Pte Roy Lonsdale was shot in the left buttock—perhaps mercifully, as his buttock would survive and the wound meant an end to his further participation in what would be a bloody and thankless campaign for the 2/13th. Roy was a seasoned performer, and had seen plenty of action in Tobruk. He had no qualms about leaving the stage to the greener performers.

While there were no mules in the vicinity, each battalion included among their ranks one pigeon, to be released on capture of the objective. The pigeon was to carry a coded message to a mobile homing loft at the 9th Division headquarters. On my side of show business it is considered unwise to work with children or animals. In the theatre of war, it's the animals that soon learn that it's never wise to work with grown men in isolated desert theatres. I once worked with a pigeon on a film shoot in New Zealand. We named it Lunch. On the last day of the shoot, we proudly announced the punchline we'd been rehearsing for months—'Lunch is wrapped.' (OK, maybe you had to be there . . .)

## Act II—The guts-eating

After surviving the day under a blanket in his hastily dug hole, on the night of 24 October Pte Livingston moved forward with the battalion to secure its second objective. They reached it at 0250 hours the following morning. There had been no opposition until the enemy woke up to the fact that the battalion was digging in, their picks and shovels glinting in the moonlight. The Germans opened up with Spandau machine-gun fire followed by heavy shelling throughout the night, and by dawn enemy troops were seen forming up, preparing for a counterattack. This day was to be the battalion's worst, dubbed 'Black Sunday' by the troops. After repelling counterattack after counterattack, the men of the 2/17th poked their heads out of their holes and counted seventeen dead and dying German rhinoceroses scattered in front of them. The Australians hadn't slept for forty-eight hours and there was no interval planned for this production.

When Rommel arrived back that evening he faced more stomach problems—the guts-eating had begun. But who was eating whose guts was the question. Sgt Fearnside notes that most Allied stomachs were in turmoil on Black Sunday. 'Could men die of madness and fear on the battlefield? A thousand deaths of madness and fear? The valiant never taste of death but once . . . Where is the valour of cowering in the dust, swamped by a fury of frightening sound?' No sleep was had on the night of the twenty-sixth as the battalion came under heavy shelling. Dawn's light revealed twelve enemy tanks poised on a ridge in front of them. Stanley was getting sleepy. Sleep deprivation is an age-old tactic of war. It creates confusion and doubt in the deprived. With no word from HQ, the front-liners had no idea whether they were fighting a winning or a losing battle. The pigeons weren't having an easy time of it back at battalion headquarters; two carrier pigeons had their basket hit. They survived, and were sent back into active service with a note: 'herewith two bomb-happy pigeons'.

At one stage in the midst of this battle, Pte Livingston found himself attached to a platoon carrier. These sawn-off tanks were little warhorses, ferrying the wounded and supplies along the line, providing backup fire for the advancing troops, or drawing fire upon themselves to protect others. The problem was the carriers were effectively only half an armoured vehicle—they resembled small lightweight tanks with the top shaved off. A sardine can with a motor. They offered no overhead protection, exposing the crews to sniper and grenade attacks and shrapnel blasts. Each carrier generally held a crew of three men—a commanding officer (CO), a private and a mechanic—and each vehicle had its own Bren light machine-gun on board. When on offensive duty in the desert, a carrier could hide behind a mound, or a pimple, with its gunner firing over the crest. In the open the crew would dismount with the Bren and open fire. Stanley's role was to man the Bren, assisted by the mechanic. The CO let them know where to aim it. The vehicles added extra mobility to the force, but rolling around the battlefield in a convertible tobacco tin made for a bumpy and nervous ride.

The battalion had moved on to different holes by 28 October, but they couldn't escape the relentless shelling. For Lt Col Simpson this period was harrowing: 'It is almost as much as human endurance can survive.' From my experience, a comment like this has never come from the leading cast, it's almost always from a reviewer. But Act II was not over yet. That night the shelling was the heaviest so far as the battalion made their way through booby traps and mines, and the barrage continued until well after dawn on the twenty-ninth, the day that Pte Gordon Oxman returned to active front-line service.

By midday the enemy were preparing another counter-attack, this one aimed in particular at C Company and including no less than fourteen German armoured rhino-ceroses. By late afternoon the tanks had effectively been beaten back. The battalion wasn't making too much progress, but they weren't going backwards either. Back in London, Churchill was wondering why he was not seeing any movement on his map. Meanwhile, Montgomery was making plans for a break-out he had entitled 'Supercharge'. That night Rommel moved more of his forces into the area to deal with those stubborn sleep-deprived Austra-lians. The next forty-eight hours saw the troops survive a *khamsin* that lasted a day, reducing visibility to 200 metres. Then followed another hectic night. It was not until 31 October that the intensity eased, and Pte Stanley Living-ston crawled under his blanket, the sounds of slight enemy activity lulling him off to sleep.

## Act III—The break-out

On 1 November, Rommel resumed his efforts to dislodge the Australians. This determined attack began at midday and didn't ease until two-thirty the next morning. As Rommel planned his next move, a tremendous barrage stretching along the entire front interrupted him. Operation Supercharge was underway and with it the Ninth British Armoured Brigade, two British infantry brigades and a New Zealand division advanced past the Australian 9th Division. Hitler ordered Rommel to fight to the last, but the Field Marshal had no intention of sacrificing his men to a lost cause. At 5.30 p.m. on 3 November, Rommel ordered a general retreat. For the men of the 2/17th, the show was over. After twelve days and nights, the curtain came down on Operation Lightfoot. Lt Col Simpson described the men's efforts as 'Homeric'.

On 6 November the battalion was moved to a rest area known as Little Italy, a slightly raised geographical feature, a pimple in the shape of a boot. Here the weary troops received a message from headquarters that answered a question many in the battalion had been afraid to voice. It was clear and concise: 9.2 per cent killed, 28 per cent injured.

# 4

## *Mayhem was only a part of it*

'Violence in large lumps fascinates only the timid; and viewers of news bulletins can sup with the devil of war every evening in their lounge and dining rooms. One lesson we all learned in the war was that mayhem was only a part of it.'

*Peter J. Jones, 9th Division AIF*

The military machine had no time to pause and reflect. Just one week after the battle ended, retraining commenced. To boost morale the troops received a letter of gratitude from Monty for their 'very fine performance'. He mentioned a few encores still to be had, and wished those involved 'good hunting to you all'.

There was an overwhelming sense of relief and something more: 'A gnawing, deep sadness affected everyone as they reluctantly considered the reality. It took at least months for these feelings to adjust.' The commanding officers' directive was that every man be occupied. It was time for the bump out. For a start, the battlefield needed to be cleared and 9.2 per cent of their mates required burial. Row after row of identical crosses presented a sobering image of these men who died together, no single act of sacrifice greater than the other. In stark contrast to these Allied military graves, Pte Jones remembers being moved by the sight of a neatly maintained German cemetery not far from the enemy front lines. He was particularly struck by the attention to detail of each individual grave. While these were only temporary burial sites, enormous care was taken with each plot. No two graves in the German cemetery were alike and there among them was the grave of a Canadian airman, complete with the date he was shot down. Half of his propeller blade made for a memorial; white pebbles formed a cross on the sand. All hell might have broken loose, but somehow, in this theatre of war, a degree of mutual respect seems to have survived.

●

The war diaries for 14 November 1942 state that there was nothing particular to report. The battalion were at ease, resting on the Mediterranean coast. As Pte Stanley Livingston breaststroked along the shoreline, at a certain hour of that day in a small cottage in Tramway Street, his father, Ernest James Livingston, died at the age of fifty-four. A few days later a violent *khamsin* raged all day in the desert. So too, perhaps, did Pte Livingston.

•

Towards the end of November, the troops received their orders for a return to Palestine. The convoy of trucks skirted the pyramids before crossing the Nile and entering Cairo. After four days they arrived at Camp Julis in Palestine, where the men were met with a generous issue of beer. Lt William Pye returned to Palestine with the 2/3rd Anti-Tank Regiment, who missed out on the beer allotment as the entire regiment were down with jaundice. Bill was not having a pleasant war. Leave passes were on offer to Tel Aviv, Jerusalem, Haifa and Cairo until 21 December, when the troops were once again in full dress rehearsal—this time for a ceremonial parade at the Gaza aerodrome set for the following day. All units were in attendance as General Alexander addressed the entire 9th Division, the assembled troops stretching for a kilometre across the airstrip. From the sky the battalion lines would have resembled a highly disciplined herd of caterpillars. Stanley Livingston was down there somewhere, and in a Salute to the Fallen, closer inspection of the twelve thousand gathered revealed that 'tears ran down many faces, but there is nothing in the book to say that can't happen, only that you must stand still'.

Christmas came and went. And so did Stanley. On the twenty-seventh he was AWL from 6.30 a.m., back again by nightfall. The only activity reported for that day was an order that all personnel were to be vaccinated and inoculated, so why do a runner? Was he distraught about his father? Was he just out for a good time? Was he simply afraid of needles? He was fined five pounds. He could have used those pounds: there was a mule-racing event on the parade ground that week, bookies and refreshments provided. Perhaps the photo was snapped here? Was Stanley a jockey? Was the wog a bookie? It's more likely Stanley borrowed a few shillings and lost them immediately. It wouldn't be the first or the last time he would lose a packet on the mules.

Roy Lonsdale was up and about again, left buttock obviously none the worse for wear, as he was reported AWL on 28 December. When he returned to duty the next day he was charged with conduct to the prejudice of good order and military discipline, and fined five pounds. For a man earning only seven shillings a day, being docked five pounds must be something of a butt-clencher.

On 7 January all other ranks were informed that the division was moving by sea to an unknown destination codenamed Operation Liddington, fuelling much debate about the destination. Some were adamant they were headed straight for Japan. All they knew was that their latest tour of duty was coming to a theatre closer to home. At least two people were not too pleased with the decision to move the troops. US President Franklin D. Roosevelt and British Prime Minister Winston Churchill were intent on changing Prime Minister John Curtin's mind. While Curtin was a minor player on the world stage, American general Douglas MacArthur could upstage the best of them. 'Dugout Doug' was keen for the 9th to play a supporting role in his Pacific theatre of operations, and without further ado plans were put in place to return the division to Australia at the end of January 1943.

When troops are on the move, all the world's a staging camp. The unit moved by truck convoy to a staging camp at Asluz. The next day the convoy left for the long trek across the Sinai to the East Bank canal staging camp. The next morning they left for Tahag staging camp near Al Qassasin in Egypt. On 24 January two trains left Al Qassasin on the four-hour ride to the Suez staging camp. On the twenty-seventh the battalion embarked on HMT *Aquitania*. The four troopships in the convoy, *Queen Mary*, *Ile de France*, *Nieuw Amsterdam* and *Aquitania*, were supported by an armed merchant cruiser and an escort of warships. The men were warned not to consider the trip a pleasure cruise, but with the thought of perhaps returning home, and with the African desert behind them, spirits were high.

A photograph shows soldiers lying prostrate, packed like sardines on the open deck of *Nieuw Amsterdam* while a melee erupts in the background. At second glance it's clear the men are all happily bathing in the sun while behind them a boxing tournament is taking place. These bouts were a feature on each ship. No doubt Pte Stanley Livingston, who fancied himself as a handy pugilist, would have stepped up for the challenge—and been downed just as swiftly. Stanley had plenty of courage, but he had a glass jaw and a nose of putty. He had dodged many bullets during the battle of El Alamein, but he couldn't dodge a left jab on board *Aquitania*. Amateur boxing was a challenge Pte Livingston attacked with passion, but his skills failed to match his passion; and by the time he reached Australian shores, the boy from Zetland had had his nasal septum crushed so often that it departed from the centre of his nose, never to return. This deficiency was put to good use by the young private, who would flatten his nose with his thumb in attempts to impersonate any number of snub-nosed officers in the vicinity. Many years later this defect would also serve as a source of endless amusement for two infant boys who would take turns poking the nose of their father with an index finger until it disappeared into his skull.

Each night, Stanley, Gordon and Roy stood on deck smoking Capstan Navy Cut tobacco and searching the skies for any sign of the Southern Cross. On 17 February they sighted Fremantle, where seven bags of mail were delivered on board to the battalion. Among them were letters for all three. It was all good news from Roy's family in Mascot, and Gordon was delighted to receive a swathe of mail from Lilly Livingston. A letter to Stanley from his eldest sister Margaret was more sombre. The death of their father had left his sisters distraught. Lilly had been inconsolable and feared the further loss of her brother, as well as his good friend and her first love, Gordon Oxman. Margaret feared for her wellbeing.

With his duty to country and empire fulfilled, foremost in Stanley's mind now was the feeling that he had been

AWL from his family in their time of great need. He was torn—he wasn't about to desert his mates but neither would he desert his family. However, they were not yet home and safe. Journalist Fred Smith's notes, dated 24 February 1943, from one of John Curtin's regular press briefings report that although the 9th Division had arrived safely in Fremantle, Curtin remained worried and had not slept well for three weeks. The problem was that if the troops disembarked in Western Australia, the force would be immobilised for months, the rail system not being up to the task of ferrying troops across the nation. They would have to continue on by boat to Sydney. A further concern was that a Japanese plane spotted over Sydney on the previous Friday night was thought to be a surveillance flight to ascertain whether the troops had arrived. Curtin insisted the return of the troops remain a secret, so although those at home knew of an imminent return of the 9th, the finer details had been denied them.

As dawn broke on 27 February, HMT *Aquitania* approached Sydney. It was a fine, sunny morning, and as the convoy edged towards the safe harbour, stillness fell over the troops. They were home. Just after midday, *Aquitania* cruised past South Head, through the great sandstone gates of the harbour. Years before, they had left these heads as young adventurers. Apart from the New Zealanders, no soldier had been further away from home during the North African conflict.

William Pye and Eddie Emmerson were in that convoy

as H.D. Wells stood on the deck of *Aquitania*, not too far from Roy, Stanley and Gordon. Wells claimed there were no words to describe the scene, before going on to describe the scene in vivid detail:

> It was the hearts saying it, for voices had stilled while the convoy slowly edged through the heads. And then as the *Aquitania* steamed past South Head we heard it. Horns of cars honking till their batteries almost became flat. People waving sheets from windows, rooftops, jetties. Voices shouting unintelligible, jumbled noise—but it was a jubilant exciting sound. Slowly troops responded, afraid at first their voices would not obey their throats . . . For those who returned—this morning was worth it. This feeling, the inadequacy of words to express it. No man can buy it, no masterpiece of oil painting can conjure it up. It can only be felt inside. Each man reacting outwardly as if it happened every day but knowing this only happens once and is then present for all time.

They had endured what no sheet-waving, horn-honking civilian could ever imagine—and made it home again.

Apart from the return of a few thousand speechless young men, life went on as usual on that Saturday morning in Sydney in February 1943. The *Herald* reported that there was to be no children's party in the restaurant at the Farmer's department store in the city that day. On a more disturbing note, especially for Stanley, there was a threat of a one-day beer workers' strike. In the lost and found column was a notice that someone had left a red bag in a yellow cab: call Miss Perry. Also lost was one cow, a brown-and-white spotted Ayrshire, in full milk. Reward. On another page was a plan to save money by shortening matches; it was predicted that by reducing the size by a mere quarter of an inch, the saving would be seven million feet of timber per annum. A meeting of the women's council of the Lord Mayor's fund announced a drive for one hundred thousand pairs of socks to be made in a new pattern. The new sock pattern would make it possible to create five pairs out of a pound of wool. There were vacancies in the Women's National Service office. Women of up to twenty-eight years were required to be trained in oxy and electric welding, no experience necessary. Lower down the page a 38-year-old Roman Catholic gent was eager to meet a lady or a widow with view to matrimony. Just below that a self-described smart, refined Protestant lady in her late fifties of good address and some means wished to meet a respectable gent. Sadly for the pair, in those days, the romantic merging of the two faiths was frowned upon, as Stanley would soon enough find out. There was also something about the Royal Air Force heavily bombing Nuremberg, and the Red Army in Russia preparing to launch an offensive on the northern and western fronts.

When *Aquitania* berthed at Woolloomooloo, thousands of men loaded with gear and kitbags filed down the gangways, attracting a crowd of a few hundred who had spotted the ships silently making their way down the harbour. Word travelled slowly in this mobile-phoneless world, and so did the people. The small crowd waved handkerchiefs and towels. As the men passed, some asked them about the desert, but there were no boasts. Many glanced down; they weren't ready to talk. Most never would be. Some of the soldiers thought that their involvement in the final breakthrough at El Alamein had been overhyped and were insistent that the New Zealanders, the South Africans and the Highlanders should share equal credit. The men were swiftly split into groups and shuttled by buses to a camp at Narellan on the outskirts of Sydney. It was a short stay; all personnel were given leave the next day. Newspapers reported streams of tough, brown fighting men on three weeks' leave pouring through the city after what one headline described as a 'strangely silent homecoming'.

Some of the men were affronted by the attitude that greeted them, claiming that locals were more than happy to whinge about conditions on the home front, the effects of rationing, the new sock patterns, shorter matches and striking beer workers, but were indifferent to the soldiers' ordeals. One veteran of Tobruk and El Alamein was disgusted by the armchair opinions of the civilian population, including one acquaintance who assured him the 9th Division would find the Japs far harder to handle than any mere German or Italian. Another returning soldier reported that many didn't have a clue who they'd been fighting over there. 'Someone asked me where I had been and I said, "Syria". He was puzzled and wanted to know whether we had been fighting the Japs in Syria! I told him we had been fighting the Vichy French. They said, "What were you doing fighting the French? Was it a brawl in the street or something?"'

While no civilian could be expected to grasp the essence of what those returned soldiers had endured, neither did the soldiers quite understand the urgency and fear that had gripped the nation while they were away. All eyes had been focused on the threat from the north; the war in the Middle East had taken a back seat. The presence of so many US soldiers signalled to the returning troops that the war closer to home was now the priority. The blissful journey through the heads was turning bitter for some, but for the majority it was enough to spend time with family and loved ones. It had been a tough couple of years, with no doubt more to come in an entirely different theatre, and out-of-town rehearsals set to begin shortly in the Atherton Tablelands in far northern Queensland.

Roy Lonsdale wasted no time in heading to the family home in Mascot. He had a brand-new wife awaiting him there—after enlisting as a single man, Roy had married on 2 November 1940, seven months before embarking for the Middle East. Making up for lost time with his bride was foremost on his mind as the train rambled from Narellan to Redfern, where he took a tram straight down Botany Road. It was the middle of the night when he knocked on the door of the barber shop, but there were no complaints from the household after they were roused from sleep. Stanley and Gordon were also on that tram. They hopped off a few stops before Roy, where Botany Road met Tramway Street, and headed for the Livingston family home at number 77. The tramline to and from the city had begun service in the 1880s, running along a single line with a loop at Gardener's Lane. Tramway Street derived its name from being a part of this loop.

Tramway Street had not always been home to the Livingstons. As mentioned, Stanley had spent his childhood in Zetland, a suburb or two closer to town yet less densely populated. It was heavy with industry, and not exactly child-friendly. Stanley and his four sisters were encouraged to go out and play on the road: there was nowhere else to play, and very little traffic. During the post-war boom of the 1920s, large-scale factories had sprung up in and around Zetland. The Great Depression hit those industries between 1929 and 1933, but they had rapidly recovered by the outbreak of World War II. By then the local municipality of Alexandria contained over five hundred and fifty factories, and was supposedly the largest industrial municipality in Australia at the time. Stanley had found employment in one of those factories before he enlisted. He had left school in 1932, at the age of fourteen, and any of the local factories were willing to take on a local boy, no questions asked. Travelling long distances to and from work was out of the question: you'd need more than a factory wage to be able to afford a car, and if you weren't near a tram or train line you walked.

Factory life proved hazardous for young Stanley; a scribbled note in his discharge papers makes mention of a pre-war crush injury to the fingers of the right hand. His palm was laced with a tangle of raised white scars, evidence that the hand had literally been ripped to shreds, devoured by a metalworking lathe. After he was rushed from the factory floor, doctors were quick to inform him that there was no way to save any of the fingers, but young Stanley insisted on keeping what was left of them. After all, he was a teenager, and it was his right hand. To lose those eager fingers at that stage of life would have been an unkind cut indeed. Stanley ended up with quite a capable claw, never shy of a cigarette, and the affliction was obviously no hindrance to enlistment. In fact, a gruesome gnarled fist most likely made a decent weapon.

Stanley Livingston was probably not a born fighter, but he would have had to learn fast on the streets of inner Sydney in the 1920s. The family occupied one of only two houses in the street, a pair of identical, decrepit terraced houses, two old molars among a row of sparkling new galvanised-iron, saw-tooth-roofed industrial dentures. Unable to afford the rent on one tooth, they moved out— to the tooth next door. The new neighbours turned out to be problematic. Not long after moving in, Stanley, then no more than ten years old, was playing in the dirt that passed for a garden in the narrow backyard. Behind him, two men, both wielding sub-machine guns, burst into the yard, sending him running for the back door, where he was met by his mother. Bridget Livingston stowed the boy under her skirt before folding her arms and blocking the door. There was plenty of room left in Bridget's skirt to harbour the rest of her brood—Molly, Lilly, Margaret and Dorothy. To a child, the thin cotton of a mother's frock is as safe as any shield, and may even explain Stanley's later attraction to well-aired blankets in times of stress. The men demanded Bridget move aside. They had no interest in her or the children; they were after someone called Squizzy. She told them firmly that there were no Squizzies here and they might want to try next door. Duly chastened, the men backed out of the yard and instigated the same move next door, by which time Squizzy Taylor, a frequent visitor to the Livingstons' neighbours, got wind of the situation, and before any blazing of guns commenced, the diminutive gangster was well and truly gone.

While his family were being harassed by potential murderers, the breadwinner, Ernest Livingston, was at work. Ernie's early years had been tough, to say the least—he'd spent much of his first decade in the care of the Randwick Asylum for Destitute Children, an institution originally set up to care for abandoned children or those whose parents were deemed 'dissolute characters'. Fanny and James Livingston were not parents of a dissolute nature; they simply had no choice, given the hardship of working-class life in inner Sydney in the nineteenth century. Their fortunes wavered, from being penniless to having just a few pennies, and on the rare occasions they managed to scrape together the means to achieve it, their six children would all be reunited at home. The records show that Ernest first entered the asylum in 1891 at the age of three, with three of his sisters. Life became even more desperate in 1894 when Fanny died after falling down a flight of stairs and fracturing her skull, leaving six children aged between two and thirteen, including five-year-old Ernest, with just their father, James, to care for them. In 1897, when he was eight, Ernest was again in the asylum, along with four sisters. Two of the girls were still there in 1901.

After this tough start, Ernest made it to adulthood, met Bridget and landed a job at Tooth and Co breweries on Broadway. He loved his job and was a loyal supporter of the company product. Ernie was always up for a liquid lunch. In fact, the only substances that entered Ernie's stomach arrived there via a straw. He had no choice, for this Tooth's employee didn't have a tooth in his head. The lowly wage of a brewery worker meant that he could not replace the teeth that had deserted his gums in childhood. Perhaps this didn't worry him too much, as he turned his gums to the art of gurning to make a bit of spare cash on the side. Gurning, for those who don't know, involves the grotesque distortion of one's facial features for the entertainment of others, and is still practised to this day. The ability to gurn is compromised by the presence of teeth, which restrict the ability of the lower jaw to swallow the top one, if possible including a portion of the nose—all done while keeping the eyes crossed at all times. Ernie the Gurner made a few extra shillings on his way home from work, stopping in at the many pubs between Broadway and Zetland. Ernie had other skills, according to his daughters, who avoided the subject of their father's gurning abilities and would instead heap praise on his delicate watercolours of native birdlife. It was the only respectful comment I ever heard about my paternal grandfather from anyone, but to my knowledge no paintings have survived.

Ernie's gurning earnings, along with his ability to mimic the calls of both native and introduced birds, enabled him to squirrel away enough money to eventually put a deposit on a house in Tramway Street in Mascot. I own a photo of Ernest and Bridget standing outside their gurning-funded home. Ernie is dressed as a Scotsman, with Bridget in similar garb—the pair apparently loved an informal dress-up. But it wasn't a marriage made in heaven; it was made in the Tooth and Co brewery. Bridget was partial to a drop herself, and every day she'd hand little Stanley a tin bucket and send him to the nearest pub, where it would be filled to the brim with ale before the slightly framed ten-year-old struggled home, trying not to spill a drop.

When not getting on the plonk, dressing up, gurning or bickering, somehow Ernie and Bridget managed to instil a strict moral code in their children, raising them as Roman Catholics. When Bridget died suddenly in 1936 at the age of forty-eight, Ernie was left with five children and no cotton skirt to protect them. His kilt would have to do. But he still had his second love, booze. In early 1942, with his only son in the Middle East and the threat from the north increasing at home, Ernie Livingston was given the duty of standing lookout for the Japanese on the brewery tower. Not long before he died, Ernie was found asleep at his post, having sampled the factory product a little too eagerly, and was unceremoniously sacked.

While Stanley embraced the dipsomaniacal inclinations of his parents, the girls embraced the spiritual side and maintained their faith throughout their lives. Somewhere along the line, Stanley Livingston lost his. Whether it was due to the trials of war, I have no idea. All I know is that Stanley was never one to rely on ethereal redeemers. Long before I met him, he had given up on ghosts.

•

Thanks to some hardcore gurning, the Livingston children had inherited a modest little cottage in Mascot. By 1943, three of Stanley's four sisters were married. Dorothy and her husband, Jimmy, were living in the family home with Lilly when Stanley returned to Sydney. Jimmy didn't fit the devout Catholic milieu. He was an SP bookmaker, a trade that was illegal outside a racetrack. Jimmy ran his bookie business from the Tramway Street cottage. He recruited local children to keep 'cocky' at either end of the back lane, on the lookout for the police. When Jimmy passed away in 1966 he had no bank accounts, but there was money stashed all over the house and a revolver on the top of his wardrobe.

On 1 March 1943, Stanley was expected home on leave, but there was no telephone at number 77, and no-one quite knew when he would arrive. When night fell, Stanley was missing, presumed drunk, and Dorothy and Jimmy hit the sack. Lilly couldn't sleep, and when she answered a gentle knock on the door her mood improved considerably to find not just one but the two most important men in her life standing before her. Jimmy wasn't quite so welcoming to the late arrivals. Generally it doesn't bode well when an SP bookie gets a knock on the door in the middle of the night.

# 5

## Three men and a barber shop

'Beware of the young doctor and the old barber.'

*Benjamin Franklin*

While the Tramway Street reunion was in full swing, Roy Lonsdale was readjusting to home life on Botany Road. The barber shop in Mascot was slotted into a space no wider than four and a half metres along a row of similar shops. Inside, two 1920s chrome and leather hydraulic-lift barber's chairs were set in front of a long mirror. Combs, scissors and hand clippers rested in glass jars full of misty methylated spirit on a shelf below the mirror. A thick pall of tobacco smoke was ever present—any man sitting on the single wooden bench waiting for a shave and a trim at the hands of Ernest Arthur Lonsdale or his son Ernest Jnr would bide his time smoking. The elder Ernest's wife, Annie Lonsdale, kept the nicotine flowing, perched at a high bench in the tobacconist booth tucked near the shop window. Ashtrays on silver stands stood near spittoons, surrounded by near misses of phlegm splattered on a wooden floor covered with discarded hair accumulated from the day's cuttings. Gentlemen of the time kept their hair short and well above the ears, ensuring the profession of gents' hairdresser remained a secure and reliable source of income.

In deference to the long tradition of barbering, affixed to the front window was a decal of a barber's pole with its familiar red and white swirl. The origins of the barber's pole icon hark back to the Middle Ages, when a barber doubled as a surgeon. The process of bloodletting required the patient to squeeze a long staff, encouraging veins in the arm to engorge and allow easier access to the vein for 'letting' with leeches and blade. Bandages used to soak up the let blood were wrapped around the staff and left out in the sun to dry. The ball on the top of the pole was originally a leech basin. Harking forward, we find that bloodletting was not available at Ernie's, but therapy of another kind was freely offered. The barber, like the taxi driver, would always lend an ear, even when burning the excess hair out of someone else's with a long wax taper. The taper worked just as well on nasal hair.

While the barber shop was a constant hive of activity, there was never a queue outside the shop. The line wasn't straight—it was scrunched up as people crowded into the tiny shop, smoking and chatting. No-one cared who was next in line. The shop was a meeting place, a place to gossip, to laugh or cry. Today, filmmakers and stage managers use smoke machines to create atmosphere.

In the 1940s it was a case of BYO atmosphere, courtesy of the cigarette. The mood was always set. The perpetual whorl of cigarette smoke acted like a social adhesive, enclosing all customers and hangers-on. In the 1940s a non-smoker was a social outcast. A cigarette held in casual disregard was never absent from the hand, a compulsory addiction. The tobacconist was the dealer. She had all the accoutrements: Tally Ho papers, slender black Bakelite cigarette holders, silvered matchbox cases with enamelled portraits of the King. It was hard to resist the sweet smell of fresh moist tobacco rolled between nicotine-stained fingers. The men congregated around the barber's chairs, leaned on walls, smoking and solving the problems of the world as a stream of local women stopped by for a chat with Annie Lonsdale in her tobacconist booth. Any advice was offered free of charge, and no doubt was of great comfort during the worrying days of World War II. From dawn to dusk, the fat was chewed and spat to the rhythmical snapping of scissors in the deft hands of the two Ernie Lonsdales.*

---

*Clearly there was a glut of Ernies around at the time. For the sake of clarity from here on in, Ernest Lonsdale the elder will be known as Ernie Snr, his son as Ernie Jnr, while Stanley Livingston's father will remain simply Ernie. To complicate matters further, there was one more Ernie. Bridget Livingston gave birth to a boy, Ernest William Livingston, on 18 September 1922. This littlest of Ernies was two months premature and died two days after his birth. As Mr Kipling wrote, 'Lest we forget'.

Ernie Snr was a man of high standing in the local community, a one-time Grand Master of the Masonic Lodge, master barber, father of seven and husband of Annie, who sat behind the tall cork-topped desk and sold tobacco and lottery tickets with her daughters Evelyn and Dot helping out while half of her sons were busy with the war. Roy Lonsdale had been the first to see active service, while his younger brother Eric chomped at the bit to go. On his return, Roy must have seen in Eric a boy similar to his pre-war self, full of the lust for adventure. Whatever Roy might have said to young Eric didn't dissuade him. Eric didn't need his arm twisted to go to war—unlike their older brother Jack, who needed both arms twisted before he finally enlisted (as will be revealed in due course). Two more brothers, Don and Ernie Jnr, were to miss the action. Don had a child and an essential business to run. He was pumping petrol while Ernie Jnr was essentially cutting hair.

All seven siblings were brought up in the confines of 1187 Botany Road. Beyond the tiny shop was a small space, ambitiously named the dining room. Here there was a gas fire and a long table, used exclusively at Christmas—a special occasional table. There was just enough room left for a Singer treadle sewing machine that had seen more action than Pte Roy Lonsdale, and induced as many injuries. Seven over-eager children had tested the treadle to its limits. When not pedalling the sewing machine they were pedalling a pianola at the other end of the room.

The only child who actually learned to play it was Evelyn, who played stride style, belting out Fats Waller tunes, much to the chagrin of her mother—young people's music. The others contented themselves with pedalling out tunes punched into the perforated brown paper of player piano rolls: 'Ragtime Cowboy Joe', 'Black Bottom', 'Toot Toot Tootsie' and 'Yes, We Have No Bananas'.

One step down from the dining room under a rusted corrugated-tin roof with a leaking skylight was the kitchen, home to a round wooden table, an Early Kooka stove, a leadlight cabinet and one tiny basin. Between the shop and the dining room a steep set of stairs led up to the sleeping quarters. One room for the parents, and the rest of the crew were jammed into another room with a closed-in verandah. Out the back was a laundry, with industrial-size deep concrete tubs to wash both clothes and children. In a far corner sat an iron-footed freestanding bathtub. There was no shower and no hot water—just a cold tub under bare charcoal-black brick walls. The toilet was an architectural afterthought, a dark hut that you wouldn't want to spend too much time in. The newspapers jammed onto a wire coathanger weren't for reading, they were for wiping your arse. The backyard was a narrow strip of bald dirt. Grass didn't have much chance after years beneath the feet of seven children, but here and there a few brave sprouts poked through, like a nervous digger sticking his head out of his doover. At the far end of the dirt was a tin shed, at one time home to Ernie Snr's pride and joy, a black

Model T Ford. Eventually the costs of bringing up a family had meant a choice had to be made, and reluctantly the Model T had to go.

I know a fair bit about the Lonsdales' place. I grew up there too.

•

The little barber shop was much like its patriarch. Ernie Snr was a slight man, not wealthy by any measure, yet immaculately dressed at all times in a three-piece pinstripe navy-blue suit, braces, silver spring-metal armbands, a shiny silver fob watch in his vest pocket and tortoise-shell horn-rimmed glasses perched on his nose. During the years of the Great Depression, wearing that same suit Ernest took Ernie Jnr in hand and wandered the beaches of Botany Bay offering free haircuts to the hundreds of men forced to sleep out on the sands while they searched for a home and a job.

One day, around about the time little Stanley Livingston was ferrying buckets of beer to his mother in Zetland, there was a knock at the door of the barber shop after closing time. Annie Lonsdale was busy checking the lottery sheets and counting the day's takings, while Ernie Snr was sharpening a cutthroat razor on a leather strop. A silhouette of a male, smaller even in stature than the small-statured Ernie Snr, could be seen through the frosted-glass door. Annie asked no questions and invited the man in: a head in need of a haircut was never turned away. As the well-dressed gent entered the shop, Annie failed to notice the blood drain from the face of Ernie Snr, who tightened his grip on the cutthroat razor. Their visitor also knew a thing or two about cutthroat razors, but that was about all the men had in common. Annie offered the man a seat in the barber's chair. Word of the highly respected barber's generous nature had spread beyond the borders of Mascot, and the man quietly but firmly explained that he wasn't after a trim, he was in urgent need of a short-term loan. Ernie Snr said nothing. Annie chastised him, 'Ern, Ern! The gentleman is talking to you.' Ernie Snr had frozen to the spot. Annie went straight to the cash drawer and sorted out the loan, then bid the man good day. She closed the door and resumed berating her husband for his uncharacteristic rudeness, until he interrupted her.

'Do you know who that was?' he said softly.

'Never saw him before in my life,' spat Annie.

Squizzy Taylor was the man's name. And as the blood returned to Ernie's face it retreated just as swiftly from Annie's. The loan was never repaid. Taylor was shot dead on 27 October 1927. Both the Livingstons and the Lonsdales were touched by the notorious Squizzy Taylor, but Ernie Lonsdale was touched for a week's wages.

●

Reassured that Lilly Livingston was in good spirits, Gordon was off to his family home in Wollongong. Meanwhile, Pte Stanley Livingston dropped in to the Tennyson Hotel to meet Roy and grab some courage before heading across the road for a trim and a shave, but more importantly to see Evelyn Lonsdale. The pair had exchanged letters throughout Stanley's time in the Middle East, but seeing her now made him nervous—he'd had plenty of time to think about this girl, still in her teens when he left, and to sort out his list of priorities. Evelyn was high on that list. As Evelyn assisted her mother trading tobacco that day, she found it impossible to avoid the gaze of Pte Stanley Livingston, now seated in the chair, his chin lathered in foam awaiting a much-needed shave. It did not go unnoticed by Ernie Snr that the young private had his eyes set upon his daughter, a quiet, intelligent girl with flowing brown locks. Ernie Snr grasped the leather razor strop and vigorously sharpened his cutthroat razor before holding the blade within inches of Stanley's neck. The young private soon turned his eyes right.

Three weeks into March of 1943, Operation Liddington leave was almost up for the men of the 2/17th. With her Stan around the house, and Gordon never far away, Lilly's condition had improved, but the thought of losing them again distressed her, and Stanley and Gordon were reluctant to leave. Roy Lonsdale was enjoying married life, albeit in the cramped upstairs quarters of the barber shop, and over a quiet beer the three of them decided to turn their leave into a stay. When the battalion returned to duty at Narellan camp at 0645 hours on 23 March, privates Stanley Livingston, Gordon Oxman and Roy Lonsdale were reported absent without leave.

H.D. Wells was also loath to return to camp. He reports that a large number of troops, like himself, extended their leave for a few days. He was fined two pounds and given a severe reprimand. Pte Peter J. Jones too found the three-week leave ended far too swiftly and the prospect of a return to duties away from those of family hard to swallow. Still, Jones and many others straggled into camp, either of their own volition or under military escort after being rounded up. Roy Lonsdale was rounded up by the military police and returned to his unit on the twenty-ninth. He was fined five pounds. The two other absconders managed to elude capture and were not present for the ceremonial parade that attracted thousands in Sydney before the battalion moved to far northern Queensland on 17 April to commence intensive training in the Atherton Tablelands in preparation for active service in the south-west Pacific theatre.

The troops were immediately subject to lectures on the tactical problems of such warfare, with emphasis on encouraging the fighting spirit. Point 30 of a training memorandum issued by Lt Col N.W. Simpson states the importance of maintaining morale, and that if the troops were well led 'their morale will be high and with all that they are more than a match for the enemy, without, they lay themselves open to defeat by uncivilised natives armed with spears and bush knives'. After studying the memorandum, the men were issued fresh supplies of tomahawks, picks and bush knives.

Major John Broadbent wrote of the training that it was initially directed to 'familiarising troops with the different types of jungle country . . . learning bush craft as it applied to such including the many personal problems of how to evade or remove leeches, know the stinging tree, sharpen and use a machete, cook the new style rations. Scrub typhus first raised its ugly head here and soldiers learned the application of mite repellent and most soldiers were extra serious about it.'

Scrub typhus and leeches were far from the minds of the two absentees. With Lilly in the safe hands of Gordon, Stanley was spending far too much time hovering around the barber shop on Botany Road. How many haircuts can one man endure in a week? Ernie Snr knew what was going on. Years behind the chair had given him a unique perspective on male vanity. Without exception, when a man was in the chair, he looked steadfastly at himself. Once in the chair, it was polite to stare. It was imperative, in fact; with scissors snapping at near light speed in and around the ear area, one false move and a man could lose a lobe. The head was to be handled by the barber only, a tilt to the left or right, but at all times the eyes of the customer were never to leave the eyes in the mirror. During a haircut, a client's eyes act as a pivot point. A barber works around the centrifugal stare of the client. The barber's chair allowed time for a man to indulge in narcissism without criticism. The fixed stare, the music of the scissors snapping and the gentle massage of the comb quiets the man-beast, and then it's all over too quickly. Especially if your last trim was the previous day. Stanley Livingston was breaking the golden rule: he was not looking at himself. His eyes kept drifting to the left to study the profile of Evelyn as she sold cigarettes and chatted with too many other young men for Stanley's liking—many of them dressed to impress in uniforms that had never left Australian shores.

Evelyn's sister Dot had not initially approved of her older sister fraternising with Stanley. He had apparently been going out with a girl called Madge who worked in the cake shop on Botany Road when he spotted Evelyn. And she had her eye on him too. 'Evelyn used to watch your father,' Dot told me. 'He always had white cricket pants on, you know, he was always immaculately dressed and Evelyn was always impressed because our boys were rough and ready.' Dot couldn't work out what Evelyn saw in him. 'Evelyn always thought what a nice fellow he was, and I said, "Oh, he's a bit too queeny for me,"' the elusive charm of Stanley Livingston remaining a mystery to her to this day. The two girls were also familiar with Stanley's father, who after gurning his way along the pubs on Botany Road often dropped in for a haircut. Dot clearly remembers the enthusiasm Ernie Livingston demonstrated as he gurned just that little bit too close to their ungurned faces for comfort.

Ernie Lonsdale Snr was a stickler for the law and did not approve of the boys going AWL, but under instruction from Annie, the only person who held sway over him, he conceded to hold his tongue and welcome them into his home. He even relented so far as to offer Stanley a roof over his head at 1187 after Stanley gave up his couch to Gordon. The two men had shared too many doovers together in the desert to split a couch on Tramway Street.

●

Ernie and Annie Lonsdale were born late in the nine-teenth century. Ernie Snr managed to avoid the conflicts of World War I: he was married, had his own business and was raring to breed. Annie lost a brother, Donald, at Gallipoli. Some years before this she had almost lost her own life. Annie grew up in the slum suburb of Padding-ton in Sydney. Her mother, Jessica, had a habit of leaning over the upstairs balcony to abuse any debt collectors or beggars knocking on the door below. One day in 1899, after hearing a knock at the door, five-year-old Annie Macleay tried to emulate her mother and leaned over the balcony to rebuke a visitor. She fell and was impaled on the iron-spiked fence below. It missed most vital organs but had that spike pierced a few centimetres further north most of the stories presented here would have been nipped in the bud. Annie Lonsdale had no qualms about flaunting that scar on her upper thigh in later life. It was pretty gruesome. No child can resist gruesome. My father had a claw and my grannie had been impaled on a fence—it didn't get any better than that. Apart from Uncle Eric's missing index finger. He'd point the stump in my face and say, 'Whatever you do, son, don't bite your nails.' I immediately started biting my nails.

Ernest Arthur Lonsdale spent half of the twentieth century keeping men's hair at bay in the shop on Botany Road while Mascot transformed around him, world wars came and went, children grew and married, then had more children who grew and married. Hair also continued to grow from men's heads, and up until the mid-sixties it was to be removed with military precision. When he was born, in 1892, Mascot hadn't even been a name on a map. The young Ernie Snr grew up in Hill End, a goldmining town in the central west of New South Wales, his parents rushing for gold like thousands of others. The tiny wattle-and-daub cottage the family lived in would in the coming century be overrun by artists. In the 1940s Donald Friend moved in, followed by Russell Drysdale, and these two boys soon struck gold without even digging a hole.

In the nineteenth century the Port of Botany was largely sand, swamp and market gardens, acres of lantana, buddleia, mulberry, flax and pines. The entire population of Sydney relied on the gardens for their potatoes. With the onset of the gold rush many gardeners left to hit it rich up north, but those who hung around had the last laugh as the price of spuds rose to twenty pounds per ton. Apart from the gardens there soon developed a mill, a candle factory, a piggery, Barney Dougherty's boiling-down works, a tannery and a slaughterhouse. There was a glue factory and a blacksmith named Joe Bogis who was also renowned for his rhubarb-growing prowess. It seems that you could buy a pig, have it slaughtered, make candles out of its fat and a saddle from its hide, then have the rest boiled down and made into glue while you enjoyed a bowl of Sydney's best stewed rhubarb with Joe, all without leaving the suburb. But back then the one thing you couldn't get was a decent haircut anywhere along Mudbank Road. Convicts had built the road, which rolled from the district of Mudbank through to George Street in the city. To get in there you had to either walk or take a market cart. By the end of the nineteenth century you could take a bus for a shilling each way, or a double-decked steam tram from the loop at Tramway Street.

Come the new century, the unused marshy land and mangrove swamps would become the Ascot Racecourse, the track soon to be absorbed into an embryonic aerodrome where the likes of Charles Kingsford Smith, Bert Hinkler, Amy Johnson, Jean Batten and Charles Ulm would practise their skills in biplanes high over Mudbank. Charlie Kingsford Smith and Charlie Ulm were regulars in Ernie's barber shop in the 1920s, dropping by for a trim before setting off on another solo adventure. I always look closely at photos of Smithy, knowing my grandad cut that hair, most likely using the same pair of scissors that later trimmed my own. A good pair of scissors was a prized tool of the trade and would last a lifetime. Kingsford Smith once had his photo taken in the barber's chair for a local news story. From then on the old iron seat was always referred to as 'Smithy's chair'.

By the time Stanley Livingston was born, horse-drawn jinkers carried the biplanes into the paddock that passed for an aerodrome. The only thing required for anyone wanting an aerodrome licence in those days was 'a surface smooth enough to allow a T-model Ford to be driven at 20 mph with the driver still comfortably seated'. Local racehorse trainers were warned against using the former racecourse, now landing strip, as a training track. Dogs and horses were also banned from crossing the strip, but the authorities had less success in halting gangs of youths who used the aerodrome as a shooting ground.

The traffic on Botany Road was about to get very busy. Smithy had seen action in World War I in Gallipoli, Egypt and France before enlisting in the Royal Flying Corps. In 1927, he and Charles Ulm took a boat to the United States with the dream of coming back across the Pacific in a plane. No-one had given this a go before. Smithy and Ulm purchased a Fokker Trimotor aircraft in Seattle, dubbed it the *Southern Cross* and, with the help of Harry Lyon navigating and James Warner operating the radio, took off for home. Eighty-three hours later, on 10 June 1928, three hundred thousand people jammed into Mascot's tiny airfield to catch a glimpse of Charles Kingsford Smith's *Southern Cross*, fresh from Oakland, California, on its pioneer crossing of the Pacific. Dot Lonsdale still remembers that day. The five-year-old couldn't quite understand all the fuss—she'd seen plenty of planes before—but she remembers the excitement, and Annie and Ernie urging her to look to the sky as the *Southern Cross* came into view and landed safely in the aerodrome that would one day take Kingsford Smith's name. He wouldn't live to see it. Smithy and co-pilot John Thompson Pethybridge were piloting a sister aircraft, the *Lady Southern Cross*, when it disappeared off the coast of Burma.

Ernie and Annie's seven children grew up playing in the paddocks surrounding the airstrip, from childhood to adulthood, biplanes to bombers. There were no fences to keep anyone out or in, much to the displeasure of the market gardeners still holding the last of their ground surrounding the airstrip. On the occasion of Smithy's arrival, onlookers stampeded and flattened the vegetables. The predominantly Chinese gardeners brought out their tomahawks and threatened the crowds, but they were out-numbered by the hundreds of thousands of people. The gardens also made excellent soft landing areas for the less experienced pilots. These were the last days of the market gardens; Sydney would soon have to look elsewhere for its spuds.

At the aerodrome there were no restrictions—visitors were free to walk into hangars and fondle the biplanes. You could even go on a joyflight on a whim if you spoke to the right person. One of the pilots once offered Ernie Snr a free ride. Ernie Snr wasn't one for heights, but he didn't have the heart to refuse the offer, so he took Dot with him for support, or more likely in the hope that the pilot would refuse to take the tiny girl on board for safety reasons and he'd be off the hook. No such luck. The pair were bundled into the cockpit and were soon spinning and looping all over the city. Dot recalls the thrill of it; she also remembers the bruises on her arms from her father's vice-like grip. 'When I think of what they used to do up there ...' Evelyn said, recalling an incident involving a one-legged flyer. 'You can imagine those little planes, and there was an alleyway beside the hotel and he told us he could turn side on and come through it and over the Tennyson Hotel. They were really daredevils. He did it. He went through the lane, turned his plane side on, and went up and over the hotel. Not a scratch. But he must have been blind drunk.'

In 1931, as the airfield shifted from drome to port, the Controller of Aviation set down a few safety rules:

- The practice of soliciting for passengers on the road leading to, or within, the aerodrome is not permitted.
- Pupils under instruction shall have their aircraft distinguished by a red streamer, and they are not to be approached closely by other aircraft.
- Persons visiting the aerodrome do so at their own risk.

Charles Ulm, in a letter to the Civil Aviation District Superintendent, showed concern:

I feel that it is quite unnecessary to bring to your attention the fact that there are very many comparatively inexperienced pilots flying from Mascot Aerodrome and if an inexperienced pilot had any engine failure just after taking off . . . it is quite possible that he would run into people playing golf on the aerodrome.

In 1938, the looming war in Europe spurred a boom in aircraft technology. Wood, wire and fabric were soon to be replaced by jet engines. Sydney Airport was about to become a military facility, and domestic aviation was put on hold. Soon the former swamp became an assembly, repair and maintenance facility for military aircraft. Four new runways were built, one of them forming a level crossing where planes competed with coal trains heading to the Bunnerong Power Station. The stage was being set for war.

# 6

## *A nip in the air*

'Fear springs to life more quickly than anything else.'

*Leonardo da Vinci*

In December 1941, as the battle-weary boys of the 2/17th Battalion rested at Hill 69 camp in Palestine, back home a new player was upstaging the Middle Eastern theatre of war. Japan was well rehearsed. Their tour of duty in the Pacific theatre opened with a pre-Christmas attack on Pearl Harbor. What an entrance. When they went on to barnstorm Thailand, Malaya, Guam and Wake Island, the Imperial Japanese Army had the Australian audience on the edge of their seats. Everyone was wondering whether the Nips were coming to a theatre near them anytime soon. Prime Minister John Curtin famously proclaimed that Australia was facing its gravest hour. Australia's 'no worries' policy was becoming a bit of a worry. The word 'invasion' was being bandied about. Those aliens H.G. Wells had warned us about were hovering in the skies just north of Australia. The war of the world had already seen Hong

Kong, Manila, Shanghai and Singapore under attack from the skies, and Australia had plenty of sky to attack from.

When Japanese aircraft eventually attacked Darwin on 19 February 1942, pandemonium ensued. To everyone on the ground, it was a clear sign that the Japanese had invaded and that ground troops would soon follow. With air-raid warning systems destroyed and further raids expected, the Royal Australian Air Force ordered all personnel to move a couple of kilometres into the bush, sparking panic as both the military and civilian refugees poured down the main road, most heading not just a couple of kilometres out of town but intent on reaching the Adelaide River over one hundred kilometres away. They were seen fleeing on 'bicycles, trucks, a road grader, an ice cream vendor's bicycle cart and even a sanitary cart'. It seemed the entire town was going AWL. The exodus became known as the 'Adelaide River Stakes'; some made it to the Adelaide River, but the overall winner was a Darwinian deserter who after almost two weeks finally limped in to Melbourne.

James Thurber once said, 'Humour is emotional chaos remembered in tranquillity.' But there was little to laugh about in Darwin at the time. Sixty raids would be made on the city over the next two years, with 243 people losing their lives on the day of that first raid. There were reports of drunkenness and looting in the aftermath of the initial attack. As women and children were boarding a southbound train at Parap station, the military police, many of them drunk, tried to calm the panicked crowds by firing shots above their heads. The government was unnerved by the panic displayed by both the military and the civilian population and decided it would be best to keep the finer details under their hats. Eventually John Curtin announced news of the attack from a bed in St Vincent's Hospital. Incursions from an overwhelmingly powerful enemy can wreak havoc on your gut flora: he had a bad case of gastro. For the benefit of broader Australia, official casualties were broadcast as a more palatable fifteen dead. The Prime Minister further informed the Australian public that 'the armed forces and the civilians comported themselves with the gallantry that is traditional in the people of our stock'.

The seemingly impossible defence of our shores was on the minds of most. There was official concern about the Aboriginal population around Darwin and on the offshore islands, and measures were put in place to shift the people south. While their safety was one issue, of more concern was the possibility that the Aborigines might reveal information to the invading force. The inhabitants of Melville and Bathurst islands were believed to be in cahoots with the Japanese due to pre-war bonding between pearlers and fishermen. This was in the face of the fact that the day after the raid on Darwin, the Melville Islanders were the first to capture a Japanese prisoner on home soil.

Sometime around the end of May 1942, five Japanese submarines were somehow not spotted lurking 80 kilometres off the New South Wales coast. These mother subs had midget subs and seaplanes secured on their decks. On 30 May one of the Japanese seaplanes flew in through the Sydney Harbour headlands, past the Harbour Bridge, took a good look at the naval dockyard at Garden Island, then swung out to get a better view of the city before returning to the mother sub without anyone taking the slightest bit of notice. The following night, residents living on the shores of Sydney Harbour were treated to a fireworks display rivalling any twenty-first-century New Year's Eve event. The city's wealthier citizens had been some of the only ones to respond to H.G. Wells' earlier warnings: many of the well-off had abandoned their vulnerable harbourside homes at the first mention of hostilities, some leaving their properties vacant, with the result that the more opportunistic squatters now had a perfect view of the fireworks from these grand mansions. They would have seen searchlights scouring the harbour, heard shells whistling overhead, the sound of machine-gun fire and the detonation of depth charges. But the aliens were not descending from the sky: three Japanese midget submarines were in the harbour, and inside each were two of H.G. Wells' aliens with one torpedo each.

One sub immediately became ensnared in a boom net while the other two tagged behind the Manly ferry. The crew in the entangled sub took their own lives by setting off a massive explosion. The general public were unsure whether the attack was genuine, and many lined the harbour foreshore to watch the show. It was not a safe place to stand, as the subs failed to hit any of their intended targets. They were aiming at the American cruiser *Chicago*; instead they hit HMAS *Kuttabul*, killing nineteen sailors. The sub that fired the indirect hit then sank of its own accord, and the third sub, crippled by depth charges, sank to the bottom, where the crew took their own lives. Many Sydneysiders not close to the harbour remained unaware of the attack.

All was quiet again until just after midnight on 7 June when the residents of Dover Heights were certain the Japanese invasion had begun as shells whistled over their homes. Rumours flew as fast as the bombs. Chinese whispers about the Japs had one report claiming that Brisbane had been destroyed, Gosford was under fire and now it was Sydney's turn. In the wrap-up, ten shells were fired. Six were duds, and no-one was killed or injured in Dover Heights. Down the road, an angry mother of a submarine, no doubt grieving for its lost children, surfaced like a great whale off Bondi Beach and attacked the eastern suburbs. Somehow, the grieving sub missed all but one person; the only reported injury was inflicted on a local refugee who had fled from Nazi Germany.

When the two submarines were dredged out of the harbour, the bodies were taken to Rookwood cemetery, where they were given a full military send-off. Japanese flags were draped over the coffins, a three-gun salute was discharged and the Last Post played. The gesture may have been intended to send a message of conciliation to the

Japanese, who were currently holding twenty-two thousand Australians in POW camps, but the funeral arrangements caused more uproar than the fact that Sydney was found sorely wanting in its attempt to defend itself against just three mini subs.

●

The attacks on mainland Australia left few on the home front in any doubt that they were on the verge of being invaded by the Japanese. Had the powers-that-be gained insight into the activities of the Japanese high command, it may have become clear that the Japanese had no definite plan in place to invade Australia at that time. It is argued that the primary reason for the Japanese air attacks on Australian military installations was to protect the waterways between the Australian mainland and New Guinea, and there was no intention at that time to penetrate further inland.

The script might have played out differently had the Japanese not hit a few snags as they moved south: namely the Battle of the Coral Sea, the Battle of Milne Bay and the Kokoda campaign. Still, the notion of imminent invasion persisted. Understandably so. When the neighbours are fighting so loudly, it's hard to ignore them. Without hindsight's great benefits there was no telling which way the tide would turn or when, or how often; and after all, we were their enemy, and this put us at great peril, whether fighting over there or holding down the fort at home.

Still, the Allied successes of late 1942 were causing some to drop their guard. At a press briefing held on 6 October 1942, Fred Smith reported that 'Curtin said he couldn't understand the mentality of Australian people. One day they were in a panic and next they wanted more race meetings.' In a further briefing on 30 December Curtin said, 'there are buggers in Australia who won't work . . . We are like people who have got contagion out of the house and just over the back fence. Apparently we are not worrying how dirty the yard is.'

For those younger civilians on the home front, Sydney was an exciting place. This isolated backwater had become something of a frontwater. The youth of the day, pumped up by the influx of exotic, cashed-up Americans and the emergence of a vibrant city nightlife it had never known, were living like there was no tomorrow. Elaine Hope was an ambulance driver in Sydney in 1942. 'It was dance, dance, dance all the time,' she said. 'I'm dancing away and there's nobody here to check whether I'm dancing too close to that fellow or to make sure I'm home by eleven o'clock. Everybody seemed in a hurry to live.' For the first time in its brief history, Sydney was happening. The American troops brought glamour, money and no shortage of charm with them. The American invasion had begun soon after war was declared on Japan. The troops hit Brisbane first, bringing with them weapons of mass production: Camel cigarettes, hamburgers, hot dogs and Coca-Cola. Curtin welcomed these aliens: 'Without any inhibitions of any kind I make it quite clear that Australia looks to America, free of any pangs as to our traditional links or kinship with the United Kingdom.'

This was the beginning of a turning away, for better or worse, from the traditions of empire, and it continues to this day. But leaping from the arms of Mother England onto the shoulders of big brother USA came with its own conditions. When General Douglas MacArthur wrapped an arm around John Curtin after their first meeting, the newly appointed Supreme Commander of all Allied forces in the south-west Pacific said, 'You take care of the rear and I will handle the front.'

The new boys on our block had plenty of money and they liked to spend it—mostly on our women. Meanwhile the old boys went off their blocks. It would appear that holding up the rear was not a position most Australian men felt at all comfortable with. Resentments emerged at home between the Australians and the US troops. The Yanks were given the best seats in restaurants and hotels, and another of their alien habits, tipping, guaranteed them attention.

Occasionally, small wars broke out. The 'Battle of Brisbane' began on 26 November, Thanksgiving Day 1942. There were approximately ninety thousand Americans in and around Brisbane at the time. No-one quite knows who cast the first stone, but the battle seems to have been sparked by an incident near an American canteen. A number of Australian servicemen and American Military Police were allegedly engaged in a verbal disagreement—

some might call it a stoush. (I have no hesitation in calling it a stoush, because I love the word 'stoush'.) When one local boy attempted to make a point by hurling a No Parking sign through a plate-glass window, the stoush escalated. Hostilities lasted for three days. A couple of months later, two thousand men went to battle in Melbourne and held up traffic for an hour. A Perth stoush drew a thousand participants in Hay Street. Newcastle was not stoush-free either: in Hunter Street, Australian soldiers wielding belts with brass buckles claimed a major victory over the soft calf-leather, tiny-buckled belts of the Americans. The US troops paid a high price at the hands of the Australians, who stood their ground, trousers at the knee, belts twirling. Eddie Emmerson, on the other hand, had no problem with the Americans. 'The Yanks were good, you could use them. In Brisbane I lined up at the brothels in Albert Street. You'd line up in the brothels and the Yanks bought your place. Oh yeah, you could use them.'

There are mixed reports of the relationship between African American soldiers and the Australians. A white American soldier allegedly single-handedly rioted at a dance hall in Sydney when the manager refused to comply with the American's request that black troops be excluded from the club. Bill Pye remembers the tensions within the American ranks. 'The Americans never had mixed units, they thought [the African American soldiers] were not active front-line troops; the white American felt so much superior to them, there was no fraternisation, they really were separated. And you . . . were very conscious of this, [the African American soldiers] were just second-class citizens. They discounted them.'

We had our own policy on such matters, a white Australian one. The White Australia policy can be traced to the resentments felt towards Chinese immigrant workers in the mid nineteenth century, as it was presumed they would work for lower wages. Come the new century, restrictions were placed on immigration. The community wholeheartedly embraced this white Australian stance. In 1919 Prime Minister William Morris Hughes boasted that the decision was 'the greatest thing we have achieved'.

The White Australia policy survived until the mid sixties, when those with suitable qualifications would be allowed in no matter their hue. Meanwhile, a couple of per cent of the Australian population were not even permitted to have their say on the issue. Around three thousand Australian Aborigines were accepted for enlistment in World War II, many volunteering as home guard. Others were refused outright solely on the grounds of race. The government was concerned about loyalty; they feared that the Aboriginal soldiers might help the enemy if offered tobacco. But once in the army, unlike the African Americans, Aboriginal service-men were accepted unreservedly into the ranks. According to Gary Oakley, Indigenous Liaison Officer at the Australian War Memorial, the Australian Defence Force was the first equal-opportunity employer of indigenous Australians. The uniform was all that mattered. When the war ended, however, it was as if they had never been in the army. After serving in every conflict, it was back to segregation, in pubs, schools and restaurants. Stanley mentioned to me a time he was training in Dubbo in 1941, where inside the local picture theatre a hurricane wire fence separated black from white. He just shook his head; he was not amused.

Other Australian residents were also suffering the effects of a war not of their making. When on 10 June 1940 Italy sided with the Germans and declared war against everyone else, Australians of Italian origin became targets for official and public suspicion. Many were interned without having committed an offence. Italian fruit-shop and cafe owners were marched from their homes and placed in cells in Long Bay gaol. Their families were left to suffer the war years under the gaze of paranoid and wary neighbours. Australians of Japanese origin were interned as soon as the Pacific War was declared. Two thousand Austro–German Jewish refugees were also interned in New South Wales. It took a while before the powers-that-be agreed that it was not necessarily in the interests of national security to imprison those who were the subject of oppression by those with whom one was fighting a war.

There was also little sympathy for conscientious objectors in those days—not good news for the local branch of the Jehovah's Witnesses, who did not believe in self-defence. As happens in times like these, rumours spread, including one claiming that the music broadcast on Jehovah's Witness radio programs contained secret messages intended for the Nazis. Meanwhile, Jehovah's Witnesses in Germany were under attack for conscientiously objecting to the war on the eastern front. Nonetheless, the organisation was banned in Australia in 1941.

In areas isolated from the excitement of the big city, there was a growing sense of unease. The government had unprecedented control over its citizens. Wages were pegged, as was pricing of goods and services. Governments decided the rates of interest banks could charge. A Directorate of Manpower was put in place to oversee strict changes to workers' conditions. By 1943, out of a population of seven million, 715,000 men and women were in the armed forces. For the rest, to find employment they would need to go to the Ministry for War Organisation of Industry. Employers in the protected industries—shipping, munitions, construction and engineering—could not sack an employee without the permission of the Manpower officials.

The official who bore the brunt of public ire about rationing and austerity measures was the Minister for War Organisation of Industry, John Dedman. Dedman alienated the majority of the public in late 1942 when he discouraged the production of non-essential items like toys and decorations; even stripes on lollipops were taboo. The terms Christmas, Yuletide, and Festive Season were banned from advertising, and Father Christmas was forbidden to appear in any window display. Dedman had effectively grinched Christmas. To keep the home fires burning, in a blaze of patriotic fervour he insisted that New Year's

Day 1943 not be classed a holiday, resulting in hundreds going AWL from the workplace. Dedman tried to boost his popularity by introducing his own range of austere fashion items, for example the Victory Suit, single-breasted with two buttons, no buttons on the sleeves, no cuffs on the pants, and a width restriction on the trouser leg. A matching waistcoat was out of the question. You could pick up a Victory Suit for seven pounds, seven shillings. Then you would need a permit to get the thing dry-cleaned.

Reductions in the production of alcohol didn't win many friends either, with hotels forced to close even earlier. Manpower raids on hotels gained media attention. These raids were often farcical, as the bureaucratic officials would not dare go in on their own, instead enlisting the aid of police and security forces.

The outlawed Jehovah's Witnesses also came under fire from Manpower's workforce regulations. Many were imprisoned for non-compliance, refusing to work in any industry that supplied war-related goods. The godless weren't faring any better—it was a confusing time to be a communist. They had been fighting fascism for years, but now Communist Party leaders feared that this war was not against the fascists but against socialism. There were concerns that conservatives on our side could form an alliance with Hitler against Russia. Only when the Germans attacked the Soviet Union did their sympathies turn towards the home team. In December 1942, a ban on the Communist Party was lifted. The party held a lot of sway with the unions. Strikes were unpopular, most people considering the action an affront to the fighting forces, but the government needed the unions onside. A discussion between the Prime Minister and Harold Wells, president of the Miners' Federation, illustrates the uneasy alliance between the government and the Communist Party. Wells reports that when he met with John Curtin, the Prime Minister said to him, 'Supposing you forget you're a communist and I forget I'm Prime Minister and we get along and talk to each other and help each other.' Wells said that suited him just fine.

Restrictions on non-essential everyday items like lawn-mowers, swimsuits and pyjamas created the perfect conditions for a thriving black market, turning ordinary folk into common criminals. Citizen racketeering was rife. The main source of illegal alcohol came from the pubs themselves. The beer was often stored in sugar bags known as 'CSR suitcases' and sold for exorbitant prices. The going rate for under-the-counter grog was five shillings for a bottle that normally cost little more than a shilling. A bottle of scotch could fetch up to nine pounds, the equivalent of around four hundred dollars today. Men who were AWL were particularly prominent among the black-marketeering crowd. To boost their labour supply, managers often employed soldiers who were AWL. The men were recruited from pubs, where the soldiers often congregated. It wasn't too hard for a seasoned pub-dweller like Stanley Livingston to pick up a couple of days' work no questions asked. No doubt Stanley worked both sides of the bar with equal gusto.

The effects of rationing had cons, but there were also some pros. Sydney's flamboyant Tilly Devine, always dressed in red to signify danger, found her services in high demand among the troops, much as Henrietta had discovered half a world away in Latakia. The authorities generally tolerated the comings and goings of Tilly's profession. However, US officials were concerned their troops might be in danger of disease and demanded certain nightclubs be closed down.

SP bookmaking also flourished, despite horse-racing being a target for government crackdowns. The racing industry was accused of diverting labour and money from the war effort, and one race-free Saturday every month was ordered, with no races during the week. In spite of this, SP bookies were kept very busy, and Stanley's brother-in-law Jimmy Hemmings was on top of the world. Jimmy would put the word out that a horse without a chance of winning was a dead cert; the locals duly backed it and lost the lot. Bookies in the Atherton Tablelands, keen for the soldiers' shillings, were having a harder time of it. Unbeknown to the bookies, the troops had access to radio equipment that gave them the winning horses before the books were closed.

The general community tolerated the black market, particularly if they could benefit from it. Shopkeepers were in a position of enormous power, and a friendly butcher could always get a little something extra for a customer for a small fee. Unlike Jimmy 'the Grifter' Hemmings, Ernie Snr viewed himself as a citizen of high moral standing, although he too may have been tempted during this era of rationing. He was keeper of one of the most coveted of black-market items, tobacco, but I can find no evidence of the Lonsdale name being tarnished.

# 7

## *The home-front line*

'Some elements were inclined to resent the barbed wire
on the beach, which to some extent restricted surfing.'
*Captain W.H.J. Phillips OAM ED*

By night, the city was cloaked in an eerie darkness. The
lighting design for the theatre of war on the home front
included the brownout, basically a dress rehearsal for a
blackout. From the top of Sydney's highest man-made
structure, the AWA tower, the view during a blackout was
disquieting. There was no sign of a city, just the glint of the
harbour and the outline of the Blue Mountains against
the sky. The overall impression was an atmosphere not of
calm but of imminence. Town names and street signs had
been removed in the hope of confusing any invader, but
it was equally confusing for a local travelling into parts
unknown. Unidentified railway stations meant only a good
guess got you off at the right station.

The building of private shelters was encouraged.
Some were simple holes in the ground, others were more

elaborate. Ernie Snr built one out the back of the barber shop and held routine drills, but often it was only Ernie Snr and the dog who crouched under the corrugated-tin humpy, fingers in ears waiting for the bombs to drop. If you had enough coupons you could always purchase one from Nock & Kirby's in George Street. The Anderson Air Raid Shelter—instructions and bolts supplied—could accommodate six persons. An aerial photo taken over Mascot in 1943 shows far too clearly a row of air-raid shelters in the grounds of Mascot Public School. In the black and white print the newly erected pristine concrete shelters glow a brilliant white, looking for all the world like the perfect target.

By far the most prevalent underlying fear for those with husbands and sons serving overseas was the arrival of a telegram. The news was never good. Ernie and Annie Lonsdale no doubt feared the postman, as their daughter Dot recalls.

> They must have worried, but life just went on with them, they never made a fuss, they just hoped they didn't get a telegram. I do remember Mrs Cragg, her son was in the navy, he was in that ship that went down, and I remember her knocking at the door, this was a bit late in the night, and I just peeped in and she was crying her eyes out, she said, 'I've lost my son.' She'd just received the telegram.

Her son George was a stoker on the HMAS *Sydney* when it was sunk in November 1941. For Stanley Livingston it had happened the other way round: he was the one to receive news of his father's death while on alien shores. Everything was how it shouldn't have been. The world was upside down. And now, in early 1943, he was back home, pretending he'd never been away.

While the rest of the 2/17th Battalion were doing the hard yards in northern Queensland, Stanley and Gordon were being fitted for a wardrobe change. During their official leave the men would have enjoyed wearing the uniform, singling them out from the rest. When they removed it they were forced to take on a different role. A sense of shame chaperoned any able-bodied young man out of uniform. The government, the press and the community conspired to coerce its members to support the war effort. With the Japanese knocking on the ceiling, the majority needed little prompting. Stanley was now playing against type. It was a hard pill to swallow. His was a crisis of duty, personal versus national. He was no coward—nor was he a deserter. He may have been AWL from the army but he had not deserted his sister. Yet without uniforms to signal their status to the person on the street, Stanley and Storky looked like people on the street. And not just any people, but able-bodied young people of the male persuasion. As they avoided the sideways glances from the public, and the full frontal stares of uniformed soldiers on official leave, the leeches in

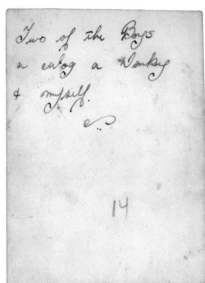

Two of the Boys
a wog a Donkey
& myself.

14

Just what did you do in the war, Daddy? And where? And with whom? And why didn't you ever tell us?

In 1941, Stanley spent his first Christmas overseas in Palestine. Here he is airing his blankets. In a few months time Pte Livingston would learn that a blanket could be an infantryman's best friend.

With no Christmas cards handy, Stanley cut and pasted this postcard, replacing the sights he'd seen with the one he'd most like to see. Never one for effusive prose, Stanley didn't give much away on the reverse side, but I think Evelyn got the message.

From left: E. Currie, S. Livingston, B. McGreal, L.G. McPhillips, F.W. Peters and A.H. Currie. There is no date on this photo, but from the look in Stanley's eye and the protective touch of his hands I get the feeling these boys might have just lived through an experience they would not be too willing to share with the rest us in future. (Incidentally, Pte Alfred Herbert Currie, on the far right, was later to find out that chronic diarrhoea was no excuse for going AWL.)

Stanley was shipped back to Australia in 1943, on board the *Aquitania*. The view from this ship was of a convoy of other ships, including this one, the *Nieuw Amsterdam*. In the background the ORs are watching a boxing match. This was a popular pastime shared by the troops, and Stanley was quick to step up to the challenge. Unfortunately, he was just as quickly put down. (Image from the Australian War Memorial.)

This was Stanley Livingston's military wallet, with his initials and enlistment number stamped into the leather. Tucked below a photo of unidentified mates is a fine lace handkerchief, a keepsake from Evelyn Lonsdale on his departure to the Middle East. It never left his side while he was away.

The Livingston clan in 1924. Front row: Margaret, Molly, Stanley and Dorothy. Back row: Ernie, Lilly and Bridget. (Far back row: an advertisement for Ernie and Bridget's favourite pastime.)

Stanley James Livingston, Catholic schoolboy and beer-bucket conveyer.

Evelyn Lonsdale, a teenager enjoying a lull between a great depression and another great war.

Billy Rudkin and Stanley Livingston, third slip and right-hand off-spinner respectively. Evelyn's sister Dot warned her about men like these, but Evelyn was easy game for a man in pristine cricketing creams with the ability to make his late ball pitch square into the corridor of uncertainty.

Ernie and Bridget Livingston
dressed up to the kilt in
Tramway Street.

Ernie the Gurner, alone
and at ease.

The barber shop in Mascot in the 1940s. Taken from the vantage point of the saloon bar of the Tennyson Hotel.

Ernest Arthur Lonsdale, apprentice barber, circa 1915.

Ernie Snr, Annie and Shiny Lonsdale on leave of their own in 1940.

Evelyn's brother, Pte Roy Lonsdale, and Pte Stanley Livingston in the backyard at Mascot, on official leave in early 1943. All smiles after having made it home in one piece after their ordeal in the Middle East.

Stanley found a reason to turn his leave into a stay.

Pte Gordon 'Storky' Oxman had his own reason: Stanley's sister Lilly Livingston.

Guilt-inducing posters like these were unlikely to have prompted Stanley to return to his unit, but an increasing unease with the trifles of civilian life after enduring the realities of battle may have provoked him to rejoin the ranks of men who understood those realities. (Image from the Australian War Memorial.)

It's hard to know when Stanley was snapped pedalling the pianola at the barber shop in Mascot. There are no known photographs of Stanley during his months AWL. In fact, the visual history of Stanley Livingston almost vanishes until the end of the war. Was it that the excitement of the first wave of the war, with the boys marching off to glory, had passed? Or had it simply been that severe wartime restrictions meant they couldn't afford film?

While Stanley had been fighting the Desert Fox, Evelyn was taming a tree-dweller.

Evelyn and Dot Lonsdale feeding hard-earned rations to the locals on the home front. A pair of uniformed predators, no doubt armed with silk stockings, hover in the background.

Jack Arthur Lonsdale, semi-eternal bachelor, gunner and runner. Even here in his enlistment photo there's some hint that this would not be the last time Jack Lonsdale would have his mug shot taken.

Evelyn and Pauline, cohorts and co-workers at William R. Warner and Co. pharmaceutical company, around 1942.

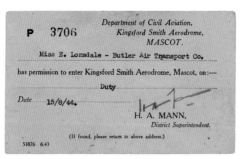

'Is this how men earn their money?' Evelyn's pass into the world of male employment, riveting bombers at Kingsford Smith Aerodrome in 1944.

Evelyn gladly changed her job, and took his pay. (Image from the National Library of Australia.)

Gordon and Lilly Oxman tie the knot at St Bernard's Church in Mascot on 15 April 1944. Pte Roy Lonsdale, Pte Stanley Livingston and his sister Dorothy were present and accounted for.

Stanley Livingston front and centre during his Pacific campaign. The story goes that this photo was taken in Borneo in 1945, and that may be so, but to my eyes that jungle looks suspiciously like the Atherton Tablelands in Northern Queensland, where the troops played a waiting game while 'Dugout Doug' MacArthur called the shots.

Gordon and Stanley after the war. Formerly brothers-in-arms, and now brothers-in-law.

Evelyn and Stanley in January 1946, post-war but pre-parenthood. I was at this time, as they say, just an itch in my father's pocket.

Dot Lonsdale on bridesmaid duties at her sister Evelyn's wedding in May 1946.

Post-nuptials, Stanley and Evelyn Livingston, with Ernie Snr keeping watch. Something in the bride's and groom's eyes attests that all had not quite gone to plan that day.

After his 1786 days of active service, Stanley soon found himself back on the factory floor, picking up where he had left off and where he would stay for almost forty more years. Here he is on a smoko at the factory in the 1950s, flanked by fellow toolsetters.

Christmas 1956. Eventually Mr and Mrs Livingston managed to go forth and multiply by two. In the driver's seat their firstborn, Brian Ernest, went on to graduate from university and become a card-carrying member of Mensa. Holding up the rear is their last born, Paul James, who managed to fail every subject in the HSC and has never yet held down a 'real' job, or gained a driver's licence. He did, somehow, manage to write this book.

the Atherton Tablelands were looking more and more appealing.

The White Feather campaign was a British innovation from the Great War. Whenever a woman spotted a young, healthy gentleman not in uniform, she was obliged to hand him a white feather, a symbol of cowardice. This affront to his masculinity was a powerful and deeply humiliating means of enforced recruitment, but ultimately lost public favour due to the feather-wielders' inability to distinguish between deserving and undeserving ununiformed males. Yet it persisted into World War II, and even on the streets of Sydney in 1943, there could still be found women armed with white feathers and not afraid to use them. I can imagine Stanley Livingston, incognito, strolling through Hyde Park, when he is approached by a young woman, normally a welcome advance, only to be presented with a white feather. This civilian gig was a tough role. Would he break character? Would he take offence, blurt out the truth and risk being mocked as a liar? And what must it have been like for Evelyn to be surrounded by other girls clinging to uniformed heroes? To protect her man, she had to play her role too.

A uniform drew women like a magnet. Perhaps it embodied a sense of security in uncertain times; perhaps it just embodied a young, firm body. Some men enlisted for the clothing alone. Others wore fake uniforms: it worked just as well. Wooing without a uniform was hard going. A single-breasted cuffless Victory Suit just didn't cut it.

For women, having a boyfriend out of uniform was a symbol of no status. Did the couple share a sense of shame? Evelyn was aware of Stanley's battle credentials, even though he spared her the more gruesome details. In the postcards sent from the Middle East he would most often mention the great cities he had visited, the same stories he told me as a small child: the wild bus rides around the mountains of Lebanon, the Pyramids of Egypt, the wogs and the mules. (Eddie Emmerson had his own method of correspondence: 'Mum used to go crook. I used to write to her and say, "Am well, hope same, love Eddie." We had a code, before we left home. It was all [based] on spirits. Like, rum was London, gin was Glasgow, or something—see, they censored your letters; you couldn't say, "I've arrived in Scotland." But you could say, "I've been out, we had a party tonight and we all got stuck into the rum."')

I would guess Evelyn and Stanley were too busy enjoying their own company to worry about anyone else's opinion. They were often seen at the Ascot picture theatre, just a few doors down from the shop. Perhaps they caught a screening of *Private Buckaroo* showing at the time. Thin on plot but big on songs, it starred the Andrews Sisters, always favourites with Evelyn, although the reviews say that comedian Shemp Howard stole the film. This would have delighted Stanley—he was big on Shemp—but the plotline of a man who tried every angle to join the army may have irked him. Donald O'Connor plays the underage lad desperate to enlist. When O'Connor finally succeeds he's off to the joys of battle. The end. Perhaps Stanley would have pre-ferred the next film on the double bill, *Ship Ahoy* starring Red Skelton, another of Stan's favourites, the comedian's red hair and rubber face reminding him of his own late father. Or perhaps Stanley and Evelyn put on their town clothes and trammed it into the city to see Frank Capra's *Meet John Doe* at the Regent. Or Roy Rogers' *Sunset Serenade* at the Capitol, or *Gone with the Wind* into its fourth big month at the St James.

•

As Stanley embraced civilian life, newspapers were cele-brating the return of the 9th Division. The last boat had now left the Middle East and the reports were full of bombast and propaganda. Perhaps the journalists were instructed to do their best to boost morale or perhaps this reporter was just in love with the sound of his own typing:

> The Australian likes to carry through any job to which he has set his hand, and because in this war trained Austra-lian Infantry proved themselves second to none among the world's most renowned armies, the men of the 9th Division probably left the scene with feelings pre-dominantly of regret . . . No explanation, however sound, can quite console them for having been 'pulled out' just when they had helped in signal fashion to win a great victory and throw the enemy into headlong flight.

Is this effusive spray the voice of an able-bodied, un-uniformed journalist fearing the white feather? The article goes on: 'They have a job to do here, in short which will demand the best there is in them.' Stanley was well aware of this, which was why he chose to be by the side of his traumatised sister Lilly in Tramway Street, swapping his slouch hat for an Akubra. You could pick one up for twenty-five shillings in the Strand Arcade. This was a fair amount at the time, but it was unthinkable for a man to venture outdoors without a hat in 1943. However, Stanley would most likely have picked one up from his old man's cupboard: his inheritance didn't stretch to twenty-five shillings.

Evelyn seemed satisfied with her plain-clothed Antipodean soldier and they shared many nights out. Stanley was eager to spend the spoils of his black-marketeering enterprises—when he hadn't already gambled them away. The good thing about having an SP bookie in the family is that you could always borrow back the money you had recently lost to him. A night out at the Tivoli theatre would have been on the cards for sure. Touring shows on the Tivoli circuit brought much-needed distraction to Australians during the years of war. Toni Lamond was seven years old and living in Melbourne when the war was declared in 1939. Her parents were already stars of the Tivoli circuit when she began singing professionally at the age of ten, working with her parents.

All through the war years I was engaged in what was called 'the war effort', entertaining at Heidelberg Hospital [in Melbourne], to which the injured troops were brought for treatment, and at Fisherman's Bend, where the gun turrets were made for fighter planes and there was a twenty-four-hour work ethic for workers, and because of this, entertainers were brought in regularly, to lift the spirits of all concerned, to entertain and bring smiles and laughter in the food canteens. So for me it was doubly exciting, as I was doing what I loved, and felt such a sense of being involved.

There were plenty of shows travelling through Sydney during the early months of 1943. Currently showing was a successful run of *Design for Glamour*, starring Roy Rene, Bob Dyer and The Crazy Builders. Coming soon was *Strip for Action* with Morry Barling, Buster Fiddes, June & Jeanette, Mascotte Powell and The Tivoli Swing Sisters. Or they could save their pennies for a chance to see my father's and my own favourite comedian of the time, George Wallace, in *Target for Delight* with The Leotards and The Three Alecs & A Girl. Or they might catch a matinee session of J.C. Williamson's *White Horse Inn*, a musical with a cast of one hundred now in its fourth month at the Theatre Royal, 'scientifically cooled for your comfort'. Failing that, there was always Luna Park, with its Big Dipper, Tumblo Bug Ghost Train, Coney Island River Caves and Floating Dance Palais. Perhaps the couple may have joined Evelyn's sister

Dot, who remembers going dancing at the 'Troc' in George Street of a Saturday night and jitterbugging the night away to the sound of a Trocadero Big Band Jazz Orchestra.

Lilly Livingston was also enjoying nights out with her plain-clothed hero. Storky Oxman stood head and shoulders above any judgemental glares. With her boys by her side, Lilly rallied, but it was only the knowledge that they were safe at home that settled her, and she panicked at any mention of them leaving again. The men were in a bind. It was nearing the end of April and they'd been AWL almost two months. Duty was calling from all sides.

•

Once satisfied that Lilly was in good shape and in good hands, the pair decided to put up their own and surrender. With a slight touch of disgust for civilian life, the two deserters dropped their day clothes and any pretence, suited up and returned to their other duty. NX20181 and NX20277 were marched into camp at Python Ridge near Kairi in far northern Queensland under close arrest on 13 April 1943. Morale had improved somewhat in this location since training had commenced, with the establishment of a mobile cinema and regular supplies of tobacco and beer. Stanley wondered what they'd been missing.

This is what they'd been missing.

Hardening up of the troops had been going on for forty days and thirty-nine nights. Lt Bill Pye, who had returned to Sydney with the 9th Division in February, duly returned from leave and headed for the Tablelands.

> I remember it took us several days, we finally got off the train, they drove us out in trucks and I remember getting off and they showed us a mark in the ground with a stick. They said, 'That's the start of your camping area.' Then we went down half a kilometre and he said, '. . . and that's the end of it'. And that's it. And all it was was bloody scrub. We didn't have tents or any bloody thing. So I went around to a civil organisation who were building things for the government and I went up there and I scrounged some nails and I went to another place where we got offcuts from a timber mill and we started sort of building mess huts and doing things and then they finally gave us tents. It was a bad start up there. We were not really adequately prepared for it.

What met the men there was similarly described by Sgt G.H. Fearnside as more of a campsite than a camp. Nothing but a vacant lot surrounded by a gnarl of tropical jungle, it appeared to him as though a small patch of New Guinea had been imported just for their personal use. The stage was set for rehearsals to commence. 'All the props were there,' he said. The jungle had been fitted with trip wires. When these were triggered, the brown-overalled broomstick troops—survivors of their past stunt at El Alamein—sprung up from the jungle floor, swung from trees or peered around bushes. After a hard day of avoiding sprung dummies, Pte H.D. Wells dragged off his boots and socks to reveal a foot covered in blood—the sock was full of leeches. The other foot told a similar story. It had been a tough day for Wells, who at one stage was submerged under a deluge of caterpillars. These bit players were great improvisers, the swarming creatures suspending themselves from branches, clustering into the size and shape of a football. It didn't take much to trigger a caterpillar bomb. Wells copped a direct hit.

Typhus mites lived in the tall kunai grass. Scrub typhus could kill, and the fatalities grew as the troops were weakened by exposure to the hardships of jungle warfare. Early diagnosis was difficult, as those afflicted could appear quite well before the abrupt onset of fever, chills and rash. For many, the disease prompted more dread than malaria. Later on in New Guinea, surrounded by mite-infested kunai grass, the thought of scrub typhus gave Pte Peter J. Jones nightmares. He feared the mites almost as much as the enemy; but whereas aircraft could be heard approaching, the typhus mite gave no warning. The poisonous stinging gympie bush also played its part. Jones describes the high price paid by some unlucky soldiers who unknowingly used its finely haired, broad leaves as toilet paper. He quotes a sufferer: 'Hairy curses tickle hairy arses.' In those first weeks of rehearsal, the unit suffered two cases of haemorrhoids, one case of a carbuncle of the lower left eyelid, four cases of scabies, three stonefish stings and one rectal abscess, courtesy of the gympie bush no doubt.

It could be argued that while his comrades had been training for battle in the tropical jungle, Stanley had been acquiring similar skills in the city. The key tactics were the same.

- Protection on the move: The tram to Mascot—it was illegal for a soldier to be arrested while on public transport.
- Protection at rest: The Tennyson Hotel.
- Opposed river crossing: Avoiding being urinated on by inebriated servicemen at 3 a.m.
- Offensive operations in jungle country: Urinating on a serviceman at 3 a.m.
- Reorganisation and capture of objective: Sober up and do it all again tomorrow.

Commanders stressed the need to avoid noise during jungle training. (A tough call when your head is enclosed in a caterpillar bomb, leeches are sucking your feet dry and your anus is burning.) When men were stationed in the desert, enemy positions were well in front of the line and any major movements were clearly visible by day, whereas in the jungle the enemy could be five metres away no matter which way you were facing. The Japanese also had a trick of memorising western names and nicknames and calling them out to confuse and mislead the troops, so the soldiers were instructed never to call to one another. They were urged to make silence a habit. Personally I hate mime, and I'll wager so did the boys in the AIF. Mind you, this silent tactic could have saved an entire 2/17th platoon whose leader had a stammer and resorted to using the word 'Whoa!' after failing to get out the word 'Halt' just before his platoon fell down a ravine during training.

No soldier in the 2/17th survived his time in the army without earning a nickname. If you didn't enlist with one, it wouldn't take long before you earned one. Storky was set from the word go. Stanley had also packed his own: it was Livo before he joined the army, and forever after; this was also passed down to his sons, and the sons of his sons. One can only imagine the Japanese soldiers attempting to memorise their lines before crying out in the midst of battle, 'Porky! Rabbits! Blue Boy! Reject! Livo! Cockroach! Storky! Cowpoke! Sniffy! Spanky! Stumpy! Soak! Paddles! Dagwood! Whizzer! Panicky Pete! Mastoid Basher!' Not to mention 'Herbie' Grooms, 'Snoozer' Doust, 'Swoon Crooner' Sheedy, 'Oily-Tongue' Larkins and 'Watering' Mellon.

●

A surprise visit to the troops by General Douglas Mac-Arthur on 5 July 1943 failed to raise their spirits. From all reports the Supreme Commander wandered around the camps and straight out again, surrounded by a bevy of photographers, one of whom allegedly fell over a stump as he walked backwards in front of the pipe-smoking general.

At precisely the time when privates Livingston and Oxman were returned to camp, the commanding officers were cracking down on a perceived lack of discipline.

'Attention is directed to the fact that the seriousness of the offence of absence without leave is not properly appreciated. And that the commission of the offence has become very prevalent. From the date of this order personnel committing an offence of absence without leave of any duration are liable to committal to trial by court martial.' Good timing, boys. A further point was hammered home to the troops in Queensland. 'A soldier is AWL when he is away from the place where his duty requires him to be.' This is a telling statement when considered in the context of Stanley Livingston's case. Where exactly did his duty lie? Would the war be lost without him, or would his sister have more to lose from his absence? Did he have a case to plead? Would it wash at a military court martial?

•

While awaiting a date for his court martial, Stanley was warmly welcomed by his compatriots, although the reunion was to be short-lived. Less than twenty-four hours after arriving at camp he received another letter from home: Lilly Livingston had suffered a further breakdown and was asking for him. Stan's duty was clear, he didn't think twice; nor did Gordon Oxman, and at 0645 on 3 May, just forty-eight hours after arriving at Python Ridge, the pair were again declared AWL.

It was not difficult to escape from the isolated camp, yet AWLs were rare in the tropics. They soon found out why. Once beyond the confines of the camp gates the going was tough, and these two were not trained for tropical jungle conditions. While it was a clear day, recent heavy rain and flooding meant the ground was waterlogged, and it was a long walk back to Tramway Street.

Queensland railways were employed extensively during the war years, with steam trains hauling men and equipment across the state. Jumping a train was hazardous in the best of conditions, but running beside one and launching one's body onto the boxcar of a steaming goods train in the middle of a rain-soaked mountainous jungle can present additional problems. After many foiled attempts, Gordon managed to grab a sliding door and scramble aboard one of the wooden boxcars. Stanley, however, was struggling to make the jump, and a dozen carriages passed before he made a successful attempt and rolled into a car. At least both men were on the same train, even though they had no idea where they were headed.

When Pte Livingston turned around to survey the interior of the boxcar, he was shocked to find he was face to face with a fully striped battalion sergeant. His heart sank, until it became clear that the sergeant hunched in a corner of the car was also AWL, and the pair shared tobacco and warm beer all the way to the border and beyond. When the train terminated in country New South Wales, Gordon was taken aback to see Stanley approaching in the company of a sergeant, but with the aid of their higher ranking companion it wasn't long before all three made it safely to their loved ones in Sydney. Lilly perked up immediately, and the boys went about the business of minding their own business and keeping their heads low.

A month later they were still in Sydney. By mid 1943, the Japanese threat was acknowledged as passed when John Curtin announced his future strategy for the Pacific theatre: 'We have established that the enemy cannot occupy this country or any appreciable part of it.' Curtin went on to say that the second phase of the Pacific war was going to be fairly long and he was determined not to make 'a bloody business of it', the idea being to attack the enemy from the air rather than 'throwing masses of infantry against them'. The news no doubt filled Stanley with a mixture of dread and reassurance. If he were to return to his unit he could expect a long campaign to come, but at least it would not be like El Alamein. Or so he hoped as he and Gordon pondered the prospects of returning to camp.

Wednesday, 2 June 1943 was Stanley Livingston's twenty-fifth birthday. The headline in *The Sydney Morning Herald* that day was '67,191 Australian Casualties of War'. So far the tally was 10,253 killed, 24,303 wounded, 10,721 prisoners of war and 21,914 missing. Stanley may have wondered if he and Gordon were included in the missing list. There were photos of AIF soldiers training for rigorous jungle warfare in the Atherton Tablelands. They didn't look too comfortable. Below was an article warning that while victory was in sight in Europe, the Pacific outlook was 'dark and full of menace', with further warning of a major attack by the Japanese at any moment. Propaganda perhaps, but it still sent a chill. A more preferable chill for the birthday boy this winter would be a spot of ice-skating at the 'Glaciarium' ice rink at Railway Square, where skaters circled a rink enclosed by poorly rendered murals of vast mountainous ridges. Come nightfall, Stanley made his way to George Street for 'the jolliest dance in town' at the Good Companions Natation Ballroom next to the GPO. It promised a swing band and plenty of partners. Stanley didn't need one—he had Evelyn by his side as they foxtrotted the night away. He would have wanted to kick on, but Evelyn had to get home. She had an early start at work in the morning.

# 8

## *Evelyn's war*

'Another fellow put the drill through my finger, silly
bugger. They all wanted to rush me off to hospital to
get a tetanus needle. I didn't want it. I was alright.'

*Evelyn Lonsdale*

John Curtin announced the compulsory call-up of women
on the night of 26 January 1943 after the response to voluntary recruitment had not met with demand. Indelicate
placement of their recruitment campaign advertisements
may not have helped the cause. Next to an ad for De
Witt's Antacid Powder ('A Friend In Need For Flatulence'),
an April issue of the *Australian Women's Weekly* featured an
ad bearing an image of a tin-hatted digger overlooking a
housewife polishing a table.

Come on housewife, Take a 'VICTORY JOB'. You'll find
it no harder than your house jobs. Easier perhaps. In fact
many war production factories, with their spic-and-span
canteens, bright music and carefully planned rest breaks

are more fun to work in than any house. Come in and have a chat with another woman at your nearest National Service Office. She'll understand how you feel if you've never gone out on a job before. Come on. Change your job for him—won't you?

With a large percentage of males removed from the workforce, and the pool of unemployed men from the depression years now employed, work opportunities for women expanded during the war years. After the bombing of Darwin, positions opened for women in new munitions factories. However, conditions were often not pleasant, with rest breaks, bright music and fun overshadowed by the health dangers common to munitions factories. To get through the day, many women workers became reliant on analgesics to relieve headaches caused by the use of nitrates in the manufacture of munitions. It was a case of a cup of tea, a Bex and then back to the production line. The image presented of triumphant, healthy, happy, shackle-breaking women labouring through the war years is in stark contrast to the reality. Much of the work was simply monotonous, and of major concern was the lack of childcare facilities. The powers-that-be hadn't thought it through, the government and their advisers being mostly males. The authorities couldn't seem to grasp the connection between the practicalities of feeding a growing family, caring for ageing parents, and holding down a job.

For those who did answer their country's call, ingrained prejudices persisted. The children of working women, dubbed latchkey kids, were often singled out as responsible for the rise in juvenile delinquency, and the absent mothers copped the blame, scapegoats for a lack of support and understanding from the authorities. While the demands of work were high, women's pay rates never quite met those of the male populations. There were exceptions: bus 'conductresses' were paid the male wage, but behind this apparently forward-thinking decision lurked an ulterior motive. The unions were worried that come war's end, if the women wished to continue working for a lower rate, employers might choose them over men. The unions wanted their members back when peace came, and at full pay.

Younger women were also coming under attack from members of a bygone generation who were concerned about the moral decline they perceived among the carefree women who strolled around arm in arm with foreigners in regimental regalia. Some in positions of authority agreed. On 25 February 1943 a headline in the Melbourne *Sun* declared 'Deputy Premier alarmed at Moral Drift'. The deputy premier of Victoria, Albert Eli Lind, called for the closing of hotels on Saturday afternoons. He warned that: 'Associated with men under the influence of drink who have been guzzling and should have been protected from getting more—I am referring to men in uniform—you will find girls of tender years. I am alarmed at the way in which we are drifting—to see these girls in the arms of men they have, perhaps, never seen before.' And by inference, we are led to conclude, would never see again.

An article in *The Sydney Morning Herald* on Saturday 6 November complained of scenes of intoxication and unseemly behaviour amid the sordid city nightlife. Under the headline 'A Disgrace to Sydney', the writer makes the following claim:

> Apart from the discredit they bring to the city and the offence they give to decent citizens, it is alarming that drunkenness and immorality should be so rife among adolescent girls and young women who are not only sowing an imminent crop of misery for themselves but jeopardising their whole future as potential wives and mothers. They are to be observed in the company of Servicemen at all hours of the night, and, according to police reports, they represent a large proportion of those who frequent shady cabarets and residentials . . . It is the 'amateurs', not the 'professionals'—to use the accepted police terms—who constitute the grave and growing danger to our social standards and to the future of our race.

This word jockey appears to be riding an extremely high horse. He gallops on: 'These [women], flattered by the attentions and money lavished upon them by men in uniform, bent only upon having a "good time," and more often than not the victims of parental neglect or indifference, have now attained numbers which appal all those who know the facts.' And he wasn't about to stop there. Perhaps they should have considered rationing printer's ink.

It is not the least of the evils of war that it inevitably induces among the less stable elements of the population a loosening of morals and the other social restraints which apply in normal times. Work and cash are plentiful, servicemen are constantly in search of female companions to beguile their hours on furlough, and unscrupulous panders make profits from providing opportunities for sordid immorality or from the sale of black-market liquor, or from both. The State Government must be given credit for some checks to the sly grog trade in the metropolitan area and for closing down several of the more sinister night clubs.

Why do I get the impression this reporter would like nothing more than a schooner of sly grog and a night out at Club Sinister? But wait, there's more. 'That only an insignificant proportion of these miscreants is apprehended is proved by the facility with which their noxious wares can be purchased and by the squalid exhibitions of drinking to be seen nightly in parks, streets, and doorways.' He certainly seems to have done his homework.

We can safely assume that these lusty trumpetings of moral decay were somewhat overstated. Yet there was no doubt that ample opportunity for sexual misdemeanours was available. Armed with accents, cigarettes and confidence, the American boys were fond of giving flowers to the local women, orchids especially, as well as their main bait, nylon stockings. Silk stockings were impossible to come by in wartime, and the girls resorted to drawing fake seams down the back of their bare calves with a black eyebrow pencil. It took a steady hand and a lot of patience to venture out in a pair of fishnets in those days.

Evelyn and her sister Dot went through quite a few eyebrow pencils. Dot remembers a date with an American serviceman named Horace.

> I wouldn't be surprised if Horace was married or had a girl at home . . . He just asked me because there was an American Ball on in Redfern and he wanted a partner. He gave me this great big posy. I couldn't find a spot to put it on my dress. When we came out to go home, there was all these boys from Redfern, 'Ah, we'll get you, Yank,' and Horace said to me, 'Quick, come on, let's run.' So we did. Every time he came into port he'd call me up, just for company.

While the Americans showered the local girls with chocolates and stockings, on a night out with a local boy you'd be lucky to get a crayon and a Polly Waffle. Dot also recalls a night out with Henry, a Mascot boy who kicked things off by presenting her with a packet of liquorice allsorts before eating the lot of them at the pictures. The Americans were ahead of the game—dating was part of their culture. They knew all the tricks: bring a gift, be attentive and appear to care. Appearances might have been deceiving but the local women didn't mind—they weren't used to being attended to. Many suspected it was all show. One woman remarked,

'I'm sure they could forget a girl as quickly as anyone else. But they seemed different; they seemed to put a higher value on the relationship. They seemed to like women's company more than Australian men did.'

All this American insincerity was a welcome contrast to the mundane and awkward manner of the local boys. As the Americans well knew, confidence is everything. In fact, many were overconfident. However, unwanted advances were stopped in their tracks. Young Australian women wore hatpins in those days and most weren't afraid to use them when necessary. The local women also had their own bait when it came to attracting the Americans. If you mixed two tablespoons of golden syrup with a tablespoon each of honey, lemon juice, and boiling water, stirred well and served hot, you would have created the perfect lure for tempting an American soldier: homemade Australian maple syrup. Some girls took advantage of the Americans' generosity on dates by reselling the prized orchids to florists the next morning at half the retail price.

In Melbourne, the young Toni 'Lolly-Legs' Lamond passed Flinders Street Station, the main Melbourne meeting place, on her way to evening dancing lessons. 'I very much took notice of the pretty girls, with flowers in their hair. They were there to meet the American soldiers, sailors and airmen. I was very interested in how they wore their hair—like Betty Grable, who was just making her name. When I was fourteen, Max Reddy [Toni's step-father] was in a military concert party which was going into the jungles of New Guinea, dangerous places like that.' He was based at Pagewood in Sydney, and because he was going to be there for a few months, Toni's mother Stella locked up the flat and moved the family to a room in Kellett Street in Sydney's Kings Cross. 'I was thrilled. I could walk around the corner, and be right there in the middle of the Cross, and see the Yanks with pretty girls (with flowers in their hair) by the hundreds, while I stood outside the milk bar listening to the jukebox. Wishing I was older!'

●

While Stanley had his days free, Evelyn was gainfully employed. Having been called up, she was in the army now. The first stage of recruitment was restricted to women aged eighteen to twenty-one. Evelyn Lonsdale was twenty-one and single and lived very close to Sydney Airport. Previously, when she wasn't helping her mother out in the shop she'd been working at William R. Warner and Co. at 508 Riley Street, Surry Hills, with her friends Heather and Joyce. 'It was like a ballot,' Evelyn recalled fifty years later, of the recruitment process. 'We all got a shock, you know, and I got my letter last. Heather and Joyce got theirs first, and off they went. And then I got one. I had to give the letter to a person in town, they had to sign it and then they sent me out to the aerodrome. The three of us finished up at the aerodrome.' Evelyn was to be trained as a riveter at Sydney Airport.

Her wartime work experience was not commensurate with that of the girls in the munitions factories. The government had targeted intelligent women in particular, and Evelyn had outshone every other student at Mascot Primary School, receiving a scholarship to attend a private girls school in the city. She'd seized the opportunity, devouring books, learning languages and gaining the respect of her teachers. It seemed there was nothing at which she didn't excel. Music was her great love, and the piano her instrument of choice. Her skills on the piano were not so much in demand when it came to wartime occupations, but her grasp of mathematics qualified her for a position making tools for and repairing military aircraft. Evelyn talked with great fondness of her days riveting bombers in the hangars at Mascot, a duty she found far from challenging.

I had a man on one side of the wing and I was on the other; I couldn't see him, all I could do was hear him. You had to be very careful, and I had the rivet gun—you had to go gently, so you didn't hurt the aluminium of the plane. But that was all there was to it. Then when he'd done a wing, that'd be it for the next few hours. Go and get lost. And I was getting men's wages, I couldn't believe it. That was an easy place, you'd sneak out and go to the canteen and have a coffee. You did so much and no more. We used to go outside and sit in the sun, and the air force boys would come out and sit with us, and we'd all be sitting there having a party. I could never figure it out. I did so little. And I used to think, is this how men earn their money? You know, I'd been working hard at the pharmaceutical company, and I just couldn't believe it.

A few adventurous women had already contributed to the history of the airport. In the 1920s, aviation was predominantly a male occupation; not being wage-earners, most women could never afford flying lessons. The Australian Aero Club eventually opened its doors to women in 1926, and in 1927 Millicent Bryant entered the domain after becoming the first woman in Australia to obtain a pilot's licence, soon to be followed by Margaret Reardon and Evelyn Follett. But it was the arrival of Englishwoman Amy Johnson at Mascot in 1930 in her 'Jason' Gipsy Moth that put paid to any notions that a woman was less of a flyer than a man. She'd travelled alone all the way from the United Kingdom. This opened the door for local girl Nancy Bird, who learned the ropes at the recently opened Kingsford Smith Flying School in 1933. The immaculately coiffed Smithy was not initially keen on the idea of female pilots, but the school needed both pupils and money, and he soon realised Nancy Bird was more than up to the task. Nancy had been saving her own pennies, and when she turned nineteen she bought herself a second-hand Gipsy Moth and set off joyriding around New South Wales. Nancy later secured a job at the airport cleaning spark plugs on Smithy's *Southern Cross*. During World War II she trained other young women hired to lend support to the Royal Australian Air Force. I have no idea if Evelyn was among her students.

With so many men out of the picture, women became more reliant on each other. Australia is yet to invent a term for the female equivalent of mateship, but during those years, women, children, single girls and grandmothers worked together to keep their families and the economy afloat. The excitements of the social scene were restricted mainly to young inner-city girls; for others it was a hard slog. For most, the war at home was a time of hardship and insecurity, and the sooner the show ended the better.

# 9

## *Run for your death*

Chico:    Hey, wait, wait. What does this say here, this
thing here?

Groucho: It's all right. That's in every contract. That's
what they call a sanity clause.

Chico:    You can't fool me. There ain't no Sanity Clause.

*The Marx Brothers,* A Night at the Opera

Undercover and unsung, the two deserters were not alone in absenting themselves without leave. Not just in this war—the practice is ancient. As long as men have been waging war, men have been actively avoiding it. The penalties could be harsh, depending not just on the nature and length of absence but on geography. Under Australian law the maximum sentence for desertion among soldiers serving in World War I was a term of imprisonment, whereas British, Canadian and New Zealand deserters could be shot for the offence. The British were not too happy with the leniency shown by Australian authorities and believed that in the interests of army discipline and equity, AIF deserters should be put down. Prime Minister Billy Hughes defied any such pressure from the British, well aware of the damage such an unpopular move might do to his reputation and his party's. Australia stuck to its guns, and refused to fire those guns against their own. The British were certainly not swayed by our decision. The shadow of such brutal punishment had some British soldiers in World War I choosing to relieve the pressure of front-line service by shooting themselves instead of the enemy. On-the-spot court martials were held at medical units as wounded men suspected of self-harm were evacuated from battle. There was little sympathy for the wounded, who were interrogated as they lay on stretchers.

By the close of World War I, the British had executed over three hundred of their own men. To add salt to these wounds, the firing squads that carried out the punishments were usually chosen from the men's own unit. Desertion is a flexible term—it can be interpreted as merely malingering, or the more serious activity of self-inflicted wounding. However, the fatal decision was not to just absent yourself without official leave, but to have no intention of returning at all.

Britain's high command in World War I were convinced that harsh measures such as these were the perfect deterrent for any lack of self-restraint in the ranks. Fear cultivated discipline. Yet to this day no Australian serviceman has ever been executed for any military offence, under our very own 'No Death' clause.

There were, of course, the famous executions of Breaker Morant and P.J. Handcock in the Boer War, but these were at the hands of the British. Australian mythical hero worship aside, the real Ed Murrant was little more than a slaughterer of innocents, including one twelve-year-old boy. There is a tradition in this country of glorifying low-life killers and con men: we revere the likes of Ned Kelly and Breaker Morant. This peculiar cultural compulsion perhaps stems from a fascination with the notion of the little battler upholding justice on his own terms. Or could it be the old chestnut of our shared convict past? It does seem rather odd that invariably, when an Australian delves into their past and uncovers no convict ancestor, it is of great disappointment to them.

In Australia, at least, thanks to the 'No Death' clause, we most certainly did believe in a sanity clause. Sanity almost prevailed in the United States: during World War II 21,049 soldiers were charged with desertion, and forty-nine of those were sentenced to death, but only one achieved that end. The case of Pte Eddie Slovik is a famous one.

By the time he was twenty-two, Slovik, a Polish-American resident of Detroit, had spent more than four years in prison for petty crimes ranging from drunkenness to disturbing the peace. He was paroled in November 1943, and before year's end he had married. For once, things were looking up in the life of Eddie Slovik. Just before his first wedding anniversary he was conscripted and sent to France. The army needed as many bodies as possible, preferably young and alive, and prison sentences were no hindrance. Eddie wasn't happy. While marching in to his unit an artillery attack sent Eddie running for cover, and he didn't stop. Separated from his unit, he joined a Canadian one nearby and huddled down in a rear position with them for the next six weeks. No charges were laid for this misdemeanour. But this slice of active service was about as much as Pte Slovik was prepared to take and he made it perfectly clear that this was the case. He admitted to a superior officer that he was scared to death and requested that he be placed in the rear. He also asserted that if the officer didn't grant this request he'd run away. Eddie then asked if that might be considered desertion. The answer was a resounding 'yes' and his request was abruptly refused. Eddie then informed a Military Police officer of his intention to desert; this time he went one step further and put it in writing. He was advised that if he destroyed the note he would suffer no consequences. But fear, coupled with a longing for the woman he loved, meant Eddie not only refused to comply, he also wrote another note, which would turn out to be his death warrant.

He had inadvertently made quite clear to all that he was completely aware of the consequences of his actions. Slovik wasn't worried—it never occurred to him that his complaints would lead to him facing a firing squad, and he had no fear of prison. Technically Slovik was not a deserter, more a man with intent to desert, but it was enough for the US Army to decide to make an example of him. Slovik was just what the military needed: a deterrent. This obscure private was killed even though his actions had endangered no-one. Slovik was guilty of blatant honesty. The argument went that he would have been a liability on the front lines; his argument was that he wanted nothing to do with those front lines. Despite pleas from his wife, it would be forty-two years before his remains were allowed back into America, by which time Mrs Slovik was dead.

While the USA only managed one execution, the Germans eliminated thousands of men for desertion during World War II. Not to be outdone, the Russians chose on-the-spot execution for anyone who turned their back to the front.

Another threat to maintaining good order in the ranks was the condition that came to be known during World War I as shell shock. Those in the British higher ranks thought it a disciplinary matter rather than a medical one. The solution? More discipline. The proposed treatment was to return the shell-shocked to the front lines as swiftly as was possible. This belief was shared by leading military figures on both sides, with the result that on the front lines shell-shocked soldiers found they were face to face with opposing shell-shocked soldiers. For some reason the Irish were singled out as particularly susceptible to the condition. The Irish were considered to be 'predisposed to lunacy' and 'emotional', and therefore of great danger to discipline. Consequently, they were appraised as suitable firing-squad material. While officials denied that the phenomenon was at all medical in nature, there remained concern that shell shock was contagious. There was a fear that whole units would collapse under the influence of lunatic shell-shocked Irishmen running from battle. A chap of high standing at the time, one Lord Gort, made his feelings known on the matter. 'I think "shell-shock," like measles, is so infectious that you cannot afford to run risks with it at all and in war the individual is of small account.'

There were two categories of shell shock: commotional and emotional. Commotional meant the result of a commotion, like being blown up. Emotional was the fear of being blown up. Either way, shell-shocked men were considered worthless and disposable, which placed them right in the firing line for execution. The renowned psychiatrist W.H.R. Rivers described shell shock as the result of the repression of one's natural instinct; that is, to flee the battlefield. I wonder how long it took W.H.R. to figure that one out. Military historian Colonel Henderson, writing at the turn of the nineteenth century, put it a little more emotively. 'The truth is, when bullets are whacking against tree trunks and solid shot are cracking skulls like egg shells, the consuming passion in the heart of the average man is to get out of the way.' You don't need to read Freud to agree with the colonel. Any soldier appealing for leniency by complaining of shell shock had their pleas interpreted as an admission of their lack of discipline, and therefore, in the minds of their superiors, they were expendable.

The solution? Shoot them. There would be no reprieve for those of a nervous disposition, especially a nervous Irish one.

●

By the outbreak of World War II the British had called a ceasefire on their own troops and focused their aim on the enemy. The term 'shell shock' was officially replaced by 'battle fatigue', which was eventually to evolve into 'post-traumatic stress disorder'. The medical profession at the time covered a lot of bases with the term 'anxiety state'. The army felt they could dumb this term down a touch more, declaring that any soldier removed by stretcher from active service after exposure to prolonged and unrelenting bombardment by other persons exposed to prolonged and unrelenting bombardment be marked NYDN—Not Yet Diagnosed Nervous. The soldiers themselves had their own name for it: shell-happy. Stage fright is the term used in my own profession, often the result of a relentless bombardment of abuse from aggressive intoxicated hecklers. Audiences have their own term for the condition: NYDF—Not Yet Diagnosed Funny.

Whatever name you gave it, no soldier was immune. Pte Stanley Livingston was no exception. According to family legend, at some stage Stanley had been taken from the line, not yet diagnosed nervous, and hospitalised for three weeks before being sent back to the front. Where this occurred is unclear, and whether it was commotional or emotional I'll never know. There is no report in the records of Stanley being evacuated in the Middle East. For Pte Livingston, the show that must not go on was obviously yet to open.

# 10

## *Gaps in the ranks*

'I was court-martialled in my absence, and sentenced to death in my absence, so I said they could shoot me in my absence.'

*Thomas Hardy*

For those Australian soldiers who prolonged their leave, the most obvious handicap was the immediate suspension of payments. Many families were dependent on the soldier's pay to supplement their income. For some it was their only source of revenue. Hundreds of other men were wrongly reported AWL, leaving wives and children with no source of income, and not a small amount of shame. Such was the situation for Pte Fullarton, a married soldier with a clean record after thirteen years of military service in both wars when he arrived home in Melbourne for two days' leave. Mrs Fullarton did not appear happy to see him. When she curtly inquired about life in the training camps in Queensland, Pte Fullarton said it was going OK. Mrs Fullarton was not OK with his OK, calling him a liar and suggesting he head straight back to the arms of the woman he had been seeing during his two-month AWL. The poor woman had been stewing for some time. The situation had come to a head when their daughter had gone to the post office to pick up his allotment as usual, only to be advised there would be no money for Mrs Fullarton. Without money and assuming she was also without a husband, Mrs Fullarton had suffered a heart attack. The private was horrified—he had no explanation for the cessation of his pay. When he tried to plead his case, his wife presented her trump card. She produced an official statement from the accounts department charging that her man had been AWL, and ordered her husband out of the house. With that, Pte Fullarton left the premises, but not to return to any mystery woman. He went straight to the accounts department and made his complaint heard. It was soon established that Fullarton had never left his unit. He returned home, but not without arming himself with an official memo from the office proving his innocence. Mrs Fullarton made a complete recovery, and so did the marriage.

For bona fide AWLs, it wasn't too difficult to obtain work in the country, as the rural industry was exempt from the necessity of obtaining labour through the National Service Office. Under the heading 'Employment of Deserters and AWL Personnel', a document marked 'secret' admitted to the ease with which men absent without leave could gain legal employment and avoid apprehension. The AWL men were not asked for identity cards, and civilians were shielding them.

While on official leave, Pte Tom Klein was helping out on the family farm west of the Great Dividing Range, near Parkes in NSW, when his father came down with kidney stones. Not wanting to leave his younger brother alone in charge of the farm, Tom applied for an extension of leave to complete the harvest. He needed a doctor's certificate and the authority of Manpower to further his application. This was then rejected. Tom was ordered to return to camp in fourteen days, at the end of his official leave. His elder brother Alan was home on leave for two days, but Alan was army through and through and refused to join his brother and remain home until the harvest was done. After the two weeks had passed, Tom stayed on the farm and lived in fear of the Military Police arresting him. He was well aware that if he were to remain absent without leave for more than twenty-one days he would be charged with desertion. On day twenty of his absence, after a hard day carting and loading 730 bags of wheat onto trucks, Tom needed to be back in camp for the 8 a.m. roll call the next day to avoid a charge of desertion. He left on a mail train from Parkes, but the line was washed away by a severe storm and another train took him via Narromine, Dubbo and Orange. He eventually reached Granville, then changed trains to Liverpool, walked to the Moorbank camp and reported to the warrant officer there at 1.30 p.m. the next day. He was immediately charged with AWL and confined to barracks.

Tom, being human, assumed the powers-that-be would be sympathetic to his case.

A week later he hit a wall—Major Wall, with a face like granite, who didn't wait for any explanations and accused Tom of being an irresponsible young person, telling him that any such person who 'defies his commanding officer's orders, and treats the army with contempt, deserves the highest penalty, not only to teach you a lesson, but also any other spirited trooper'. Tom wasn't a happy spirited trooper; he snapped at Wall, who snapped back, 'Will you be tried by me, or a court martial?' Tom chose a court martial. Wall turned to his aide and said, 'Stamp his papers deserter.'

●

While in the confines of close arrest after their recent AWL, Stanley and Gordon would have found themselves among friends. Quite a few of the boys from the 2/17th Battalion didn't make it back to camp until the winter of 1943. Pte Alfred Henry Harrison was a Roman Catholic born in the same year as Stanley, and judging from the somewhat undisciplined handwriting on his attestation form, Alfred's enlistment had most probably been assisted by generous amounts of alcohol. After enlisting at the same time as Stanley, Alfred left for the Middle East in late 1940, contracted a bad dose of the mumps on arrival, then spent eight months in Tobruk, whereupon he was wounded in action but stayed on with his unit. He then copped a stray shrapnel blast, leaving him with first-degree burns to the right leg and right elbow.

Pte Harrison arrived back in Australia on 27 February 1943, the same day as Stanley, took his Liddington leave and didn't return to camp until 11 June. Alfred was not a newcomer to AWL. He had eight charges to his credit, mostly small offences, a day off here and there, and after what he had been through, surely he had earned the right to take the odd break. For his latest absence he was court-martialled on 19 July, found guilty and sentenced to six months' detention. It would appear Pte Harrison was not comfortable in the detention centre, and by the end of August he was AWL again. This time he made it back by 2 October 1943, just in time to embark for Port Moresby. He was home again for Christmas, and that's where he stayed, remaining AWL from 25 December 1943 until his arrest on 22 May 1944. He escaped from custody three more times between June and October. He had proved himself a loyal soldier in the battles of the Middle East—the man was no coward, so surely he had a reasonable excuse?

In his defence, Harrison told the court:

In civilian life I am a farmer. It is a rented farm and it belongs to my parents. I have a brother and two sisters. My brother is eighteen. He was in the army but he is discharged now. My father is dead. Prior to his death he was seriously ill for a long period. During the last two years he has been ill at different times over that period for about twelve months. With my brother in the army that left my mother and two sisters to run the farm and one of the sisters is going to school. My mother and sister had applied for help to run the farm but they could not get it. It is a dairy farm with about seventy cows. They had to milk the cows on their own. I decided that as they could not get help, it was my duty to go and try and give them a hand.

It would appear that once back on home ground, Pte Harrison was torn between duty to country and duty to family. The end result for Harrison was that on 23 October 1944 he was sentenced to two years' detention to be followed by a dishonourable discharge, which meant that his application for his hard-earned campaign medals for service in Tobruk and the Middle East was refused. In 1949 Harrison was still trying to clear his name. Following a request from the Returned and Services League as to the nature of Harrison's dishonourable discharge, a letter from the central army records states that 'by reason of his numerous Army convictions he is deemed to be incorrigible'.

Pte John 'Jack' Wilson was a 2/17th soldier from B Company who found himself at the centre of a major but little-remembered event that occurred on the home front. The 28-year-old had embarked for the Middle East in October 1940, some eight months before Stanley. Wilson saw action throughout Tobruk as well as El Alamein. He also arrived home on *Aquitania* and took more leave than was on offer. He returned to the camp at Narellan in June after a total of fifty-four days absent without leave. He pleaded guilty and was sentenced to nine months' detention.

Wilson's reputation preceded him. His previous convictions included the following: sentinel sleeping on his post, striking a superior officer, conduct to the prejudice of good order (five times), two previous counts of AWL, failure to appear on parade, drunkenness, disobeying lawful command with wilful defiance, and stealing regimental mess property. All in all he had racked up one hundred and sixteen days' detention while in the Middle East. He had covered most offences, except for one: desertion from battle. Wilson was no shirker on the front line. Lt Col John Broadbent, commanding officer of the 2/17th, would later describe Wilson as 'an audacious soldier, rather than a courageous one', who always required 'a special measure of attention'. It was while serving his detention that Wilson's audacity landed him in a far more serious predicament. On 19 October 1943, after serving four months of his sentence, Wilson was court-martialled again, a new charge added to his list: mutiny.

What would later be referred to as the Grovely Mutiny occurred in E Compound at the 2/1st Australian Detention Barracks at Grovely, in Brisbane, on 7 October 1943. At the time, he still had five months of his sentence to serve. Wilson pleaded guilty to 'Joining a mutiny to resist by combining with other soldiers of the AIF then under sentence, his and their superior officers in the execution of their duty'. He was sentenced to be imprisoned with hard labour for five years and to be discharged with ignominy from His Majesty's Service. Wilson was accused of being one of three ringleaders of the mutiny, along with privates J.J. Derrick and A.L. Chalmers. The charge of mutiny has a ring of notoriety to it, a legendary term, mostly associated with bearded men on boats. But there were no oceans near Grovely. So what exactly did this mutiny entail? Basically the charge against Wilson was: 'When on active service, causing a mutiny in His Majesty's Forces, in that he . . . addressed other soldiers under sentence then assembled, in mutinous language, by advising them not to turn out for parade in consequence of which language they . . . and other soldiers under sentences refused to fall in on parade.'

The mutinous language consisted of two sentences: 'We have complaints, but what guarantees do we get? How do we know that our complaints will be rectified?' Hardly an offence of Fletcher Christian proportions. It appears Pte Wilson was guilty of no more than engaging in a stop-work meeting. He was guilty of speaking up. Audacious? Yes. But mutinous? A cause for ignominious discharge? And just what was Jack Wilson complaining about? In early November 1944, a year after her husband had been sentenced to five years' imprisonment for mutiny, Lily Wilson, wife of Jack and mother to their two children, read that there was to be an inquiry into the case. She wrote to the acting Prime Minister of Australia, F.M. Forde, also Deputy Prime Minister and Minister for the Army at the time, in regard to the severity of her husband's sentence. In the six-page letter, neatly handwritten on lined note-paper, Lily states her case with the utmost courtesy.

Dear Mr Forde,

I hope you will not think it presumptuous of me, for writing you a personal letter, I just want you to under-stand my feelings toward your position, in having my husband's case reopened . . . I want to explain about that bad record, as you described it of my husband. The worst offence being to hit a sergeant, well, I have a letter from him telling me he hoped I would not think that he had made that charge against Jack, as he was a mate of his. He said he had told the two M.P.s to 'skip' the charge, but of course they like to show how important they can be I suppose, anyway, the boy is very sorry that this charge is being held over Jacks head . . . Mr Forde, if you could just talk to my husband for ten minutes, you would have the faith in him that I have, of course I know you are much too busy to bother over just one soldier, but I think if I made that plea to our King, to just give the minutes of his time to a soldier who had fought for him and been recommended and done numerous other things that have never been in the papers he would answer my request, I know he would. Jack is very popular . . . I have heard the following phrase dozens of times since the boys returned from the Middle East; 'Wilson, is not just one soldier, he is eight rolled into one, the gamest bloke that ever went onto a battlefield.' Referring back to those convictions, one was having a button on the tunic undone, and simple little things like that ... I know the army has to be severe, and discipline maintained but, have you ever been late at the office on unimportant days ...

Lily maintains his earlier two charges for AWL were nothing more than being late for roll call and underscores his courage on the battlefield. She argues that the nine-month detention for his AWL on the home front was not just, that he was never AWL to start with.

Do you think they deserve detention after what they have suffered, it was reading this mornings paper and feeling for the boys, that I suddenly realised my husband has gone through some hell & suffering too, that I there upon sat down to write to you. Mr Forde, when the case reopens, I want you to know, that we all have the highest admiration and esteem for you, and do not hold you responsible for what has happened to Jack. I have in fact cut your photo out of the paper to paste with one of your letters in my scrap book of cuttings about the case, which I am keeping for my two sons benefit so that some day they may read about what their father did, it may discourage them to enlist in any further wars we have, I pray we do not, but if democracy is the way my husband was treated after fighting for it, well we will always have wars. I do hope my letter hasn't bored you ... I felt I had to sit down and let some of it out on paper. I had once considered being a journalist, but I got married instead.

Lily, the ideal of the devoted wife, paints a very different picture of the audacious private, and F.M. Forde responded with sympathy for Wilson's plight. On 21 November he replied to Lily Wilson:

> The circumstances which have caused you to commun-
> icate with me are very much regretted. You will, no
> doubt, have read a statement in the press to the effect
> that I have arranged for the appointment of a Judge of
> the Supreme Court of South Australia, Mr Justice G.S.
> Reed, to conduct an inquiry into the case.

*The Canberra Times* announced on Wednesday 29 November that 'The enquiry into the case of Private Jack Wilson, who was sentenced to five years imprisonment for mutiny at Grovely detention camp, will commence in Sydney today'. On 23 December the same newspaper, reporting on the inquiry, revealed that Pte Wilson's brigadier commander described Wilson as a brave man under fire who did his duty well. But Lt Col Noel William Simpson was not so kind. He had recommended Wilson be discharged on the grounds that the private was an inefficient soldier of no value to the army or the country in general. So far the score was Wilson 1, Army 1.

The inquiry resumed in the new year with the Melbourne *Argus* reporting on 17 January 1945 that Wilson had stated at the inquiry that on the night he began his detention, the staff of Grovely detention camp were obviously half-drunk and roaring like maniacs. He denied all charges of promoting trouble or inciting others. He stated that he, J.J. Derrick and A.L. Chalmers were thrown into a six-by-eight-foot verminous wooden cell, with no straw in their palliasses. He said he knew trouble was brewing before the alleged mutiny but he kept his head down. Wilson 2, Army 1.

The score went up again on 20 January when *The Canberra Times* reported that ten of the Grovely staff were known to inmates as 'the Bloodhounds of Jerusalem' and that soldiers at Grovely learned early not to complain. The plot thickened when *The Argus* picked up the story on the twenty-third with reports of independent allegations of persecution by the guards. Leslie Milton Giles, who had been detained at Grovely for 147 days, made the most startling allegation. He stated that when thirty-nine members of the 9th Division arrived in the camp to serve their sentences, the staff came out of the sergeants' mess roaring and screaming, and repeating over and over that they hated the 9th Division. Were the conscripted guards jealous of the fierce fighting these men had seen? Having never seen action overseas themselves, were their actions the result of resentment or shame? Or were they just permanently drunk?

Giles further stated that when the prisoners left the trucks the guards came at them, punching and bashing them and pushing them forcefully over barbed wire.

Anyone who said they returned to Australia on *Aquitania* was knocked to the ground and kicked. Grovely detention camp was certainly not the place Stanley Livingston would wish to wind up after his court martial. There were further reports that prisoners were stripped naked and forced to stand for hours under the shower in a form of vertical waterboarding predating Guantanamo. Guns were fired towards prisoners, and everything was done to intimidate them. Another ex-serviceman, Jack Bright, said the guards did their best to make the camp a hell on earth for those under sentence. While the guards gloated, the prisoners had to live in vermin-infested cells, and the conditions were unsanitary and deplorable.

The tables were turning in the Army vs Wilson case as the press revealed more of the realities of life in the Grovely camp. Word even spread to Grovely itself. On 26 March *The Sydney Morning Herald* reported another uprising by soldiers detained at Grovely. A mass escape attempt resulted in the facility being set on fire. The same article reveals that as a result of Justice Reed's interim report, Pte J. Wilson, Pte J.J. Derrick and Pte A.L. Chalmers had been released from gaol on 4 March after serving two years of a five-year sentence. Justice Reed found that they had not been the ringleaders of a mutiny. In December 1945, *The Canberra Times* reported that the Minister for the Army, Mr Forde, had not yet acted upon a recommendation that the three servicemen implicated in the Grovely mutiny should be given honourable discharges. The article further attests that the men were having difficulty in civilian life because they could not produce an honourable discharge, and were denied rehabilitation rights and gratuities and their children were denied dependants benefits.

Meanwhile, Lily continued her correspondence with Forde. She was not one to give up easily. In *The Sydney Morning Herald* on 23 March 1946 there appears a tiny article of just one paragraph, reporting that the sentences of discharge with ignominy for privates Wilson, Derrick and Chalmers for their part in the mutiny at Grovely had been revoked. The men would now be merely discharged. It had been quite a battle for the merely discharged Pte Wilson. Still, his kids got a great scrapbook out of it.

# 11

## *Absent friends*

'Similar to the military's complete disdain for any individual characteristics is its refusal to recognize the supremacy of a man's duty to his family.'

*Robert Fantina*

Contact between the four companies within the battalion was common. The monotony of daily life for the average soldier meant there was plenty of time for making friends. And on the battlefield, you needed as many friends as you could get. Relationships forged in battle conditions were magnified by the absence of family and friends. In many cases these relationships surpassed those at home. Independence became dependence, and on the front line your life depended on those by your side. Individual survival was contingent on the group's effort, and the smaller the unit, the stronger the bonds. The notion of mateship in this instance is peculiar to the conditions, and has no equivalent in ordinary civilian life.

Desertion from the field of battle was extremely rare

among Australian soldiers in general, and although a frequent and generally minor offence, going AWL away from the front line was also not the regular practice of the majority. Most men of the 2/17th returned to camp after Liddington leave in early 1943. This is not to imply they were indifferent to family strife; leaving their family for a second time would have been heart-rending. Many were no doubt satisfied their families could cope well enough without them. The evidence given at court martials by the men of the 2/17th who did absent themselves shows that in most cases they did so because their loved ones were struggling. Many women were reliant on husbands and sons to send portions of their meagre wage. It is small wonder that once out of the immediate line of fire and back on home turf, those men with families hit hardest by the effects of war saw where their duty lay and acted upon it. Leaving a gap in the ranks for any considerable amount of time generally meant something was seriously amiss in the private lives of these privates.

•

James Arthur Andrew Ellicombe was a B Company private in the 2/17th who failed to make his presence felt after Liddington leave. It was mid May when he arrived back in camp, where his court martial was scheduled for the twenty-sixth. In his defence, Pte Ellicombe stated that he'd received word that his mother had been taken ill, and on returning home he found out that she had broken down after his younger brother, also in the army, returned to camp from his leave. Two of his superior officers were called to give a character witness and both spoke well of him, one nominating Pte Ellicombe as a courageous soldier whose conduct left nothing to be desired. This didn't help his cause. He was sentenced to suffer field punishment for ninety days and forfeit ordinary pay for the same period.

With both her boys back in camp, Mrs Ellicombe didn't fare too well either: she ended up an inmate of the Rachel Forster Hospital in Redfern. She was in good hands. This hospital combined medical care with intensive family counseling for women, having being founded in the 1920s by six women who were forced to complete their medical training overseas, after it was deemed improper for the women to treat patients in a public hospital.

Another 2/17th private, Sydney Vivian Edward Quillan, was court-martialled on 31 May after overstaying his leave for less than a week, yet he received the same punishment as Ellicombe: ninety days' field punishment and forfeit of pay. His story was much the same. While he was on Liddington leave his mother had become seriously ill and was on the verge of a nervous breakdown. He stated to the court, 'I stayed on longer than the leave I was given hoping she would improve, but she didn't.' The harsh penalty may or may not have had to do with half a dozen previous AWL offences.

Pte Percy Field also failed to return from leave; he

went missing for a month and a half. At his court martial on 8 June he had nothing to say in his defence, so one can only speculate that Mrs Field was doing just fine. The only word Percy said during the trial was 'Guilty', and then he began his sixty days of field punishment. In regard to being punished in the field, the men could be relieved they weren't serving in World War I under British command. In that conflict, Field Punishment Number One was a severe disciplinary measure often handed out for nothing more than a bout of drunkenness. The soldier was bound to a fixed object, whatever was handy—a pole, a gun wheel—and left there for a couple of hours each day. The practice gained the nickname 'crucifixion'. If the offence had occurred near the front lines the soldier would sometimes be bound facing the enemy lines. The term 'picquet' was still being used in World War II in regard to field punish-ments. This was originally a medieval method of torture. The guilty party was positioned with his heel balanced on a spike in the ground, then one of his thumbs was strung up over his head, forcing him to balance between thumb and spike. Resting weight on the foot would risk impalement, while relieving the weight might wrench the thumb out of its socket. By World War II, picquet meant no more than kitchen cleaning duties. However, deten-tion centres, like the camp in Grovely where Pte Wilson had served time, were never a pleasant experience. Eddie Emmerson described the detention centres as 'bloody hell holes, proper gaols where you were locked up and treated like dogs. But if you got CB [confined to barracks] it was alright because you done [your time] at home. It's only if you got something heavy that you got dumped [in detention]. But otherwise you got fined so much and three weeks' CB. But you weren't allowed to leave the camp.' Forfeit of pay was often the heaviest toll, especially with those at home relying on the soldier's income to make ends meet.

●

Pte Morris H. Hurel made it back to camp on 8 May, extending his leave by about six weeks. He pleaded not guilty. Pte Hurel would have been one of the most eager to get to shore as *Aquitania* steamed through the heads. His daughter was born while he was in the Middle East, and he'd received word that she was not doing well. The baby had a rare condition, recorded in shorthand on the court-martial record as 'Interaption of the bowls'. Intussusception of the bowel was most probably the case. Whatever it was, it was serious, for when Pte Hurel arrived home to see his daughter for the first time, she was being rushed to hospital. He remained by the infant's side until she was released from hospital. The baby was still quite ill and his wife had been receiving a pension for bad nerves while Pte Hurel was overseas, and he had no intention of leaving them in this state. When he felt confident they could survive without him he returned to the camp at Narellan, but the unit had already relocated to far northern Queensland. In spite of his wife sending a letter to the commanding officer confirming the circumstances and pleading for leniency, the man was sentenced to sixty days' field punishment and the equivalent time in lost pay. Pte Hurel's history may have returned to haunt him: in early 1942 he had been charged with altering a leave pass and supplying false information via telegram and given twenty-eight days' detention.

Pte Reginald Alexander Tait only committed any offence once, but he undertook a wide range of offences. Pte Tait's priors included one conviction each of AWL, failing to appear at parade, drunkenness, receiving stolen property, and conduct to the prejudice of good order and military discipline. It seems Reggie was only willing to try anything once—except for AWL. On 6 June he was court-martialled for a second time, having returned to camp on 23 May after being absent without leave for twenty days. Pte Tait's wife had taken ill, and he had taken off. It would be a while before he'd go anywhere again, as he received 120 days' detention. Another first for Pte Tait.

Pte Stanley James Glynn chalked up three AWLs and was court-martialled on 19 June for his fourth. He had extended his leave until the end of May. Stanley James Glynn's father—like that of Glynn's 2/17th comrade Stanley James Livingston—had died while he was in the Middle East. Pte Glynn had plenty to say for himself at the trial:

> I have a property of ninety acres of land, forty acres under orchard. I found the orchard in a bad condition when I returned from overseas. I am married. I have two

brothers and seven sisters and mother. My eldest brother is a cripple and my younger brother is in the army. My sisters are all married and are not on the property. During my 21 days leave I was ploughing and improving the property. There was no-one working on the orchard when I went back to it.

In this instance the court was lenient and fined him fifteen pounds.

Also absent until the end of May was Pte James Gibb Hamilton. His record until then was squeaky clean. His statement at court martial on 17 June is affecting:

I was overseas for approximately seven months. My wife's condition during that period was nerves and (she was) very hysterical, a child was born on the 2nd January 43, during which my wife had a very hard time during her confinement. The child was born two months premature. My wife's condition improved considerably during the time I was on leave upon my return to Australia. With me going back to camp my wife again became nervous and hysterical. When I went absent this time I found that her condition was the same—very hysterical.

Pte Hamilton was fined ten pounds.

Pte Patrick William Murrell made it back from leave by 2 April, only a week overdue, but soon left again, not to return until 18 May. He had this to say in his defence:

The reason I did not return to camp on the 24th March 1943 from Liddington Leave was that my mother was ill. My mother was still in hospital when I returned on the 2nd April. After returning to camp on 2nd of April I was granted leave for two days at Morpeth. I did not return at the end of that two days leave as my mother was in hospital and very ill. My mother has not recovered and is still very ill.

Pte Murrell's mother was suffering from sugar diabetes and high blood pressure. He was the only family member around to care for her. His only brother was in the army and his sister was dead. He had already served overseas for two years and four months and was an original member of the 2/17th. His record was almost unblemished, and as far as blemishes go, his first had been negligible. 'I missed a leave bus returning from Jerusalem to Julis camp and got back about 18 hours later. That is my only offence since being with the 2/17th.' Pte Murrell was court-martialled the same day as Pte Glynn, who received only a fifteen-dollar fine. While Murrell's tale is no less tragic, and the fine for his one previous misdemeanour had been two pounds, the court sentenced him to suffer sixty days' field punishment and forfeit all pay.

An even more disquieting case is that of Pte Mervyn Patrick Pollard, who was AWL for no more than a month. He had been receiving increasingly disturbing letters from his wife since he returned from the Middle East. He told the court, 'I applied for leave and it was refused. My wife was very sick. She seemed to want me home. I have three children. My wife was trying to look after them by herself while she was sick. I produce letters from my wife to that effect. I have twins six years old and my other child is nine. They live with my wife alone.' A section of one of Nell Pollard's letters clearly demonstrates why her husband felt the need to leave camp. 'The doctor changed my medicine today. I hope it stops the pain in my head which is becoming unbearable. I hate to worry you with my troubles dear, but sometimes I think death would be easier for me.' She signs the letter, 'Lot of love and kisses, your loving wife, Nell.' And just below this, in a child's hand: 'love to daddy— jeff, john and peter xxx.' Even though the letters become increasingly distressing, the court sentenced Pte Pollard to sixty days' field punishment without pay.

Pte Alfred Herbert Currie, who appears in a wartime photograph alongside Stanley Livingston, fought hard to prove his case when he was court-martialled on 25 June. He had been AWL for just over a month when he returned to camp on 3 May. Unfortunately, the lieutenant he had served under as a stretcher-bearer at Tel el Eisa did not give him a good rap. When asked why he thought Pte Currie was not up to standard, he nominated the time and date of an incident when Pte Currie allegedly refused to assist in carrying a certain Sgt Powell when the sergeant was wounded in action.

Pte Currie cross-examined Lt Barry Waterhouse himself, and from the court transcript you get the impression that

Pte Currie fancied himself as a budding barrister. He went in hard.

| | |
|---|---|
| Pte Currie: | Is it not a fact that I was in hospital with chronic diarrhoea when Sgt Powell was wounded? |
| Lt Waterhouse: | As far as my memory serves me you and Pte Martin were the two orderlies ordered to carry Sgt Powell. |
| Pte Currie: | If I said that I left the unit the day before Powell was hit and I met him in the C.C.S. [Casualty Care System] would that be incorrect? |
| Lt Waterhouse: | I think so. |
| Pte Currie: | You are not certain. |
| Lt Waterhouse: | No, I am not certain. |
| Pte Currie: | Then what you have told the court may be wrong. |
| Lt Waterhouse: | ... No. |

Pte Currie had the lieutenant on the ropes and probably had cause to think he'd struck a blow for justice. Obviously he was no Horace Rumpole because the court took no notice of the private's performance and sentenced him to 120 days' detention. In fact, Pte Currie had succeeded in proving his innocence in regard to the accusation that he was a neglectful bearer of stretchers. No less a power than Major General G.F. Wootten was of the opinion that the court should not have accepted the oral evidence of Lt Waterhouse that the accused was of bad character and should therefore pass sentence ignoring such evidence. And so they did. What Pte Currie had failed to comprehend was that he was actually on trial for AWL, and to that charge he had prepared no answer.

Some of the 2/17th boys chose to just go quietly. Pte Douglas John Barnard, after surrendering on 6 June with six previous AWLs under his belt, went through the motions and was sentenced to six months' detention. Pte Norman Arthur Turner turned up at the end of June and received nine months' detention. He had nothing to say for himself either. Pte Lloyd Morgan Campbell was far chattier. AWL until 6 June, when asked to state his case Pte Campbell gave his entire life story:

I am an only son. My father died while I was young. During the five years prior to joining up my mother and I have been ill-treated by my stepfather. It was not until three years ago that I knew he was my father. He broke up several homes and was undermining my mother's health. In 1939 he joined the army and sailed with the 6th Division. After he had gone, I was only sixteen, and got my mother's permission to join up. I served with the unit and had no convictions, going through every action with them, and came back with them to Australia. My father returned about three months before I did. I found out he hadn't changed a bit and my mother's health was still suffering so I went to Victoria Barracks and saw Capt. Borden. I explained my case to him and he told

me to apply immediately for compassionate leave which
I did . . . When I received word my mother was still ill
I just left.

For his efforts he received seventy days' field punishment.

Pte Alfred Frederick Clifton Drew never left his unit,
but his is a curious case and provides an insight into the
machinations of high command. He faced court martial on
23 June on one count of conduct to the prejudice of good
order and military discipline. He was accused of being the
author of written correspondence containing statements
calculated to bring into disrepute the military forces of
the Commonwealth of Australia. You would be forgiven
for assuming from this dire accusation that Pte Drew may
have been an enemy spy. The letter was addressed to a Mrs
A.W. Drew—his mother. Or so he told the court. But who
knows what was going on in the calculating mind of this
unscrupulous agent provocateur. His platoon commander
stunned the court when he lifted the lid on the character
of the real Pte Drew.

> I have found him rather an erratic sort of chap. Some
> days he will talk a lot and complain about different things
> but nobody seems to take much notice of what he says.
> At other times he will be very quiet. But he had never
> given me any trouble as far as conduct goes. I am of the
> opinion that some of the things he says are more or less
> on the spur of the moment and he doesn't seem to realize
> what he's saying. With reference to these two letters,

he came to me a few days later and said 'I hope sir, that you don't think I was taking a dig at you' or words to that effect.

Either Pte Drew was a master of disguise and deception or he was guilty of nothing more than writing a letter to his mum. Here are the relevant highlights of the letter in question. I'll let you be the judge.

> My Dear Mum, Dad & Sister,
> Just a few lines, folks, hoping they find you all in the best of health and spirit back home. I am just the same, doing ok, as army life goes and I can't give any complaints. Thanks so much for the cake, mum, it came to hand on Friday and it was cut into twelve big slices yesterday for the boys in the tent. It was a beauty, couldn't have been better and was enjoyed by all who part took [sic] with a cup of tea ... Anyway, thanks once again, it was lovely and enjoyed by all, I'll send the tin back.

God help us if any of this got into enemy hands. But this mysterious emissary of the 2/17th didn't stop there.

> Having some miserable days here lately, a little more rain than usual and wind with it, too cold for shorts and shirt, I've got out the long trousers. That Newel person has just walked in, getting in the way and making a nuisance of himself as usual. He looks extra well, and so do the rest in fact, I saw Roy this morning, gee he's getting a big bugger ... The boys are in great spirits today, they

had their prayers answered. Last night we had a lovely fire and all stood back and watched it go and did it go. It was an elaborately built grass hut which took weeks to build and to decorate for our wonderful officers to have as a mess, well it's a mess now, down to the ground, just a charred skeleton. They spent a lot of time and money on it and then last night they had a party, made all the noise in the world, which we would have been crimed for, but at the hour of 12.20 am she was blazing nicely, gee it was a great sight, it lifted the morale of the troops 100%. Yes it's an officers war, you have no idea of what silly, childish acts some of them come at.

Having unleashed the dirt on the officers he then took aim at a higher power.

Another godsend today was not having to listen to our blubbering padre ... in peacetime I'm doubtful he'd qualify for a church gardener ... Well folks I'll say cheerio, hoping this is not cut about too much but it isn't giving away secrets, just a few true facts.

With lots of love to you all,

Your loving son and brother, Alf xxxxx.

Perhaps his platoon commander didn't think Alfie was having a dig, but the court was not amused, and decreed that Pte Drew suffer sixty days' field punishment and forfeit of pay. Of interest here is the mention of 'that Newel person'. There was only one Newel in the 2/17th and that was Stanley Livingston's great friend Stanley 'the Count' Newel. I'd say there was no doubt Stanley Livingston knew Alf, and I'm pretty sure they would have got on like an officers' mess on fire.

●

Another Jack—Jack Arthur Lonsdale, son of Ernie Snr and brother of Evelyn—also had a case to answer. Jack Lonsdale, with his arm well and truly twisted, joined the Citizen Military Forces on 1 September 1941. Unlike the AIF, the CMF were commissioned to defend only Australian shores. When Japan entered the Pacific stage, the CMF were tasked with defending Australian territories in Papua and New Guinea, and eventually their duties extended to the entire south-west Pacific area. In uniform but lacking the shoulder patch of the AIF, the CMF men were cruelly labelled by some as 'chocos', or chocolate soldiers. Often this was enough to nudge a soldier into joining the AIF. In Jack's case, it would take a lot of nudging. Jack was enjoying protecting Australian shores. His main task was to patrol the shores of Botany Bay, rifle in hand but no bullets. All the same, the uniform did its job and before long Jack's army threads had caught the attention of a young woman by the name of Grace.

Jack's routine patrols were rudely interrupted on 20 November 1941 when he was determinedly nudged, possibly by his conscience or more likely in an effort to impress Grace, into joining an expeditionary force raised for service outside the Commonwealth. He was given a loaded gun, with a pointy thing attached to it, and knew that at any given moment he could be placed in the line of fire. The new uniform and loaded gun must have impressed Grace, for they were married soon after. Jack remained in Australia until mid 1943, but soon the timorous Gunner J.A. Lonsdale was bound for New Guinea. Family lore holds that when Jack disembarked in New Guinea he wasn't too interested in being a part of the show, and on befriending a troop of American airmen within hours of arrival he hitched a lift on their Douglas C-54 Skymaster straight back to Mascot that same day.

Much as I hate to break the lore, and especially since it is a tale that resembles in no small manner the Uncle Jack I would grow to know and love, the records tell another story. Jack appears to have remained in New Guinea until early 1944. There are scant details of what he got up to over there, but it is not too much of a stretch to assume that at some stage around April 1944 he may well have hitched that lift back to Sydney. Something went missing from the war records after April: that something was Jack Arthur Lonsdale. Gnr Lonsdale was declared an illegal absentee from 2 June, and the army saw no sign of him until almost a year later when he surrendered to the Military Police on 4 May 1945. His whereabouts during this time were confirmed to me by his sister Dot over coffee and sponge cake in late 2012. It seems Jack had been holed up in a small closet under the stairs at 1187 Botany Road, Mascot.

The Military Police eventually tracked him down, and paid a visit to the barber shop on 4 May, where they convinced Annie Lonsdale that if her son gave himself up (rather than if they simply leaned over and opened the closet door themselves) it would be in the boy's best interests in the long run. Jack could hide from the army, but not from the wishes of Annie Lonsdale. She opened the closet door, Jack surrendered, and he was immediately charged with desertion.

Some mothers weren't so ready to give up their kin. A paper entitled 'Harbouring and Assistance of Deserters and AWL' describes one such incident.

> Evidence was called that the Provost who were in possession of warrants for the arrest of two members, called at the Defendant's house one evening, and proceeded to make a search. The Defendant, who was the mother of the soldiers in question, raised no objection to the search of all rooms except one, in which she stated there was nobody present. The Provost, however, searched the room, and found in it a cupboard. They succeeded in partially opening the cupboard, and therein was one of the soldiers, who at that date had been absent twenty-one days. The mother then attacked the Provost, and, as they were dubious as to their right to use force, they allowed themselves to be pushed and bustled out of the house. They posted a man at the front and rear, and obtained the assistance of the civil police. On arrival of the civil

police, a further search was effected, but the man had escaped, it being believed that he made his way into other parts of the house, it being a tenement dwelling occupied by several households. The mother . . . after having been warned, made a voluntary statement, in which she admitted that her son had been in the cupboard when the search was made, that she knew he was there, that she had pushed the Provost away from the cupboard, and that she knew at the time that both her sons were AWL. Despite this evidence which was given at the prosecution, the complaint was dismissed.

The soldier, having been absent for more than seven days, could be deemed a deserter, but the police magistrate held that there was not sufficient evidence to prove beyond reasonable doubt that the mother knew that her son was officially a deserter.

On 15 May 1945, Gnr Jack Lonsdale was court-martialled at Paddington in Sydney. The charge: desertion from 2 June 1944 to 4 May 1945. It wasn't looking good for Jack. He had a string of prior convictions, three previous AWLs, one charge of drunkenness, and a charge of 'failing to appear at a place'. The place was probably New Guinea. Jack had a bit to say at his court martial. He'd had plenty of time under the stairs to contemplate his plea. Jack took a deep breath, and spilled his guts.

I am NX56248 Gnr Lonsdale, Jack Arthur . . . I am a married man and my wife left me before I joined the

Army but since being in the army I have been corresponding with her trying to get her to come back and she has refused to come back. All the time I have been in the Army I have been worrying about the position with my wife and it has effected [sic] me to the extent I suffer from insomnia and I was also unable to eat. Finally I became run down and then I was taken to hospital and had my appendix and tonsils removed and I was still run down after that and I went AWL to try and straighten things out with my wife. I was unable to bring about a reconciliation and she served me with a divorce petition so I came back to the army. I had no intention of deserting.

Jack glanced down, and without lifting his head, raised his large brown eyes, much the way a puppy does when it's just been caught having a crap on the carpet. (Of course I have no evidence to support this observation, but believe me, I knew this man, and I have no doubt this was the case. None whatsoever.)

Q: Did you apply for any leave before you absented yourself?

A: Yes.

Q: And that was refused?

A: I applied for leave before I was sent to New Guinea and the officer told me the unit was going away. [I was told] to stay with the unit—the trouble started before I went away.

Q: Did you apply for leave immediately before you absented yourself?

A: I was granted sick and compassionate leave from New Guinea and I absented myself from that leave.

Q: What work were you doing while you were away?

A: I was helping my father in his barber's shop.

Q: The whole time you were away?

A: Not the whole time. I was more or less trying to find out what my wife was doing most of the time.

Q: What were you being paid for that work?

A: Just a few shilling a week for helping him out.

Jack did a good job of circumnavigating the truth without actually setting foot on it. There is the slightly soiled white lie of being married before joining the army, and then the fact that Grace had left him almost immediately after the wedding in late 1941.

Those puppy-dog eyes didn't do Jack a lot of good. Gnr Jack Lonsdale was declared not guilty of desertion but guilty of AWL and sentenced to eighteen months' detention. The detention centre would have seemed like luxury compared to the closet under the stairs. When the war ended a few months later, Jack was still serving time. Gracie, as it happened, had abandoned him for another uniform. Her own. Former Mascot milk-bar manageress Grace Florence Lonsdale became Pte Grace Florence Lonsdale and served on continuous full-time war service with the Australian Army Medical Women's Service AIF from 17 May 1943 to 24 January 1946. She never left Australia, but served for 1365 days at the Australian Blood and Serum Preparation Unit in Sydney Hospital. Jack never saw Gracie again.

# 12

## *From the Pimple to Scarlet Beach via Dead Man's Gully*

'Whoever said the pen is mightier than the sword obviously never encountered automatic weapons.'

*Douglas MacArthur*

Seventy days had passed since Stanley and Gordon had jumped the train from the Atherton Tablelands, where their unit remained in full training. Having embarked on their second homeland AWL before a court martial could be called, they had reached 109 days absent since the end of Liddington leave in March. That's a touch more than the twenty-one days required for a charge of desertion. It was early July when rumours reached the boys that the battalion was about to leave Australia.

Lilly Livingston had been overjoyed to have the men back by her side, and Gordon Oxman was in no doubt that this was the only place he wished to be. He made it clear with a proposal of marriage that was accepted without hesitation. This sparked the germ of an idea in Stanley's mind in regard to young Evelyn Lonsdale, even though he was aware that the coupling of a good Church of England girl and a wavering Catholic boy could raise a few eyebrows. (It has always intrigued me that something that is frowned on can at the same time raise eyebrows.) Should both nuptials eventuate, Stanley Livingston, Roy Lonsdale and Gordon Oxman would some day be brothers-in-law as well as brothers in arms.

An official record dated 28 January 1943 entitled 'Disposal of Personnel Awaiting Trial For A.W.L.' states that 'Frequently a member who has been AWL for a substantial period requires hardening training before he is fully fit for front-line duty.' With rumours circulating of the unit moving north at any moment, any hardening of Gordon and Stanley would have to be swift. But hardening of the men was not the only concern. 'Where personnel are returned to New Guinea to a unit which is engaged in active operations in a forward area the unit would find it a most inappropriate time to deal with the offenders and very probably in such cases considerable delays would occur . . . Many members awarded substantial periods of detention would have to be returned to the mainland to serve those sentences.' The question now was whether Stanley and Gordon would even make it overseas at all. At the time that the boys decided to return to active service, army officials were still debating the issue. 'It is also suggested that it may not be desirable to return to New Guinea a soldier who by reason of the fact that he is under arrest and awaiting trial cannot be regarded as D.P.I. and is not available immediately to reinforce his unit as a fighting member.'

•

On 13 July at 1130 hours, Pte Gordon Oxman and Pte Stanley Livingston marched through the convict-erected sandstone walls of the Moore Park Road Holding Centre in Victoria Barracks, Sydney, and surrendered. Many before them had received severe sentences for far shorter periods of homeland AWL and the pair had no idea what they would face when they returned to camp. A court martial no doubt, but would their private act of honour result in public dishonour? Was this the end of Pte Stanley Livingston's military service? After being held in custody, the pair were returned on 26 July at 2330 to their battalion in a tented camp in Dead Man's Gully, north of Cairns on the coastal strip near Trinity Beach. Now in its final stages of training, the battalion had become a first-class unit adept in all areas of jungle warfare.

The following morning they were awakened by the camp loudspeakers blasting out a song, 'Beautiful, Beautiful Queensland'. Pte Livingston wondered if this was a part of the training and suggested they would have no problems with the Japs as this tune should have the enemy retreating before the sun rose. The training had been intense, and as the battalion prepared for embarkation it was noted that the men had never been fitter, except perhaps for privates

Oxman and Livingston, who had essentially spent the entire training period AWL. Four days later, Stanley and Storky were on the move, but they were not ushered into court. On 31 July 1943 the battalion, including the two privates, embarked from Cairns on SS *William Ellery Channing* with little fanfare and no loved ones to wave them off. The general population had no idea these troops were heading into action. The troops themselves knew this was the real thing, but they too had no idea where they were heading.

Most bets were on New Guinea. The word among the men was that General MacArthur was intent on making his triumphal return to the Philippines an American-only affair after the Japanese had taken the upper hand and plenty of American POWs earlier in the campaign, and Australians would be left with so-called 'mopping-up' duties closer to home. 'Wither on the vine' was the phrase used to illustrate MacArthur's plan to deal with any isolated Japanese troops left behind as the enemy were forced back. This dismissive phrase underestimated the fighting spirit of the Japanese, who had no intention of withering. The Australian troops would require more than mops for the job ahead. Pte H.D. Wells felt the troops were prepared 'like sheaves of wheat to be fed to the mill—some would be ground to flour'.

Pte Livingston was without question apprehensive as he lay below the deck of SS *William Ellery Channing* while they approached the daunting terrain of the New Guinea coast. As he rubbed his unshaven chin, he contemplated whether he feared the bayonets of the Japanese as much as the cutthroat razor of Ernie Lonsdale. Or the judgement of a court martial. What would prison be like on a Pacific island? Or would they be sent straight back to the mainland? (Perhaps to Brisbane, where a mutiny in Grovely was brewing.) Would ignominy be involved? To distract himself, he wrote home to Evelyn, describing her eyes as 'two spoonfuls of the blue Pacific', a line he'd appropriated from the 1938 movie *The Girl of the Golden West* starring Jeanette MacDonald and Nelson Eddy. Unfortunately for Stanley, Evelyn had seen it too—through almond-brown eyes. I guess two spoonfuls of almonds doesn't quite cut the mustard romance-wise.

After disembarking at Milne Bay on the south-east tip of New Guinea on 4 August, NX20181 Pte Stanley Livingston was held in close arrest until the eleventh, when he and Gordon, as well as other stragglers and assorted deviants who had also been along for the ride, were court-martialled in the field.

●

From the Australian Military Forces Form of Proceedings for General and District Courts-Martial on 11 August 1943:

NX20181 Pte Livingston, Stanley James of 2/17th Aust Inf Bn being duly sworn makes the following statement: 'The reason I went AWL for the first time was that my Father died just before I returned from the Middle East. There were a few matters unsettled and I had to finalise them. In the meantime my young sister had a breakdown in health so I stayed on for a while longer until she became a bit better and then came back to camp. The reason I went AWL for the second period was the fact that my sister had another breakdown after I had returned to camp. My mother is not alive.'

Question by the defending officer:

Q: When did you first become aware that your sister had a breakdown?

A: When I returned to camp there was a letter awaiting me from my eldest sister, saying that my young sister had a breakdown and was asking for me.

In the case of Pte Stanley Livingston, the accused was found guilty on both counts of AWL and fined the sum of twenty pounds. On top of this he was ordered to forfeit all ordinary pay for ninety days, a fair price, he reckoned, for lifting the spirits of his little sister and spending precious time with Evelyn.

At the same hearing, Pte Gordon Grant Oxman, himself duly sworn in, made the following statement. 'The reason I went AWL for the first period was because I was suffering from pleurisy and I reported to Dr Sheehan and he gave me a certificate that I was unfit to return to camp.' He was then asked what treatment Dr Sheehan had given him, to which he replied, 'He told me to stop in bed and have plenty of rest.' For deserting a second time Gordon explained that 'my mother was ill. She had fallen down some steps.' It seems Gordon neglected to mention he was desperately in love with his fellow accused's sister and refused to leave her side. Unlike Stanley, Gordon had chosen not to appeal to the hearts of his superiors, perhaps fearing a more severe punishment for such a basely human and non-military response, although he did manage to get the 'unwell mother' angle in there at the last minute. Gordon had all bases covered. The court found that Pte Gordon Oxman was also guilty on both counts, and he too was ordered to forfeit ninety days' pay. But there was no twenty-pound fine. Instead Pte Oxman was sentenced to ninety days' punishment in the field. And from one glance at the fields surrounding Milne Bay, it was clear this was not going to be a walk in the park.

Perhaps if he'd played the love-of-his-life card the plea might have garnered more sympathy. As it turns out, neither party received such severe punishments as some of those handed out during the court martials on the mainland in May and June. Perhaps the army was in need of more bodies in New Guinea and the two privates arrived just in time to bulk up the numbers? Whatever the reason, after being given his light sentence Stanley Livingston was free to face the enemy with precisely zero training in jungle warfare. After months of jungle training the unit was described as finely honed, but there were at least two unhoned units now facing an unfamiliar landscape and an unpredictable foe. The only good news for Stanley was that he was a world away from what had become an increasingly alien civilian life. He could drop the act; he was among friends now.

A year earlier, on 25 August 1942, just as Stanley was getting his first taste of battle in the Egyptian desert, the battle of Milne Bay was in progress. The Japanese, flushed with a run of successes at this stage, underestimated the strength of the Australian force defending Milne Bay— for the first time in the Pacific campaign, Allied troops effectively defeated the Japanese and drove them back. The Japanese expansion began to shrink, but it was a long chase back to Japan, and years of jungle fighting lay ahead.

The campsite at Milne Bay was now a mess of barbed wire and bomb craters left over from the previous show. Pte Peter J. Jones remembers his first night at Milne Bay under a one-man mosquito-net frame, camped close to a dry pebbly creek. Conditions were mild and balmy until midnight when monsoonal rain swept in and filled the creek bed with a metre and a half of water. Many men had bedded down in the cosy-looking creek bed the night before. They made it out but lost all their personal items. The drenching monsoonal rains would be a constant daily occurrence in the months ahead. H.D. Wells said the rain was so heavy you could almost slice a path through it with a machete.

Bill Pye was just outside Port Moresby, where the view was not much better:

We went to what they called Pom Pom Park, and it was almost the same as the tablelands, it was just land [with no buildings], and we went off scrounging around and we got galvanised iron and all sorts of things, and again, we finally got tents but it was a bloody silly bloody thing . . . we sat on our arses there, we didn't have a role at all, and then finally we were sent back to Australia. I was in charge of the rear party, I had trucks and guns and everything else and tents, we had to have all the stuff folded up and you had to take it to ordnance and then they counted it all off and one of my sergeants came back and he says, 'Hey, do you know what, sir? All those bloody tents that we're folding up and all the guy ropes, you know what they're doing with them?' He said, 'They count them off then they take them around the bloody back and they burn them!' It was ridiculous because we had waited so long to get them and they were so precious and then all this bloody rigmarole of having to count them and when they got them they were destroyed.

Bill's troops assumed this was yet another example of the army 'buggering people about'. Bill put it more philosophically, using his best military slang: 'Snafu—situation normal: all fucked up'.

As usual the ORs camped at Milne Bay remained in the dark about the details of their mission. By mid 1943, General Douglas MacArthur was dictating the terms to Australia's General Blamey despite any reservations Blamey may have had. The mission was to recapture a chunk of the eastern mainland of New Guinea. Milne Bay would be the training area for Operation Postern, an amphibious landing assault on the Huon Gulf, not far from the village of Lae, an area still held by the Japanese. The 9th Division were given the task of capturing Lae. The men would soon learn that they were in training for the first amphibious assault landing by Australian troops since 25 April 1915 at Anzac Cove, Gallipoli. After a full-dress rehearsal, casualties were already being reported, although no human enemy had been encountered. Tiny armies of bacteria and small infectious secret agents were already on the march. There were numerous cases of scrub typhus and furunculosis (boils). A thigmotactical response troop of anopheles mosquitos was lying in wait. The only protection against malaria was a daily issue of Atebrine tablets. It was rumoured that the pills could make a man sterile, but the troops took them anyway, and, in the words of Pte Peter J. Jones, 'eventually got malaria almost to the man'.

Operation Postern began on 2 September 1943, when the 20th Brigade of the 9th Division embarked in convoy for Lae. The convoy of US naval ships left Milne Bay and headed north-west, hugging the coast of New Guinea. Leading the way were two APDs (armoured personnel destroyers), one carrying Pte Stanley Livingston, Pte Gordon Oxman and the rest of the 2/17th, with Roy Lonsdale and the 2/13th Battalion alongside in the other. From their most recent intensive training, the men knew they would be amphibiously landing somewhere, and once at sea they were informed that they were to come ashore on two beaches, codenamed Red and Yellow. The beachfronts were around eight kilometres apart and 25 to 30 kilometres east of Lae. They were to expect a Japanese welcome on Red Beach—in strength. There were no roads between the landing beaches and Lae, just the jungle and five rivers. Their first objective was to capture the beach and penetrate inland.

When night fell the engines were silent. On 'battle eve', H.D. Wells sensed a stillness in the men, who talked in low voices. The troops did not sleep well, not unusual given the circumstances. Prior to battle, soldiers often could not hold back the need to urinate—a practice also common in my own profession. First-night jitters can be messy: the performer on one side of the curtain outnumbered by a hostile audience on the other. The final call is made, and the players, bladders and bowels safely evacuated, go out to their potential deaths.

When the warning alarm sounded just before dawn, most were already awake. Allied bombers swept the area as five destroyers, part of the fleet of one hundred vessels, sped forward, turned parallel to the shore, and began their bombardment of the area surrounding Red Beach, clearing a path for the infantrymen. H.D. Wells recalls seeing his fellow troops clambering down scramble nets draped down the side of a destroyer, men being tossed against the sides like prawns being shaken from nets. The men carried tinned rations to last two days, mess gear, a towel, anti-mosquito cream, toilet tools, spare boots, two pairs of socks, a singlet, a shirt, one pair of underpants, a pair of trousers, a mosquito net, groundsheet, blanket, steel helmet, knife, rifles, wound dressings, ammunition, a water bottle and a grenade—all up around 30 kilograms, about half of what they'd carried into El Alamein. Slipping from the net would ensure a swift journey to the sea floor.

LCPs (landing craft personnel carriers) tethered to the ship lurched below. As dawn broke, the men squatted in the barges as they headed to shore. In one barge a 2/13th private, J.W. Holmes, crouched while his sergeant, 'Bill the Goose', 'ordered us to fix bayonets and partially squeeze the split-pins of our grenades'. I imagine J.W. also partially squeezed the last of the urine from his bladder, and to use one of Stanley Livingston's favourite sayings, in doing so he would not have been Robinson Crusoe. Near the shore the barges cut the engines and then slid towards land, where ramps were dropped and the men tumbled out and raced across eighteen metres of wide black sandy beach and into the thick tangle of jungle. This was to be no rerun of Gallipoli—no shots were fired.

The first wave, including Stanley and Gordon and the recently promoted Lance Corporal Roy Lonsdale, had arrived at their objective relatively unscathed. Others were not so lucky. Within half an hour nine Japanese 'Betty Bombers' (Mitsubishi G4M1s) and Zero fighters flew low over the heads of Stanley, Gordon, Roy and J.W. Holmes, machine guns firing at an unknown target. Veterans of the Middle East didn't fail to notice that a red disc on their underbellies had replaced the black cross of the German bombers. Not far from the boys, H.D. Wells looked up through the trees as the bombers dived towards Red Beach. He watched as they swooped towards the beach, where the men of the 2/24th were exposed. 'Like large silver birds they sped onward, dropping their eggs of death.' The American destroyers ensured their visit was short—the planes were scattered, but not before a large number of men from the 2/24th had been killed.

By last light on 4 September, with 7800 troops landed, the advance towards Lae began. While enemy resistance was light, the jungle tested the men. Although the khaki uniforms of the desert were now replaced by jungle green, no-one would have noticed as the men became caked with mud from day one. Within days large numbers of men from local villages arrived in the area to offer support. They were organised into carrying parties. Their knowledge of the jungle was invaluable when it came to obstacles like the Buso River, 50 metres wide and travelling at a rate of twelve knots. Determined enemy fire from the far bank didn't help matters. By forming a chain holding each other's rifles, the men made the crossing.

On 16 September, the 'silent' 7th Division were the first troops into Lae, approaching from the opposite angle to the 9th. When the 9th arrived not long after, the 7th were happy to gloat that they had won the race to Lae against the 'glamour' 9th. What they didn't find in Lae was any sign of Japanese resistance—the town was there for the taking. The expected battle did not eventuate, but the Japanese were not far away. With the Allies advancing, the Japanese had decided resistance was futile and withdrawn towards the town of Finschhafen. There had been eleven thousand Japanese troops in the Lae-Salamaua area at the time: they lost over two thousand men during the march on Lae, while the 9th Division lost seventy-seven. A dozen of these were from the 2/17th battalion. For most 2/17th soldiers it was a battle against the elements, and dumping their mosquito nets and groundsheets on landing to ease their burden hadn't made the going any easier. On 20 September, troops were able to rest while their officers decided how they would approach the tightly held area surrounding Finschhafen.

The capture of Finschhafen required another amphibious landing, and the 20th Brigade, comprising the 2/17th, 2/13th and the 2/15th, were selected for the job. General MacArthur was adamant that just one brigade would do the trick, but General Blamey was not so sure. Japanese numbers were unknown, but with the enemy on the run, confidence was at an all-time high among the Allies—so high that this time they were to land in complete darkness. Intelligence reports suggested that they should expect a welcoming party of just three hundred and fifty enemy around the Finschhafen area; as it turned out, the actual enemy numbers in the area were approximately five thousand. The 20th Brigade were to land at Scarlet Beach on 22 September, only six days after the capture of Lae, and advance to Finschhafen. There was no time for rehearsal.

Scarlet Beach was a small indentation between two well-defined headlands approximately 600 metres long and ten metres wide at the far northern mouth of the Song River. The convoy left Lae at 1930 hours on 21 September. Gordon, Stanley and Roy were side by side again throughout the still, quiet night as the convoy was shadowed by enemy aircraft. Once again, Roy Lonsdale and the 2/13th Battalion and Gordon and Stanley in the 2/17th would head to the beach first. The objective for the 2/17th was to capture the northern headland; the 2/13th were to capture the southern headland.

Reveille was at 0245. Unlike the situation at Lae, the troops could not see any sign of the coastline in the darkness. They could barely see the destroyer alongside their own, and worse, they couldn't see if there was an army waiting for them onshore. The Americans were eager to land before first light and get their ships out of there. The men were served breakfast, or 'the Last Supper' as some called it. After breakfast, bladders were evacuated and made safe for landing. After a burst of speed the orders went up: 'Lower barges, get ready to land, away the landing force.' Scramble nets were hung over the destroyers' sides, and the men made their way down to where the landing craft waited. Weighed down with their packs, the 'prawns' gripped the net. It was 0440 hours when the sixteen cramped, flat-bottomed barges that made up the first wave headed for shore. Stanley, Gordon and Roy stared ahead, but it was too dark to see the shoreline.

With visibility so low, one of the barges veered left, causing a domino effect. At the same moment, 4500 metres from shore, five American destroyers began bombarding Scarlet Beach, firing over the top of the landing barges into the jungle, immediately drawing return fire directly from the beach. Fear gripped the men in the barges. Scarlet Beach was occupied, and the occupants weren't happy to see them. H.D. Wells counted at least eight machine guns firing directly at the landing barges. The confusion and the darkness meant most landed far to the left of their intended positions, and the order of landing was jumbled. Some barges were grounded on coral beneath the cliffs, impeding the function of the ramps. Once on the beach, the troops answered the fire. Many now held thoughts of Gallipoli and feared the consequences of a botched landing under enemy fire.

It was only the darkness protecting them now. Many men who had fallen into deeper water had to be dragged out, submerged under heavy packs. With the first wave in disarray the second wave were left vulnerable to attack. Machine-gun fire poured into the landing craft. Once ashore, the men struggled to climb the ten-metre sloping bank. The incline was not expected; it hadn't shown up on photographs. The Americans fired into the treetops near the shore to clear any snipers, the shells passing just above the Australian troops' heads. Those who made it into the jungle had to deal with the darkness as each man held on to the muzzle of the rifle of the man behind so as not to become lost. The Japanese holed up in the jungle intended to inflict as much damage as possible with machine-gun fire onto the landing parties before retreating to more strongly held territories. Troops on the beach lay flat on their faces in the sand. Some would never get up. Despite the confusion, by 6.30 a.m. the Japanese were gone. Twenty Australians were killed on Scarlet Beach. Stanley and Gordon survived intact, but Lance Corporal Roy Lonsdale lay flat on his face. He tried to get up, but he had been shot in the leg. Roy had been wounded in the opening act, again.

Sgt Jack Littlewood, also in C Company and a good friend of Stanley Livingston's, remembers the landing:

> Bang! We landed on the rocky point, ramps went down, the port side onto rocks and the starboard into the water. There was a Jap bunker in front of us firing away . . . number 1 Section went on to the rocks, No 2 into the water . . . On landing we went in two hundred yards or so to wait for orders to move which came the next day. The Yanks came and put up their camp. They asked us to breakfast the next morning and put us first in line. What a breakfast of flapjacks and bacon! Bad luck orders came through, we had to move before lunch.

Unlike on the homeland, in the fields of battle the Yanks were a welcome sight, far better equipped than the Australians and more than willing to share. Eddie Emmerson recalls:

The Yanks were good blokes. I remember once in Finschhafen, I got into a depression and there was a group of Yanks there and they had better food than us, and so we could always get a feed, so I was having a feed ... and a bit of stuff [fire] started coming over the top ... Any rate, the Yanks were feeding us up well on creamed ham, instead of rotten old bully beef, and suddenly it started to get a bit warmer and then it got red hot and I always remember this one Yank, and he says, 'Well Aussie, it's time I went and got my gun.'

Bill Pye was getting on well with the Yanks in Port Moresby:

You could trade with them, some of our cooks were making sly grog and they were selling this to the Americans and we were getting confectionary and cigarettes back, so we were grateful to the Americans for the pictures and their canteen and so on, we were envious of them. And we thought they were a slovenly lot, you know—even though we were up in the tropics, you wore your uniform the way you were supposed to wear it, whereas the Americans, they just put it on to cover up their nakedness, they didn't give a stuff, they were a very sloppy crowd.

On 23 September the advance down the coast to Finschhafen continued. By the twenty-fourth the task was proving arduous, the men stumbling and sliding down hillsides as they moved across the precipitous terrain towards Finschhafen. Across the Bumi River they faced the enemy, whose heavily protected pillboxes looked formidable. And so did the river. The crossing was not made without casualties. On 29 September they faced the wettest day since landing. The harsh conditions were taking their toll on Pte Gordon Oxman, and the next day he was evacuated with severe asthma. Gordon's claim at his court martial that he had been suffering from pleurisy was no lie, and the conditions in New Guinea no doubt inflamed the inflammation.

With Roy wounded and Gordon evacuated, Pte Livingston was left heading for Finschhafen without the support of his two best friends, although he still had 'the Count' to count on. Despite fierce Japanese resistance, the 2/17th entered Finschhafen on 2 October. Once again, the Japanese made a hasty retreat, leaving maps and equipment. Many of the Australian troops felt jubilant, convinced that the work of the 20th Brigade in New Guinea was all but over. They had captured Finschhafen eleven days after landing awkwardly in the dark on Scarlet Beach. But the Japanese had retreated to regroup again, heading in the direction of Sattelberg, a mountain peak dominating the coastal strip. There were reports from the local population that this position was receiving strong enemy reinforcements. The show wasn't over yet.

# 13

## *Destroy all monsters*

'The makeup of every beast is different—some people
can laugh in hell and others can't.'

*Eddie Emmerson, 2012*

There was hardly a moment's rest before the troops
embarked on their toughest challenge of the campaign so
far. The Japanese had left in a hurry and were in a hurry to
return. They wanted Finschhafen back. There were still five
thousand of them in the vicinity and more were arriving.
When the actual numbers of the Japanese became clear,
the 20th Brigade were finally given some much-needed
support, and the 24th Brigade were sent in to bolster them.

Their next stop would be Sio on the north of the Huon
Peninsula. Between the brigades and Sio was mountainous Sattelberg, which was tightly held by the Japanese.
Between themselves and Sattelberg was a steep track
leading to the small village of Jivevaneng. Only twelve
months before, Pte Livingston had held a front-row seat
in the battle of El Alamein. Now he was engaged in a

battle just as fierce, in conditions that couldn't have been more different. The enemy was only metres away in some instances, and hidden in undergrowth. This was a test for the nerves.

By 7 October heavy rain had filled the defence areas with water—the place was a quagmire. There were frequent close-contact battles with Japanese on the muddied tracks, and heavy fighting continued over the next few days. The determined Japanese were coming out of the woodwork in small groups and attacking at close range. The torrential rain seemed to be siding with the enemy. At dawn on 8 October the troops were becoming frantic, emptying their trenches of water as they came under fire. The conditions were so bad that no vehicle could get through, leaving the troops without rations and with none on the way. All Japanese advances were repulsed on 9 October and Lt Col Simpson reported in his war diary that 'the enemy caused us no trouble during the morning but our stomachs did'. The following day the Japanese resumed their attacks on a number of fronts. The 2/17th Battalion was split up to cover a vast area of thick jungle as shells and mortar bombs increased in intensity. Unlike the desert where frontal attacks in battalion numbers were achievable, here the companies and platoons were dispersed, their progress painfully slow, generally uphill, and dangerous.

Pte Livingston had spent time with the carrier platoons in the desert, and he knew his way around a Bren gun.

He once told me about a time in New Guinea when he was manning a machine-gun post and decided to take matters into his own hands. Squatting behind a Bren in a slit trench, Stanley was perched on a high ridge with a good view over the terrain when he heard the sound of a bomber approaching. He watched as an enemy aircraft appeared directly ahead of his position. There was no way he could be spotted from the air, so it posed no threat to him. But Stanley realised he posed a threat to it, and taking the initiative he opened fire as it passed overhead and brought the plane down. Expecting congratulations all round and perhaps a promotion, Pte Livingston was instead shouted down by his commanding officer for risking giving away the company's position to the enemy. That was the last time Stanley took any initiative, perhaps the last time in his life.

Meanwhile, B Company had been under enormous pressure holding the tiny but tactically important Jivevaneng village where the battalion would finally regroup on 11 October. At 0445 hours on 16 October, the 2/17th were attacked in force. Their positions were heavily shelled and mortared, the bombs exploding in the trees above, showering shrapnel downwards. A barrage of three-inch mortars is not for the squeamish—you can hear the sound of the mortar descending and the closer it gets to its target the louder its peculiar whistling sound becomes. Lying in a slit trench no more than 30 centimetres deep and 180 centimetres wide, it would be easy to feel you'd dug your own shallow grave.

The attacks continued throughout the day, and at 1515 a heavy bombardment was aimed at the battalion headquarters. The enemy were as close as five metres. C Company was brought in to an area of exposed land near the headquarters and they remained in their holes all day. Stanley Livingston occupied one such hole. The battalion was surrounded on three sides. Continued attempts by the Japanese to dislodge the 2/17th were repelled. Unlike the Tobruk siege, this small-scale version was accessible in and out only by foot, and in the midst of sniper fire. The men had only one choice: to fight their way out. The intention was to give the enemy no respite, and over the following days they attacked the enemy on all sides, using small patrols to locate and assault enemy positions.

In the desert, patrols were generally nocturnal; in the jungle this was impossible. Day patrols were arduous and hard on the nerves—with the ever-present danger of ambush only metres away, the troops did a lot of listening. Jungles are noisy places, and the confusion of tiny sounds can cause trigger-happiness, which on patrol could be lethal. No doubt at the front of every soldier's mind was the knowledge that this enemy was not fond of taking prisoners; if you found yourself cornered, it was generally believed that surrender was not a choice. As a result, the Australian soldiers were given licence to respond in kind. To Peter J. Jones, 'The claustrophobic jungle imposed a stealth and furtiveness not conducive to the spirit of chivalrous opposition that characterised the conflict in

Africa. Neither did the perception that the Japanese soldier, although brave, was in no sense "honourable". The jungle war lacked mutual respect.'

Early in the war the Japanese were assumed to be inferior soldiers and treated with disdain. The tables soon turned when the troops were faced with the sheer brutality and skill of this enemy. By 1942, the tables had turned so far that Australians at home and on the battle-fields viewed the ever-encroaching enemy as an invincible force of military supermen. The fear of these sadistic and ruthless killers who showed no mercy mixed with the nightmarish terrors of jungle warfare fuelled the myth of an unstoppable foe. Creating demons is an old human habit. Perhaps by imagining an enemy that is either less than or more than human, the act of killing becomes more palatable. In the Middle East the perception of the Germans approached respect, and the Italians were seen as something of comic relief; the Japanese, however, were perceived to be an alien species.

Clichés about enemies aren't necessarily always accurate, as Pte Livingston discovered. He shared with me the occasion when he witnessed, at close hand, another side to this enemy. While on patrol somewhere in that jungle, Pte Livingston became isolated from his patrol group after venturing too far forward. He made his way back with painstaking stealth, hoping the enemy wouldn't hear his thumping heart. Creeping slowly forward holding his rifle and bayonet before him, he suddenly came face to face with a young Japanese soldier, also with rifle and bayonet in hand. Both men froze, and stared at each other for some time. It was as if they could read each other's minds. Stanley took one tentative step to his left and his opponent did exactly the same, as step by step, bayonets at each other's chest, they semi-circled each other before silently backing off, their eyes fixed on one another the entire time. For both soldiers this action would most probably have been considered cowardly, and not within the rules of war. But each man recognised something in the other's eyes. Possibly it was nothing more than the mutual mirroring of utter heart-stopping fear. My father spoke of this in his matter-of-fact manner, passing the incident off as a humorous anecdote, but technically the soldiers were following orders: on contact with the enemy, do not take prisoners. Neither did.

Another of Stanley's anecdotes highlights the closeness of the fighting in the jungle. With no enemy in front of him, Stanley had dug out a shallow trench at dusk, only to wake in the morning to find himself once again face to face with the enemy. A Japanese soldier had dug his own trench overnight without either party noticing they were only metres from each other. Stanley never told me how that one ended.

Sgt Eddie Emmerson cites fear as the instigator of a horrendous experience in the jungle:

Fear is a thing that people don't understand, fear is frightening, you can't speak. I remember once at Sattelberg, I had some blokes around, there was a few Nips about, and . . . I went to one of the lads about two o'clock in the morning to see how he was, and he says, 'I'm alright,' and then a bloke walked out into a bit of a clearing, and I says, 'Challenge him, you know, scream out to him, halt, the old story, halt or I'll shoot' . . . and . . . he's just stood there, and I said well you can't shoot him for that, you know, so I says, 'Challenge him and give him a proper warning,' and he screamed out to him, 'I'm going to shoot,' and he ran, and I says, 'Let him have it,' and with an Owen gun he stitched him right across the chest, so I says, 'Bloody good shot, son, good shot!' Went and picked him up, it was one of our own blokes. And what we think happened was he realised where he was, could not speak and in absolute fear decided to run, and once he run that was it. You cannot speak. You can't hide it. That was bad, especially congratulating the bloke on how good he shot.

J.W. Holmes recalls that on finding a wounded Japanese face down on a track, he immediately took out a shell dressing to tend to the soldier's wound. Holmes insists this was not a compassionate act, that the taking of prisoners was a means to extract information. As he tended the prisoner, a lance corporal stepped up and shot the prisoner through the head. 'Leave the wounded alone,' he said. 'You run the risk of a Jap bursting his grenade on you both.' From a distance it is easy to pass judgement, to recoil in horror from what seems a callous safety measure. Sgt G.H. Fearnside puts it bluntly: 'Civilisation steps back a pace or two when one goes soldiering in the jungle.'

•

The twenty-third of October was the first anniversary of the battle of El Alamein, and now many of those same men were forcing another determined enemy back. The battalion had been in close contact with the enemy for most of the month and the troops were exhausted; it would take days for casualties to be evacuated. There were no reported cases of NYDN, but two men were given sedatives before returning to action. The rest were suffering from diarrhoea. Eventually the soldiers received supplies of sulphaguanidine tablets and soon after that the 'uncontrollable prolapsing of the anus relented'.

On 3 November all resources were thrown at the enemy to remove the last pockets of resistance. The attack began at 1330 and the fighting went on all afternoon from a range of only 20 metres. Cpl Mayne Ready remembers the day well. 'The most vivid memory I have of Jivevaneng was the final C Company attack. The memory of men moving silently forward to face, suddenly, a terrific barrage of fire from the enemy at close range; of men going down and not getting up . . . I remember men diving forward a yard at a time, the continuous chatter of machine guns and ceaseless bursting of grenades and darkness suddenly falling, and rain.'

It rained without let-up the night of 3 November and filled any hole up to a metre—not too handy if your slit trench is only 45 centimetres deep. By the morning of the fifth the enemy position in front of C Company was quiet. Jivevaneng had been held. The next day was a day of rest. The troops washed clothes that had not been removed for weeks. Stanley had missed the siege at Tobruk but survived this one. Thirty-five men from the 2/17th did not.

The battalion history records that during the journey from Scarlet Beach to Jivevaneng the troops endured the worst operational conditions in the history of the battalion'. Although lives lost in New Guinea were half those of El Alamein, one soldier reported that the fighting was 'harder and more nerve racking than any ten days at Tobruk or El Alamein'. Not everyone agreed. Eddie Emmerson described the desert as 'a terrible place . . . it's like an ocean. It's just the same as being dumped out in the middle of the Atlantic. 'Cause there's no landmarks . . . and you'd get out in the night, you didn't know where you were, and if you went the wrong way, bad luck.' All Eddie had was the stars to guide him. 'I knew enough to make sure that I knew where they were, as you went, because otherwise there's nothing. It's just a black void . . . and moonlight—what's there to show up in the desert? Just more sand.' At least in the jungle, there was somewhere to hide.

Of course, this aspect of the jungle was a double-edged sword, and to others the jungle was pure hell; it conspired to unnerve a soldier, the assault as much mental as physical. With no horizon to scan, the element of surprise meant troops were constantly on edge. Stanley's war record contains a confusion of hand-scribbled instances of evacuation during his time in New Guinea—most were for infections, some had no explanation. While I cannot pinpoint a three-week absence, it seems highly likely that given the conditions of this jungle campaign, it was here that Pte Livingston's stoush with shell-happiness occurred. Although in the desert the shelling was relentless, a soldier was always aware that he was flanked by kilometres of supporting forces, whereas the jungle made for isolated, claustrophobic battle conditions. At times a man was a pack of just one, inching forward, always listening. The uncertainty was nerve-racking in itself. The possibility always existed that the enemy were not only nearby but on all sides. 'Some desert veterans suddenly found campaigning intolerable, and gave the reason as being "the hunting, hiding, listening part" of jungle warfare.'

At night, a soldier's ears were all he could rely on; the jungle provided an orchestra of minuscule sounds, any one of which might be the enemy. Tales of kamikaze pilots had the men on edge, and many grew to fear the sound of any passing aircraft, another potentially deadly noise to add to the jungle's arsenal. Pte Peter J. Jones describes the jungle as a cocktail of real and imagined dangers, and claims that the 'myriad tiny movements of the jungle's non-human citizenry' sent many on sentry duty trigger-happy. The Japanese had a habit of launching solo assaults under the cover of darkness. H.D. Wells recalls receiving orders to fire at anything that moved after dark. He offers a concise explanation of the soldier's predicament: 'One never spends seconds on thinking before the art of self preservation takes over.'

Jones describes the cumulative effect of torrential shelling: 'some of the men showed strain ... in their empty-eyed vacancy and unnatural quiet'. Those taken from the action Not Yet Diagnosed Nervous were treated in field hospitals, with no escape from the landscape that was at the root of their problem.

Eddie Emmerson always knew when a mate was in internal strife: 'Once you seen him catching flies you knew he was bomb-happy.' When Sgt G.H. Fearnside was evacuated with malaria he encountered an acquaintance sitting cross-legged at the foot of his bed. 'His right hand was held out in front of him as he sat there patiently, like a fisherman on a river's bank, which indeed he believed himself to be.' Fearnside adds that every one of the doctors in that particular facility ended up in a straitjacket and was shipped home.

In the early 1940s any kind of non-physical therapy

was viewed with suspicion. In the early days of the war, medical officers were encouraged to 'detect and bash back the neurotic'. As the war progressed, opinion gradually shifted, and the work of psychiatric advisers began to be heeded. Yet there remained a fear that 'over-enthusiastic psychiatrists might start a landslide which might sweep away a goodly proportion of the essential manpower through a broadened channel leading to the way out'.

Call it battle fatigue, shell shock or post-traumatic stress, the condition was a manifestation of a kind of internal AWL. The flesh may have been willing but the spirit had deserted it.

●

After being relieved on 6 November, the battalion moved five kilometres down the Sattelberg track where they were ambushed by malaria and dengue fever, with evacuations daily. Eddie Emmerson was philosophical about it. 'Of a morning you could decide what you got. See, the anopheles mosquito bites with its bum up in the air, and the dengue one is grey stripes and normal-looking so you could hold your arm and say, what'll I have? I've had 'em all.'

Gordon Oxman had been trundled from field hospital to field hospital since the end of September, and with no improvement in his condition, on 25 November he was discharged to Sydney. The jungle had won. Pte Oxman was back home by the twenty-ninth and was reported

AWL for the entire day. No doubt his asthma hadn't stopped him making a detour from the hospital to Tramway Street. He was fined two pounds and one day's pay.

Meanwhile, the battalion stayed in reserve until well into December. While they were out of the main action, the jungle kept fighting back. On 9 December, Stanley was evacuated suffering tinea from the waist to the feet. Somewhere between the feet and the belt was the groin, an area fellow tinea sufferer Peter Jones describes as 'a region poorly designed for discomfort'. The battalion moved on 24 December, marching through stifling hot head-high kunai grass to the tiny village of Hubika. The stench of decomposing bodies surrounding the area made for an uncomfortable Christmas, Stanley's fourth with the battalion. There would be no feast this year: the portions were so minimal that someone called for a microscope. More troubling to Stanley would have been the absence of even a single bottle of beer.

A series of long marches up the coast of the Huon Peninsula followed in January 1944. There was very little enemy contact but the going was tough over ragged coral ridges and deep gullies, rough enough for Stanley to be evacuated again on 7 January with general dermatomyositis, which manifests as scaly eruptions and muscle weakness, leaving him out of the march until 16 January. Stanley was probably lying on a bunk in an ill-equipped CCS (casualty clearing station) tent on 11 January while the men of C Company were marched down from the high ridges to clean and wash on the beach. Around 6 p.m., as the men relaxed in the water in the cool of the evening, their clothes drying on the sand, two aircraft passed overhead, then turned and strafed the beach. Sand and water flew as the men took cover as best they could, their best probably being no better than Pte Livingston attempting to hide under a blanket on an airstrip in Egypt. The planes came in for a second time low over the sand. From this angle the men on the ground saw that they were US fighters. You can't really blame the Americans: soldiers on both sides of the war looked the same naked. The pilots realised their error, waggled their wings in apology and sped off. Fortunately they hadn't managed to hit any of the one hundred sitting ducks on the beach.

Stanley returned to the battalion just in time to secure its next objective, Sio Mission, captured with a minimum of fuss. So ended the 9th Division's New Guinea campaign. January had been bruising on the battalion even though it saw little action. The 2/17th suffered 298 casualties—291 due to illness, scrub typhus, malaria, dengue fever and tinea of the groin. Eighty-six per cent of the 9th Division troops were evacuated at some stage during their time in New Guinea. Malaria accounted for almost half. Roy Lonsdale, already wounded in action for the second time, also added malaria to his list of wartime maladies.

February was described as almost a pleasant month in New Guinea, with the battalion resting on the Masaweng River. With little training to keep the men occupied, it didn't take long for the river to be denuded of fish, as the preferred fishing method involved the use of grenades. On 26 February the battalion was moved to the Song River. It was to be their last stop before embarkation to Australia on 2 March 1944. After six months in the jungle, Peter J. Jones was struck by the realisation that he had been in 'one of the most abundant and beautiful places on earth: florally, arboreally, faunally, and aviarily'. There had been little time to appreciate the view.

The battalion embarked with sixty-three fewer men than when it arrived. The troops were showing the strain, appearing lean-faced and thin-framed when *Klipfontein* steamed in to Brisbane in early March. Jones described his own appearance as being similar to the 'skeletonic portrait of Joshua Smith' by William Dobell—the painting had won the Archibald Prize amid much controversy in January, and there had been animated debate among the troops on the nature of art as black and white newspaper images of the painting were handed around. Jones also noticed that after months in the jungle many of the men had developed a stoop. 'Perhaps the undergrowth, sometimes only centimetres overhead, encouraged stooping; or could it be that the darkened jungle, with its mysterious menace, induced the kind of watchfulness that is accompanied by hunched shoulders and furtive glances? Or was I merely going "troppo"?'

On the day before Stanley disembarked in Brisbane, Pte Gordon Grant Oxman was discharged from the army after being classified as medically unfit for further military service. His discharge, on 8 March 1944, was honourable. For Gordon the show was over. Pte Stanley Livingston, however, still had a few more scenes to steal.

# 14

## *Present and accounted for*

'Men become tired of war and armies which are always in action tire as well.'

*John Baynes*

It had been just over a year since *Aquitania* steamed through Sydney Heads. The returning men had said little on that journey and little was said as many of those same men arrived unannounced and unrecognised in Brisbane on 9 March 1944. The previous homecoming had been muted by feelings of reunion and thanksgiving. This time around the men were muted by exhaustion. No soldier escaped the physical consequences of the New Guinea campaign, and any psychological damage was understated in the official histories.

Gordon continued to suffer the effects of chronic asthma, but nothing could disguise his delight at being discharged into the arms of Lilly Livingston. St Bernard's Church in Mascot was the venue for the wedding, slated for 15 April. Stanley and Roy were present and accounted for, being officially on leave, and the event went off in full Roman Catholic style. Everyone noticed a change in Stanley: his usual good humour was absent, and apart from fleeting moments of cosiness in the company of Evelyn, he was ill at ease. When leave finished at the end of April, reported incidences of AWL were far greater than for the previous homecoming. This time, Pte Stanley Livingston was not one of them. If a home can be described as a place where you feel free to be yourself, even if being yourself means not feeling yourself, then for Stanley, the army was home for now.

Training began in May in a new camp at Ravenshoe in the Atherton Tablelands. Stanley didn't last long here, but this was no AWL: he was carried on a stretcher from the camp on 8 May. For the next three months he lay in hospital with, among other complaints, malaria. He wasn't alone. Peter J. Jones felt a sense of anticlimax on his return from the New Guinea campaign. Friends and family noticed his lassitude and pallor, and only an hour after returning from leave Jones too was on his way to hospital with malaria. He was reunited with a lot of his mates in the hospital, where he described a two-way procession of men from unit to hospital and back. Daily evacuations continued throughout May, the numbers at times exceeding those returning from leave. Roy Lonsdale was another victim. Roy had embarked from Port Moresby and arrived in Townsville on 21 March. Having fully recovered from the gunshot wounds that had taken him out of the action on Scarlet Beach, he had contracted malaria; in addition, soon after returning he landed in hospital suffering contusions and lacerations to his leg. Perhaps he was in too much of a hurry to get off the boat. He was laid up for five weeks, give or take the odd day off for a wedding, before rejoining his unit in June. Before long the dormant malaria flared up again, and Roy was back in hospital by September.

Those still standing began training, once again having no idea for what or for where. There was also uncertainty at the top levels in regard to Australia's future in the war. Some rumours had it that they would be joining the Americans as they marched into Japan. Their uncertainty was to last for quite a while.

Stanley was well enough to return to camp in August in time for an assembly of the entire division, where the troops were addressed by the Commander-in-Chief of the Australian Military Forces, General Blamey, Lieutenant General Morsehead and Major General Wootten. The troops welcomed Morsehead and were blasé about Wootten, but it was Blamey who drew the most pique. One soldier described him as 'a fat, over-fed phrasemouthing parasite'.

•

While the 9th had been busy capturing Lae, Finschhafen, Sattelberg and the Huon Peninsula, General Douglas MacArthur had been 'island hopping' northward. 'Dugout Doug' had taken the reins and was galloping towards Japan. It appeared that after so much hard slog, the Australians weren't being invited to share the spoils. Our use-by date was up. The general public, the troops and even the government were perplexed about Australia's present role in the Pacific War. While the Americans headlined in the north, Australian troops were restricted to smaller venues closer to home in the still-lethal but less glamorous Pacific theatres. General Blamey seemed to be copping most of the blame. This is perhaps somewhat unfair, as the reality was that no matter what Blamey's intentions were, he stood at the feet of a giant in MacArthur, and Blamey's hands, along with John Curtin's, were tied. Australia had played a strong supporting role, and for years it had been crucial to the plot. But with the end in sight, MacArthur craved the spotlight.

With mopping up Japanese elements withering on vines in New Guinea, Bougainville and Borneo the best MacArthur could offer, by mid 1944 an ample section of Australia's most experienced fighting force were left thumb-twiddling in northern Queensland. The press were frustrated by the dearth of noble deeds they could blow out of all proportion. The newspapers had fulfilled their role as eager propagandists, albeit under heavy censorship by the government, and now they wanted their share of glory and triumph.

It was clear to most that the Allies had effectively won the war in Europe, and with the threat of a Japanese invasion now past, civilians were growing weary of continued restrictions and war itself. Curtin stuck determinedly to his guns, remaining committed to the war effort and to the Australian troops. Not surprisingly, the Labor government solidly lost a referendum in 1944 aimed at allowing them to control post-war prices. The waiting troops did not take too much interest in the debate. The interminable waiting had induced in them a subtropical coagulated ennui. The lack of action, a mulling on the past, no power over their future and a sense that the war was petering out kept morale down. Rumours of impending new campaigns were so frequent troops began to ignore them.

Still suffering the effects of malaria, Roy Lonsdale was discharged from the army on 7 December 1944, the reason for discharge being that he was required for employment in an essential occupation. This essential occupation remains something of a mystery. Perhaps Ernie Snr had used his rank in the Masonic Lodge to pull a few strings? Roy had punched above his weight and gone down more times than most—perhaps it was time to throw in the mop. Or maybe he actually was required for employment in an essential occupation. Whatever the case, luck had never been on Roy's side, and his family would have dreaded him taking up his mop and marching into a new theatre. This weary Rat of Tobruk was going home. But the Tennyson Hotel was still minus one, and Stanley James Livingston would not be home for Christmas, his fifth away from family, and by all reports his most disappointing.

By early 1945, it was clear Australia would play no part in the recapture of the Philippines, with MacArthur now planning his long-anticipated glorious victory parade into Manila and not one Australian invited. Cinderella would not make it to the ball. Training resumed in February 1945, with the ORs still in the dark about why they were training at all. On 11 March a little light was shed when the men learned of pending embarkation. Two months later, on 6 May, the troops embarked from Townsville on *David C. Shanks*. Pte Livingston had been on home soil for fourteen months with not one AWL or any other offence to his name. Was this a soldier who had now found his place in the army, surrendering to duty and authority? Or had he just had a gutful?

The general feeling among the troops was that this was going to be the last big show, the final act. A history of the battalion reports that morale was high, but for the five-year veterans, the mood was somewhat damper. Being a hardened veteran did not by definition make for an easier journey this time around. For the seasoned performer it was a numbers game—they'd been dodging bullets for years. The gut feeling was that the more time you spent among stray bullets, the closer you came to the one with your number on it. As the ship passed by the coast of Finschhafen, it moved closer to shore for the benefit of those who had fought there. Stanley Livingston may have preferred a wider berth; a lot of numbers had come up on those shores.

They were on board only a few days when news broke that the Nazis had surrendered unconditionally. The war in Europe was over. Newspapers described scenes of mass jubilation in Sydney on the afternoon the announcement was made. Thousands jammed into Martin Place and a snowstorm of paper fell from surrounding buildings. Standing knee-deep in shredded paper, complete strangers linked hands and sang 'Polly Wolly Doodle'. The AWA tower was brilliantly floodlit, in stark contrast to the brownouts of recent years. The party continued long into the night, extending into Kings Cross. It was noted in *The Sydney Morning Herald* on 9 May that the soldiers present seemed to be the most reserved. Celebrations on board *David C. Shanks* were also tempered. Their war was still very much alive.

On 16 May, the battalion arrived at Morotai Island in northern Indonesia. One soldier on board would always remember this island. A Japanese POW being held on Morotai would eventually migrate to Australia and marry the daughter of a 9th Division soldier, Pte Ralph Hopkins.

By late May all ORs were informed of the nature of the coming campaign. Australian troops were ordered to focus their mops on Borneo and the Netherlands East Indies. The 9th Division was to be split into two groups, the operations for this particular theatre being OBOE-1 and OBOE-6. The 26th Brigade were given first oboe duties—to secure the island of Tarakan—while the 20th and 24th took on sixth oboe, the recapture of North Borneo. No other oboes were mentioned in the orders.

Stanley, ever a fan of rhyming slang, made the comment, 'I didn't mind playing the oboe, I just didn't want to get shot in the orchestra stalls.'

On 2 June 1945, Stanley's twenty-seventh birthday, he boarded HMAS *Kanimbla* and joined a convoy of eighty-three vessels headed towards British New Borneo. The birthday boy's part in this show was to assist in capturing Brunei Bay. The 2/17th were to make their entrance with an amphibious assault on Green Beach and capture Brunei Bluff. Over fourteen thousand 9th Division troops joined the party with Stanley. On this island he was by no means Robinson Crusoe.

After two previous amphibious landings, Stanley was well acquainted with the choreography. On 10 June, after eight days on board and 1700 kilometres travelled, the convoy arrived at their destination at 0800. After sharing the compulsory nervous cigarette below deck, the troops received their landing orders. Pte Livingston stood by as the scramble nets were draped over the side; already a massive air bombardment was raining down on Green Beach and Brunei Bluff. It did the trick. The landing barges made it to shore about a kilometre too far east but there was no opposition and all objectives were achieved by 1230. Everything was going to script, apart from a bit of upstaging by a couple of the 2/17th boys. After landing, the first shot fired was by John 'Basher Lug Slug' Sugden into the face of no enemy, but he almost took out his good mate 'Bateye' Shepherd. Meanwhile, 'Lusty' Layton got a bit lost as he wandered neck high in the swamp. He eventually caught up with the battalion at day's end as they advanced towards Brunei Town.

The next morning, with C Company in the advanced guard, none other than Supreme Commander General Douglas MacArthur dropped by to congratulate the unit and wish them luck: he just happened to be in the area checking the vines for wither. With their luck freshly wished, they made for Brunei Town. By late afternoon they were forced to take up a defensive position. There was enemy movement ahead of them—what rotten luck.

It was a nervous night's sleep and the going was tougher the next day. As the battalion negotiated mined roads, pockets of enemy fired on them from the thick scrub surrounding the track. As the terrain became thicker, so did the enemy presence. Mortar bombs headed their way, some hitting their mark. At dawn on 13 June an airstrike intended to decimate an enemy position ahead of them fell dangerously close. A second strike forced almost an entire battalion of enemy troops to withdraw. A good thing too: it would have meant fierce close-contact fighting for the 2/17th had they remained. More bullets dodged. By 1445 hours, the town of Brunei was secured.

On 15 June, the battalion were paid a visit by the local Dyaks, the spear-carrying, head-hunting, poison-dart-shooting men of Borneo, who marched in from the jungle carrying several Japanese hostages bound to poles, a gift for the Australians. The Dyaks, with their jungle knowledge and stealth tactics, were a curse to the Japanese. Although of small stature, these men were a fearsome sight, with coins and other trophies of war worn in their ear lobes, waist-length hair, teeth replaced by jewels or brightly coloured stones, and their necks and arms covered in tattoos, generally images of birds. The hogtied Japanese were extremely happy to be delivered to the Australians, rightly confident the troops would not remove and smoke their heads before mounting them on spears. It is not the best tactical move to alienate a people who know the terrain like the back of their hand and have the nasty habit of relieving you of your head if you upset them. It comes as no surprise that these particular prisoners were very forthcoming when it came to giving up information.

On 16 June the battalion advanced towards Tutong by motor transport. No enemy contact was made and Tutong was secured the same day. This advance was recorded as one of the fastest made by land forces in the South Pacific area. It's amazing what infantrymen can accomplish when you give them trucks and remove all traces of a deadly enemy presence. In civilian terms it's called driving along a road.

The Sultan of Brunei accompanied by his Sultana arrived by canoe on the seventeenth to express his gratitude to the troops. A detachment of the 2/17th was provided to guard the Sultan. Stanley never mentioned guarding any sultans, but he never let up with the sultana jokes. (One thing Stanley was well known for: if something amused you once, he figured it would amuse you for a lifetime. Withered fruit were a particular favourite of his, and we kids were always up to our apricots in date jokes.)

This campaign was proving easier going than previous ones, but still the men had no idea of what was ahead or how long this mopping-up would continue. Some speculated that it would take years to flush out the remaining Japanese left to roam the Pacific islands.

Their next mission was to liberate the oilfields in nearby Seria. They advanced on 18 June and by mid-afternoon reached the oilfields. While the outer fields were intact, those further on were burning fiercely. The enemy were there, but not in battalion force—just small groups and isolated snipers, many half-starving. The next day they were gone. The locals provided the information that the Japanese had withdrawn from the area, but not before slaughtering many Indian POWs in a compound nearby. The locals now refused to approach the place, turning away from the bones of POWs that lay near burnt-out galvanised iron. The men had been herded and forced at bayonet point, bound, beheaded and set on fire. The Japanese were unrelenting in fighting a losing battle.

Meanwhile, forty-five oil wells blazed out of control, sending black smoke thousands of feet into the sky. This would take some serious mopping. The scorched earth left by the Japanese spread 800 metres inland for around three kilometres along the coast. The noise of the blazing wells was intense and the night burned bright as day. The battalion spent the next three months fighting the fires using mud, water and steam to quench the flames and secure the valves. Dangerous conditions, particularly for those wearing asbestos safety suits.

The wash-up for the campaign had been an advance of 120 kilometres in twelve days, capturing along the way Brunei Bluff, Brunei Town, Tutong and the blazing oilfields of Seria. Swift and successful it may have been, but six men of the battalion did not leave Borneo alive. Still, from here on, the Japanese gave up on recapturing Brunei. They withdrew inland, a dangerous move into the heartland of the Dyaks, who literally preyed on the retreating Japanese. The jungle and its inhabitants took over mopping-up duties.

While OBOE-6 had suffered relatively few casualties, the troops from the 26th Brigade in OBOE-1 had drawn the short straw. The battle to capture the island of Tarakan had cost 250 Australian lives. It was by all accounts a bloody affair, and unfortunately the aim of the enterprise (to open the airfield on Tarakan as a base for ongoing operations) was not implemented, mainly due to the damage done by the preliminary Allied bombardment.

Bill Pye had been involved in the battle of Tarakan but escaped any harm, and was currently not too far from Stanley in the port of Weston in British North Borneo. The general idea at Weston was to work their way up the railway line clearing Japanese. Bill took the first train from Weston to the town of Beaufort—there were no locomotives so they fitted railway wheels to jeeps:

The Japanese had landed in Borneo without any resistance, so there hadn't been any damage before we went in to land, and then we went in, and we destroyed the aerodrome and blew up all the railway bridges. We destroyed the railway bridges! Bloody unbelievable, so when you got to Beaufort you had to take the stuff off the trains and get into barges and then take it across to the other side and then you went on to Papar and there's another river and you had to take it off and take it out [load onto barges] again, and then go inland to Tenom, which was the end of the interior railway line. Anyhow, soon after we'd landed I took this train up, and we didn't have any resistance on the way to Beaufort, but because we were bombing, strafing there, the people were leaving their villages, and at Weston we had hundreds of people pouring into it with no accommodation and no food and it was a hell of a bloody mess.

●

News of the death of John Curtin came through on 5 July. He did not live to see Japan's ultimate surrender, nor would US President Roosevelt, who had died on 12 April. Both deaths were blamed on the stress of managing their nations throughout the war, but Roosevelt's may have been helped along by his ongoing battles with angina, coronary artery disease, atherosclerosis, high blood pressure and congestive heart failure. Churchill was still standing but he was no longer Britain's leader, suffering a landslide defeat after a general election held on the same day as Curtin's death. The old warhorse would have to cheer on from the sidelines the victory he had instigated and fought for.

Back in Brunei, with no enemy in the vicinity, attention was turned to local reconstruction and maintenance. The troops swam by day, and there was a mobile cinema for the night's entertainment. Many recall pleasant times in the area, the local children being a constant source of amusement, as was the introduction by the adults to the native wine, saki. One soldier recalled an old Dyak coming into view carrying the head of a Japanese soldier: the head was smoked in celebration and much saki was consumed. A further anecdote attests that 'Bubbles' Andrews drove everyone mad playing the same record over and over on a gramophone until it broke down, and life was pretty peaceful until 'Shell Head' Mathews and 'Gundi Guy' repaired it.

Among the same collection of anonymous personal anecdotes was this paragraph: 'Ring-a-Dang-Doo Ring was the cook (or thought he was). He had the cheek to yell out, "Come and get it or I'll throw it away." Pat Green carried out a bit of bookmaking on a commentary given by R.C. Ford. Jack Littlewood and Stan Livingston were worried about the five year plan.' The five-year plan had been announced by the Australian government in late May, proposing that those who had served in the Australian Forces for more than five years would be made eligible for early discharge. There was much scepticism about the chances of the government actually implementing the plan. Stanley and Jack would have been banking on it. Sgt Jack Hadfield Scargill Littlewood was the elder of the two friends, twenty-nine years old on enlistment and married with three children. He had enlisted ten days before Stanley; the pair had seen action in the earlier theatres of the Middle East and would be together at the end. Jack racked up a few minor AWLs before being made sergeant, which probably endeared him to Stanley and the rest of the ORs.

After the war, Stanley spoke more of Borneo than anywhere else. He talked freely of the jungle, its remarkable wildlife and his fondness for the locals. It occurs to me now that this was the end of his journey. Any bullet with his name on it would have to wait. He had time in those final months to relax, and smell the bamboo. He was officially at ease.

●

D Company had set up their headquarters in a small Dyak hut on the jungle-lined bank of the Bakoeng River, near Baram. In the evening the troops would sit around a small wireless set and listen to news from Radio America. On the night of 6 August those huddled around heard news of an atomic bomb dropped on Hiroshima, with enthusiastic commentary by the American announcer, who omitted no details of the horror unleashed. A few days later the same announcer was delighted to report that a 'Fat Man' had fallen on Nagasaki. And that, as they say, was that.

The show was all but over. There was a sense of unreality about the impending end of the war. It had gone out with a bang, or two, but that was not the general feeling in Seria where Stanley was waiting out the end of his war. The cursed thing had dragged out, and the danger was not over. The men were advised that should the Japanese surrender, military discipline would not be relaxed. The present danger was whether those remaining isolated Japanese would even know of the end of the war, whether they would believe it, and whether they would surrender without a fight.

On 13 August 1945, the troops were issued orders to cease offensive operations. On the fifteenth, VJ Day came with confirmation that Emperor Hirohito had accepted the terms of surrender. The fighting was officially over. Exhilaration among the troops was tempered by reflection. Peter J. Jones wrote home from Tarakan that day that the Japanese surrender had 'seemed anti climactic to me after we heard that a Jap city, once flowing with the life of a quarter of a million people, was laid waste and lifeless, with a single man-made piece of jetsam called an atomic bomb'. J.W. Holmes too wrote home on the fifteenth, 'The War Is over! It is hard fully to comprehend what that means. No one is surprised. No one appears excited. Tommo says, "No one is excited and it's not very much to our credit either." It shows our minds have become warped and numbed. I don't think he is right, really.'

# 15

## *The ordinary trenches*

'War does not determine who is right—only who
is left.'

*Bertrand Russell*

On 12 October 1945, after five years and seven months,
the 2/17th was declared a redundant unit. J.W. Holmes
remembers how it felt when the 2/13th received the news
that their battalion was removed from the Order of Battle:
'It seemed impossible to believe that something so proud,
so alive, so vital, should suddenly become unwanted.
This formality brought to many a sense of loss; poignant,
unwelcome and unexplained. It was over, and as individuals we went home.'

It wasn't quite over yet. The troops still had more
waiting to complete before discharge. The five-year plan
meant that older vets were the first to leave. Pte Stanley Livingston was on that list, but even so, there was a waiting list
for boats, with delays of up to four weeks. Pte Armstrong,
a five-year veteran of the 2/13th, was furious about the

delay. He called the wait a bloody disgrace, and chastised the army and the government for not supplying boats. 'The bastards find them easy enough when there's a blue for us to go into,' he wrote in his diary while fuming in Labuan.

After the show, Bill Pye was asked to remain and join the British Borneo Civil Affairs Unit (BBCAU). He agreed, and was promoted to the rank of captain, before being briefed by a colonel, Bill Stanner, a former professor of anthropology at ANU. 'He said, "I've got a boat down in the river here and it's got a crew on it, and I want you to travel up the Weston Coast and call in at every village you can get into and talk to the native headmen and to the Chinese leaders and impress upon them the importance of planting rice seedlings because they are going to need rice at the moment."' Bill set off and at one port he went ashore and asked if there were any military people present.

They pointed out a house to me and I went down and there was this fellow there, Bill Money, he had come back from the First World War and settled in New Guinea and had plantations and also had an aircraft, and he'd made a business out of this, and when the second war came, he enlisted, and because he had this experience with the natives they put him in this area. He said to me, 'How did you get here?' And I said, 'On a boat, down the river.' 'Christ,' he said, 'I've got 20,000 bloody people here and we haven't got any tucker. I'm going over to bloody Labuan to blow shit out of them.' So he went down and got in the boat and he gave me the keys and said, 'There's an office down there and I'm leaving you in charge.' Well, I didn't see him for some days, and we had all these people there. Anyway, he went over [to Labuan] and organised them to send a lot more food over. I stopped there, and Bill Money was an amazing fellow. He was much older than me and he was pretty scathing when he first ran into me. 'What the bloody use are you going to be to me?' he said. 'What can you do?' And I said I can adapt myself to most bloody things. 'Good,' he said. 'There's a piano in the front room— go and tune it!'

The mopping-up in Borneo was messy, according to Bill Pye:

The villagers had deserted their properties as the army was moving up the railway line taking village by village, and that was a dreadful thing too because the troops were not instructed to leave property alone and the people who had lived throughout the Japanese occupation, well, we went ahead, and when we came across a house, they [our boys] knocked it down, took the floorboards to sleep on, killed the chickens and ducks and ate them and destroyed the property as they went, and if they came to any place where it was difficult to get over they chopped down the rubber trees, and when the planters came back they were weeping because the rubber trees had taken years to grow . . . we did incredible damage, we were never instructed to look after the natives. So they had lived all through the Japanese occupation and then they had run away from their homes because we were bombing them, and they went back and found that we had destroyed all of them.

To this day Bill Pye thinks about these actions. 'In many cases we caused greater loss and hardship than the Jap occupation. As a civil affairs officer [CAO] I saw and heard so many accounts. I wonder if any real compensation was ever given?'

As a CAO, Bill was transferred to Jesselton, along the northwest coast of Borneo. Australian civil affairs officers did an outstanding job of rebuilding the shattered communities, providing hospitals and schools. But after fifteen months Bill felt his work was most probably done.

By that time they were bringing people back who had worked in Borneo before the war, who had escaped and got away, and we were working seven days a week and they started bringing in these planters and administrative officers and they had quite a different attitude, they had a five-day week and they were saying, 'Where's the club? Oh, the club's been destroyed? Goodness me. And where's the golf course? And the tennis courts? Oh dear, dear, dear.' They gave me the shits!

Not long after that, Bill was on the first ship home to Australia.

Pte Stanley Livingston's ship finally came in on 15 October. He embarked on the *Robert T. Hill* at Labuan for Morotai, where he joined other five-year veterans aboard HMAS *Kanimbla* on 22 October.

He arrived in Brisbane on the thirtieth and caught the train to Sydney. The theatres of operations were now closed. During the 9th Division's lengthy season, including encores, those killed, wounded or captured numbered around twelve thousand men, accounting for almost a quarter of those who'd served in the division.

•

Back home, everyone had been waiting for the final curtain. The last act had lingered far too long. There had been little thought for the thousands of Australians still fighting and dying in the last stand; with a Japanese surrender imminent, Sydneysiders didn't bother waiting for the official announcement, and VJ Day partying began at 5 p.m. on Wednesday 15 August and lasted for three days. A reported one hundred and fifty thousand people turned out in the Sydney Domain, where radio station 2GB had set up its vaudeville stage in front of the Art Gallery. Jack Davey entertained the crowd with songs from both world wars sung under a sky-high 'V' beamed from searchlights on each end of Martin Place. Amid rocket fire and flares from warships on the harbour, gold searchlights hit the tops of buildings. The AWA tower featured a huge red 'V' against its blue steel. Trams were stopped in the eastern suburbs but people were happy to walk to the harbour foreshore. Around eleven o'clock a column of people, fifty in all, marched down Pitt Street carrying an effigy of a Japanese. They halted at the Pitt Street end of the Cenotaph and proceeded to burn the effigy. As before, a snowstorm of paper rained down on the crowds: shredded telephone directories, naval blueprints, top-secret documents, Manpower forms and applications for loans formed a carpet of paper. In William Street, a lone old man harangued passers-by with his proclamations of the perpetuity of wars and the rigours to come. No-one heard him. It was a bad day for the cynic. As on VE Day, newspapers reported that men in uniform were noticeably 'quieter, but no less happy'. The next day, under the headline 'Delirious Joy in Australia', the official police estimate of the crowds gathered in the city the previous night was reported to be over a million.

It would take some time before the realities of war reached the general public, yet there were some who were not so quick to celebrate, among them the relatives and friends of the twenty-two thousand who had disappeared into Japanese prisoner-of-war camps in 1942. Almost eight thousand POWs were dead, and many continued to die even after peace was declared. The appearance of those who survived the camps was alarming. On their arrival home, dozens of ambulances lined the wharves to take them to hospitals. To those there to welcome them, waving flags seemed a pitiful means to cheer these vacant-eyed men who did their best to return a smile.

After the party, the Americans went home, taking thirteen thousand Australian women with them. Rationing continued, public transport was a shambles, power blackouts were frequent, and continued petrol rationing meant peace had come but prosperity was far from assured. A million Australians had taken part in the armed forces, and as demobilisation took place, it was deliberately drawn out to prevent overcrowding in the labour market. A campaign directed at women gave them a less-than-gentle reminder of their responsibilities now that the men had returned. They were encouraged to vacate their jobs and concentrate on creating homes for the men. Government propaganda aside, making room for the boys seemed to most women the decent thing to do. The nation certainly owed them at the very least a living. Still, the government gave little thought to supporting the women whose lives had been turned upside down for the war effort.

Evelyn retired from riveting duties. Apart from briefly taking on a part-time stint as a TAB clerk in Kogarah in the 1970s, most probably to keep an eye on her husband's earnings, she never again rejoined the official workforce. In the early 1980s I took her to see an American film called *Rosie the Riveter*, a documentary on the lives of American women working in factories in World War II. As we wandered down George Street after the film, I asked her what she thought of it. Evelyn politely thanked me for taking her, but insisted her reality bore no resemblance to that presented in the film. The film lamented the fact that after the war women were forced back into the home. Yet as much as she loved her job, Evelyn insisted she and her girlfriends had no hesitation in stepping aside for the boys. 'You were finished as soon as the war finished,' she said. 'When the men came back from the war they all got their jobs back, we got letters to go back to our old jobs and that was all there was to it.' Evelyn chose not to return to her old job at the pharmaceutical company. 'It was too easy doing that [riveting] than to go back to the other job. Working at the aerodrome was heaven after that.'

After their return, many of the men had no intention of rushing back to work. Blending back into normal society was a trial for some and many took extended leave on their own account. After six years of absence from the civilian workforce, readapting wasn't easy. Apart from the nervous effects of war, recurring bouts of malaria dogged many men. Often a man suffering a sudden attack in the street was mistaken for a drunk: frequently they were drunk *and* having an attack of malaria. Long-distance courtships, like Stanley and Evelyn's, had been conducted primarily through letters. Many other men returned to children who didn't recognise them.

Peter J. Jones had problems adjusting. He was especially concerned that the 'prolonged lack of female company, especially of my own age, had made me embarrassingly shy and self-conscious. At parties soon after the War I some-times deserted the company for an hour or so in order to recover some composure.' Another fly in his post-war ointment which Jones believed hardly deserves mentioning, deserves mentioning. Because Jones had joined the army at a tender age, with little in the way of life experience, on his return his parents failed to understand he was not a little boy anymore. They had missed his crucial years of transition to manhood, and they obviously felt that loss. They didn't want to give up the child in Peter so easily.

G.H. Fearnside wondered what the future might hold, and if he would cope. He trusted that a return to old friends and family and the memories of an innocent childhood would see him through. The freshly demobilised Norm Pope put it more bluntly. 'You just wandered about and tried to pick up the threads that you'd lost over two or three years . . . People didn't fall over you the way you expected them to.' For Norm the transition was far from smooth. 'I'd sit down at a table and I'd just feel like throwing everything and going somewhere . . . You have got to experience it to know what it was like.' Nyorie Davies, a former member of the South Australian Symphony Orchestra who was recruited to tutor air force recruits in basic mathematics during the war years, summed it up for many: 'We lived our early manhood and womanhood with fear, loss, uncertainty, terrible responsibilities . . . It was a tragic and hard rite of passage. We will never forget it, and it should not be forgotten when we're gone.'

●

On 14 November 1945, Pte Stanley James Livingston ceased to be a private. On his certificate of discharge, under the heading 'Disability' are the words 'General Debility', giving some hint as to the state Stanley was left in when hostilities ceased. This general term hides a fuller story, one the army has a history of glossing over. There were no official programs in place to ease the men back into society psychologically. Instead, efforts were focused on clearing a way back into the workplace, which had more to do with boosting the economy than any individual's spirits, and now he had to get used to being an individual. Stanley Livingston was officially demobbed. A man without a mob. He was no longer an 'us', he was a 'him'. Before that, the last time he'd been a him was in 1940, aged twenty-two. He was now twenty-seven. He had not been himself for 1786 days, his 'Total Effective Period', as the army would have it.

Stanley arrived back in Sydney to no fanfare, and home was not as he had left it. Both his parents were now dead, all of his sisters were happily ensconced in marriages, Roy was married, Gordon was married, there were children on the way. Tramway Street belonged to Dorothy and Jimmy, who unhesitatingly accepted him back into the old family home, but this was another world, and another Stanley. He was out of sorts. He still had a home at the Tennyson Hotel, where many other recently discharged, generally debilitated single friends sat and swilled to six o'clock. Evelyn the ex-riveter, and the newer, quieter version of Stanley Livingston, sans uniform and not quite so dashing, were working through the new him and the new her to see if there remained any possibility of forming an 'us'. Evelyn was twenty-four and had survived her war well, but she shared one thing in common with Stanley: all her siblings were married. Being twenty-four and single in 1945, she was on the verge of old maidenhood.

'Populate or perish' became the post-war shibboleth for Australia. Evelyn, for one, was prepared to do her duty. Stanley needed to lift his game or risk losing the spoils of peace, but unfortunately his games were two-up, poker and an attraction to the horses that landed him in trouble more than once. Fortunately, his bookie of a brother-in-law Jimmy kept that gun on the top of the wardrobe, and the debt collectors at bay. There was a dark cloud over Stanley; his lack of ambition both personal and professional was palpable. Dark clouds aside, a working-class boy wasn't one to brood; his job was to breed. In early 1946, Stanley secured a job as a toolsetter in the Westinghouse factory in Rosebery, a short walk from Tramway Street, and then he asked Evelyn Lonsdale to be his wife. She agreed. She wouldn't even have to change her initials. The date was set for 4 May 1946. That they would marry in church was a given in those days, but choosing the appropriate venue presented a problem. The daughter of a high-ranking Freemason was to wed the son of strict Roman Catholics. A marriage made in limbo.

The Lonsdales were a practical lot, not given to metaphysical reflection. On their enlistment forms the boys dutifully wrote C of E, but this was mere formality. The Lonsdales were Church of England Lite. Meanwhile, Stanley, while brought up Roman Catholic, had somewhere along the way strayed from the path. Most likely Stanley's four devout sisters, fearing for their brother's soul, influenced the final decision. The Livingston sisters were not taking any chances: the venue for the nuptials was to be St Mary's Cathedral, Sydney's Roman Catholic HQ.

Photographs of the big day belie the facts. Behind the beaming couple, there's Gordon and Lilly, and Ernie Snr and Annie, the epitome of parental pride, flanked by their own brood and a sea of less familiar faces. Inside the church, however, the atmosphere had been less congenial. It was a large turnout. Seated in the epicentre of Roman Catholicism in Sydney, those gathered there that day watched the bride walk down the aisle on the arm of her grand-masonic father. Stanley was waiting, sober, at the high altar. When Evelyn arrived, the bride and groom were swiftly ushered by the priest from the altar and shepherded through a back door. The pause that followed was beyond awkward.

These days there are three wedding areas in St Mary's: the cathedral itself, the cathedral crypt, and the Lady Chapel behind the high altar for smaller weddings. The area where Stanley and Evelyn's knot was tied fits none of these descriptions. The couple were led to a small room in the rear of the church the size and proportions of a broom closet. The reason for this was that it was a broom closet.

Complete with brooms. When the priest asked whether anyone here present knew of any reason that this couple should not be joined in holy matrimony, requesting them to speak now or forever hold their peace, not one broom spoke up. In no time at all the pair were led back, and it was announced with little ceremony that they were now man and wife. So it came to pass that Stanley and Evelyn were joined in unholy matrimony.

Mixed marriages were perfectly legal in 1946, but frowned upon, and the furrowed brows of the holy powers saw fit to remove any semblance of ceremony from such a ceremony. No-one had warned the couple—or anyone else for that matter. It was a demeaning and humiliating start to the marriage. Whether it had happened right there in St Mary's, or in the trenches, or earlier, there was no doubt that Stanley Livingston's Catholicism well and truly lapsed. The marriage was off to a rocky start, and before long Stanley was spending more time worshipping at the bar of the Tennyson Hotel, completely off his faith, than at home with his bride, home being 1187 Botany Road, Mascot. The crowded little shop was now even more so with this latest married couple, and, with Jack Lonsdale, one confirmed bachelor fresh out of prison to complete the tribe.

The government were pushing home, family and marriage as the key to progress. Building one of these happy homes was not so easy. Australia was experiencing the worst housing crisis in its history. A depression and a world war had virtually brought construction of new housing to a halt. This was one reason the couple moved into the barber shop; another was Stanley's increasing apathy.

By 1950, with most of the Livingston and Lonsdale couplings producing copious issue, Eve and Stan needed to populate soon, or perish. In 1952, Evelyn was rushed to hospital with excruciating stomach pain. She was found to be suffering an ectopic pregnancy, a life-threatening condition, especially in the early 1950s. Doctors insisted that much of her reproductive equipment would need to be sacrificed to save her life. Evelyn could be stubborn and resolute, even when racked with pain. The ectopic pregnancy removed, she arrived home, the bulk of her breeding apparatus intact, and two years later, on 14 December 1954, a son, Brian Ernest Livingston, was born. Fourteen months later another boy muscled in on young Brian's turf at Botany Road. His mother wanted to call this second-born Roydon, after her two brothers Roy and Don: Roydon James Livingston—a fine name for a writer. At the end of the day, they settled for Paul.

# 16

## *Memoirs of a pacifist smoker*

'Don't let schooling interfere with your education.'

*Mark Twain*

Stanley Livingston had a new role: fatherhood. One of my first hazy memories after arriving on this planet is being held in my father's tattooed forearms, where snakes curled around swords etched with words I was as yet unable to decipher: Death Before Dishonour. All I was able to do was poke and giggle at these inked souvenirs of war. One in particular always held my attention: a furry shape on the back of his left hand, only a couple of centimetres wide but in a most obvious position. It looked like a circle that had lost its way. I would later learn that it was the result of a late-night visit to a tattoo artist somewhere between the Suez Canal and Lebanon. Fuelled by the local beer, Stanley had insisted on creating and implementing a design of his own. He took the needle in the lathe-crushed fingers of his right hand, and in honour of his beloved Evelyn, valiantly attempted to depict a small heart on his left hand. What he woke up to the next morning was an unruly scab resembling a ringworm infection. Still, it was the thought that counted and Stanley wore this flawed little heart just below his sleeve for the rest of his days.

Those crushed fingers were a source of endless fascination. Stained a golden tan through decades of hand-rolling tobacco, this tips of three of them were as hard as rocks and bereft of nerve endings. Needles, nails and razor blades inserted into fingertips and presented to unsuspecting infants induced at once shock and delight. And this was twenty years before Freddy Krueger. Only one finger remained razor-blade free; like the fist-flattened septum in his nose, the tip of the third finger on his right hand held no bone and with a pinch the fingertip collapsed. It was like squashing a bug. Hours of fun for all the family.

Barely able to assume the bipedal position, cradled in two hairy arms held apart by a blue singlet, I distinctly remember my father singing to me. The words escaped me but the tune never left. As I hummed it to him in later life he instantly burst into song in his passable tenor voice.

Close your sleepy eyes, my little Buckaroo.
While the light of the western skies is shinin' down
    on you.
Don't you know it's time for bed, another day is through.
So go to sleep, my little Buckaroo.

Stanley always loved a western, and he'd appropriated the tune from one of his favourites, the 1937 flick *The Cherokee Strip*. He also revealed that at the time he had taken a few liberties with the lyrics, and as my young eyes closed, the last subliminal line I would have heard was, 'Go to sleep, you little bugger you.'

I was bilingual by the time I was five. I had to learn to speak fluent Stan. His archaic dialect generally went something like this: 'I'm feeling a bit butcher's hook so would one of you god-forbids grab some Oscar Asche, get on your Jimmy Pike, go down the Rosewall and Hoad and have a Captain Cook for some Jack and Jills. I'll be on me Pat Malone having a Danny La Rue in the Edgar Britt-house if you want me.'

Rough translation: 'I'm feeling ill. Could one of you kids grab some cash, get on your bike, go down the road and have a look for some pills. I'll be on my own having a spew in the toilet if you want me.'

My father spoke English on occasion, but rarely did he stray from his native tongue.

●

The barber shop had barely changed since the war, and in the early 1960s every man still required a regular haircut, short back and sides. Cutthroat razors were sharpened on whetstones, honed on leather strops; combs were disinfected in jars of metho; uncurled flypaper strips buzzed with dying insects as the scissors of Ernies junior and senior clipped their way through the years. Barbering remained a reliable profession. While the pair of Ernies manned the barber's chairs, Annie and Evelyn womaned the tobacconist booth. A glass and timber cabinet behind them held all the latest accoutrements for the modern male: Brylcreem, Californian Poppy, pipes, pipe-cleaners, pouches and tins of tobacco (Borkum Riff and Prince Albert), squirrel-hair shaving brushes, King Gillette blue razor blades, and a jar of lollies for other people's children just out of arm's reach: freckles, milk bottles, Metro gum, fake teeth, bullets and jersey caramels. Torture.

Annie and Ernie Snr had watched the bulk of their children grow up, marry and create babies that boomed, but this little nest was far from empty. This Tardis of a shop seemed far bigger on the inside than the outside. As a boy I witnessed an endless cast of larger-than-life souls come and go: salesmen, ex-boxers, magicians, prospectors, the literate and illiterate, saints and scoundrels. The only thing they had in common was hair in need of cutting. By the mid-sixties total occupancy was steady at seven: Annie, Ernie Snr, Stanley and Evelyn, their two children, and Jack Lonsdale, the heartbroken deserter, living in an alcove on a fold-out canvas bunk, only metres away from the stairs under which he'd hidden during the war. Stanley rode an old Speedwell bike to his work. He never owned a car—he didn't need one. The six o'clock swill had ended in 1955, and Stanley was living within spitting distance of the only journey he made apart from the ride to work: the short walk across the road to the Tennyson Hotel.

Spittoons were a thing of the past by the time I made my entrance, but old habits die hard, and many men continued to expel huge gobs onto the tiled floor. As a boy it was my job to sweep up the hair at day's end. Using a broom with soft black bristles, I would sweep the offcuts into a hirsute mountain larger than myself, a veritable Cousin It of a pile. The job was made harder by bristles getting stuck in pools of spit. The hillock of hair was taken down the back and burnt off in a 44-gallon drum, the smell of the burning hair competing with the waft of unrefrigerated fish from the fish and chip shop on the right, and the stench of vegetables rotting in the sun behind the fruit and vegetable store on the left. The two Ernies were surrounded by Nick the Fruiterer and Con the Fishmonger.

Our family no doubt added to the olfactorial environment as we had no shower, no running hot water, and hands and face were washed once a day in the small sink in the kitchen. The old round wooden table was still in the kitchen, more splinter now than wood; the Early Kooka gas stove hadn't moved; the old leadlight cabinet had shed more of its lead; the corrugated-iron roof had lost most of its nails and leaked when it rained—or, more to the point, rained when it leaked. The so-called living room still contained the pianola and the pedal-powered Singer sewing machine whose treadle my brother and I gave a good thrashing. The glass-topped table was the only object in good condition, kept as it always had been for Christmas feasts.

The bathroom, or more to the point the room with the bath, still housed the concrete industrial tubs we had bathed in as infants. Their high grey walls unnerved us, but they were never as scary as that old claw-footed bath surrounded by cobwebs and blackened brick walls. The entire household bathed once a week, in the same water, boiled in a new addition: a gas copper that held enough water for one bathful. All hands took turns ferrying buckets of scalding water to the tub. Then it was adults first, one by one, until it was our turn. Playing with my boats in tepid water shared with my brother was less than relaxing, especially as we were surrounded by numerous black-eyed spiders and the odd cockroach. The toilet hadn't been cleaned since the war, and it wasn't clean then. It remained a lonely outpost, dark and ridden with spider's webs, the bowl the colour of neglected teeth. The old coathanger and newspaper hadn't yet been replaced by soft tissue. I'm sure a close examination of my anus would reveal ink traces of all the news that mattered from the fifties and sixties.

The all-pervading smell was tobacco smoke. I've never smoked a cigarette in my life but in my youth I passively inhaled a nimbus of the stuff. There was no warning not to—in fact, I was actively encouraged. As I sat cross-legged among discarded hair on the floor of the shop, the men would hand me a fag, but never offer a light. These were training cigarettes. Sitting there in my very own child-size blue wife-beater singlet, I was one of the men—all I needed was fire. I wasn't allowed to play with matches, just cigarettes. We could even purchase candy cigarettes with a raspberry-tipped lit end to suck on, but I never had the urge to light up. I did, however, remain a heavy passive smoker for most of my adult working life, working small clubs well into the nineties before my lungs were saved by a quantum shift in public perception. Quanta are fairly quick to shift when people start dropping dead, and change can be even swifter when governments realise how much it costs to keep those blackened lungs inflated. Yet to this day, if I get my hands on an increasingly rare cigarette, I'll sit cross-legged on the floor, snap it in half, and savour the smell of the raw weed. Mind you, the owner of the cigarette generally isn't too happy with me.

Jack Lonsdale stank more than anyone. A chain smoker working at the Botany tanneries, he constantly reeked of cured animal skin, beer and tobacco.

While we had no shortage of smells, what we didn't have was carpet, a car, a phone, light fittings (just bare bulbs swinging from frayed cords), a television or a washing machine, and we had just the one electric power point. With the onslaught of modern electric appliances in the sixties, a tangle of extension cords and double adaptors grew to startling dimensions on the grey splintered wooden floor. A hole in the ceiling, which doubled as the upstairs floor, carried a cord to where a further mound of double adaptors powered Hornby trains and Scalextric race cars, to the delight of my brother and myself. With no other heating, an open fire in the main upstairs bedroom was put to good use, as were the wooden crates used for kindling courtesy of the fruit shop next door. No wonder the fruit lay rotting on the ground in the sun. The barber shop itself was our playground. When it was closed I'd sneak into that closet under the stairs and read by torchlight from a haystack of *Parade* magazines featuring women's bare breasts. Black strips covered any hint of a nipple but it still made me the hero of the day when I smuggled one to school.

In the 1960s, Botany Road was the gateway to the city, and anyone of note arriving at the airport had to travel past the shop. We had a good view from the upstairs window, or you could join the crowds lining the streets to catch a glimpse of visiting luminaries. I sat on my uncle Jack's shoulders in a cloud of his cigarette smoke as Lyndon Baines Johnson, the President of the United States of America, drove by, stopped at the corner of King Street and Botany Road, emerged from his car only metres away and waved to the adoring crowd amid a shower of ticker tape bearing the slogan 'All the way with LBJ'. I was so excited I almost extinguished Jack's cigarette.

I had been well aware of the president's impending arrival. My fifth-grade teacher, Mr Amos, had been gearing up for it. He suggested the whole class go out into the school paddock where we were to create a big sign to welcome LBJ. Mr Amos wrote his proposed message in white chalk on the blackboard: 'Go home Yankee imperialist and warmonger'. My classmates and I dutifully copied down the slogan. When we arrived home and were asked what we'd learned at school that day, most of us wanted our parents to tell us what an imperialist warmonger was. Not long after that, Mr Amos went AWL from Mascot Public School for good. No doubt he was discharged with ignominy. Looking back now, I feel privileged to have had my fragile eggshell mind subverted by Mr Amos.

The Royal Family drove by too many times to maintain interest, but I do remember being blessed by the Pope in 1970. Super 8 footage shot at the time clearly shows myself and Colin Davis, the local paperboy, standing in the centre of Botany Road as Pope Paul VI was driven by standing in an open-topped car, blessing Colin and me among others as he passed. On other days, open-backed trucks continuously rolled by, packed with freshly shorn and bleeding sheep on their way to the city abattoirs. Blue-aproned men dragged bloody carcasses from their vans across the pavement to the sawdusted floor of the butcher's shop. Nick the Fruiterer entertained the local children by sawing the heads off his chickens with a bread knife, the scampering headless chooks terrorising the uninitiated.

When the Beatles drove past, we were too busy watching their progress live on our recently acquired black and white television to bother wandering to the window. Television arrived in Australia the year of my birth, but it remained for several years a luxury only for the wealthy. I will never forget the day Uncle Jack dragged a small wood-framed television up the stairs and into my grandparents' bedroom. After locating a spare double adaptor, Jack plugged it in and there in glorious black and white was Killer Kowalski pinning Dominic DeNucci to the canvas with a step-over toehold. My brother and I were hooked.

Before the idiot box entered our lives, a favourite entertainment was sitting at the upstairs window on Saturday afternoons, perched with my grandmother, Annie, observing the idiots across the road at the Tennyson Hotel. At around five o'clock, a stream of men made their way out after a day of holding up the bar, heading home to their wives for tea. Most of the men we knew—they all had the same haircut. There was a ladies-only saloon next to the men's, but we rarely saw anyone enter or leave.

On one particular Saturday, the men needed to negotiate roadworks outside the pub. A large trench had been dug only metres from the door of the saloon bar. Those not prepared, which was most, tumbled out of the bar and straight into the trench. Every time a man went down, my grandmother would let out a squeal and clap her hands. Eventually Jack stumbled out, heading home for a feed. He staggered forward, seemed to sense something, then staggered back, paused for a moment to focus, then staggered forward again. Somehow he teetered on the edge again and again, until at last he plummeted head-first into the hole. 'Lord love a duck!' Annie shrieked, with glee rather than concern. On reflection, I wonder why this woman didn't call out a warning to her son. Perhaps it was to teach him a lesson. Perhaps he deserved it. This was the longest time Jack ever spent in a trench in his life, but eventually he emerged; bloodied but unperturbed, he gathered himself, as a drunken man does, and crossed the road grinning from ear to ear. When Annie opened the front door to her bloodied, battle-scarred son, Jack glanced down and, without lifting his head, raised his large brown eyes, much the way a puppy does when it's just been caught having a crap on the carpet.

When sober, Jack was like a second father to us boys. When he was drunk we were wary—he seemed a lot happier but we sensed he wasn't really being Uncle Jack, and we kept out of his way. Only much later did I consider that a single man, well into his fifties, still living at home with his mum and dad, with no room of his own and only a canvas bed for a possession, might feel on occasion the need to indulge in a beverage.

Every working day, Stanley Livingston awoke at 5 a.m., made his own breakfast, got on his pushbike and rode to the factory in Rosebery. He started at seven and knocked off at three, but he was never home before six—he was at the other office across the road. Stanley was a tool-setter but I never saw him set a tool. I was familiar with the factory from a Christmas party held in the canteen each year for all the workers' children. My father once showed me around the place out of working hours. We passed hundreds of lockers where all those blue overalls lived until we came to the empty factory floor. It was vast. There were approximately three hundred lathes set row after row, and it was Stanley's job to set and see to the wellbeing of these machines. It was completely silent at the time—I could only imagine the cacophony as hundreds of men worked the lathes.

While Stanley slaved away, I was down the road at Mascot Public School, the same school my mother and all her siblings had attended. The old air-raid shelters were still standing, grey with age and less of a target, some open on one side, some enclosed by hurricane wire, a cage for kids. We ate our school lunches in them on rainy days. I didn't much like school. Bullying was rampant, but that was mostly limited to the teachers. I was thrashed with a cane on numerous occasions before I reached the age of ten. My parents never laid a hand on me but those teachers did. When they weren't whipping you, they'd be propelling chalk dusters in your direction, or, my least favourite, dragging you out of class by the ear. I can still hear that peculiar crackling as cartilage was wrenched from skull. Apart from Mr Amos, who never laid a finger on any of us, they were callous monsters and monstresses. Ink wells, blue ink and blotting paper spelled trouble for a left-hander. No matter how carefully I wrote, the movement from left to right meant there was nothing left on the page but a blue smudge, which also appeared on my palm. My father had elegant handwriting and my mother's was almost calligraphic. Appreciation of the written word and language was common among my parents' generation. It wasn't considered unmanly to write lyrical words in a fine hand. To the men of Stanley's day, poetry was an accepted tool of courtship, whereas a boy spouting poetry in 1963 didn't make too many friends.

As the 1960s progressed, the face of Botany Road changed. An arcade replaced the Ascot Cinema, and something called a supermarket took up the space of half a dozen smaller shops and sent others out of business. The barber shop held on like a loose baby tooth. As long as Ernie Snr was still breathing, the shop would survive. I remember Ernest Lonsdale's last day on earth. Stanley and Jack carried him from the backyard clutching at his chest, before laying him out on the small bench in the shop. My brother and I stood silently by. I was eight years old. I don't recall feeling any panic or sadness. Just before Ernie Snr breathed his last he beckoned his two grandsons over and asked those gathered around—Evelyn, Annie, Jack and Stanley—to move away. Ernest Lonsdale had a message to impart to us two boys, not meant for anyone else's ears. I recall moving over to my grandfather: he was struggling for breath but he could still speak. He drew us close to him, and moments before he died, Ernie quietly whispered sage advice into our young ears—words meant for us to carry throughout our lives. No-one else in that room heard a thing, and neither my brother nor I will ever reveal what was passed on to us . . . because neither of us can remember what he said.

I remember Annie cradling his head, and then he was gone. He died in the arms of Annie Lonsdale. She was wailing—I'd never heard anyone wail. She had lost the man she loved right in front of her eyes on a worn wooden bench, the bench where he had greeted thousands of customers as they waited for a trim and a shave from Mascot's master barber. The year was 1964. From all reports it was a large funeral. My brother and I weren't invited: children were not welcome at funerals in those days. Our cousin had to babysit us. Apparently over a thousand people turned out to see Ernie off. The traffic lights were turned off and the road blocked as the hearse was driven slowly down Botany Road where it stopped outside 1187 and the driver got out and saluted the barber shop.

Perhaps it was fitting that Ernie died at that time. He didn't quite live to see the demise of his cherished profession, lost to the hands of hairdressers. He had watched as men's hair encroached past the ears, but it had not quite yet reached the collar. Ernie Jnr wholeheartedly carried on the tradition with his mother, Annie, in the tobacconist booth, but before long, men's hair had ventured far below the shoulder and customer numbers diminished.

Annie Lonsdale was born before the first aircraft left the ground, and she died nine days after the first man stepped on the moon. When Annie died quietly in her sleep in her bed above the shop in 1969, the barbering business was all but over. Hair had now reached the waist on some males—a musical was named after the stuff. My own hair was by this stage parted in the middle and tickling my shoulders. I hadn't sat in the barber's chair for some years. I was a modern teenager, a traitor to the family profession. The little loose tooth was about to be extracted. Evelyn, Stanley and we boys were the first to make a move. Evelyn had used her hard-earned riveting wage wisely and invested in a block of land, although at the time she'd bought it it was a block of swamp on the outskirts of the city in a suburb called Sans Souci. The block had cost her all of fifty pounds, a fortune during the war years. By 1970 the block was surrounded by middle-class nuclear families in what had become a sought-after beachside suburb. With Stanley's war service loan, a double-fronted brick-veneer home was constructed and we left the old nest. I despised the suburbs. I missed the everyday circus of the barber shop, but for Evelyn and Stanley, who were not getting any younger, it brought a certain amount of comfort and security. Not to mention hot water, a bath, a shower and a toilet inside the house.

I missed Jack: he'd taken his canvas bed elsewhere. Jack had quit the tannery, secured work at the airport and purchased a small ground-floor apartment just a few hundred metres from the old shop. To everyone's amazement, Jack remarried in 1991, at the age of seventy-four, to a woman called Ruby. Jack and Ruby shared the little flat in High Street. Not surprisingly, the marriage produced 'no issue'. Jack was the exception to the rule to the very end. For the most part of his life an unmarried, childless, alcoholic low-income-earner, his body gave up the ghost in 1997, yet his liver had shown no sign of surrender. He beat the odds, and cheered the lives of two little surrogate sons along the way.

Ernie Jnr soldiered on for a while in the barber shop with his wife, Nellie, in the tobacconist role, but there was no future to be had. In early 1972 he packed up his scissors and closed the door at 1187, the last Lonsdale to do so, and moved back home to Revesby.

By the time we moved to the suburbs, the war in Vietnam was hitting its peak. It didn't bode well for my brother and me. Working-class boys were top of the conscription list. Stanley was adamant we were not going to war. He was no conscientious objector, just a father determined his boys were not going to go through that particular South-East Asian hell. He swore that if we were called up he'd build a cave under the house and hide us there. He didn't need to. Gough Whitlam put an end to conscription in December of 1972. My brother had just left high school; I had another year to go. I was slightly disappointed. I fancied the idea of an underground cave.

# 17

## *Don't give an old digger the gripes*

'I'm heading for the last roundup
There'll be Buffalo Bill with his long snow-white hair
There'll be old Kit Carson and Custer waiting there
A-riding in the last roundup.'

*Gene Autry*

One day in 1973 as I sat in the lounge room watching television, Stanley pulled a handkerchief out of his pocket, coughed into it, and a mouthful of blood spilled out. He became very quiet and very pale. My brother and Evelyn took him straight to hospital. I stayed home—surely it was nothing, just a little blood. Stanley arrived at the hospital, made it out of the car, walked through the doors to emergency and collapsed. He had suffered a major heart attack, complicated by complete renal failure. He was dead by the time they got him inside.

Stanley had chosen the perfect place to die, because

the emergency staff at South Sydney Hospital managed to revive him. I saw him not long after, lying in intensive care, more tubes coming out of him than electrical cords from a mountain of double adaptors. He couldn't speak. He wasn't expected to survive. Some time later, his sisters called in a priest to issue the last rites. Apparently at the sight of this priest, the near-lifeless body of Stanley Livingston rose out of bed, pulling tubes from the wall and sparking alarms; like Frankenstein's monster he clasped his hands around the priest's throat and almost strangled him to death. I wish I'd seen that.

His condition remained perilously unstable for eight days before he was transferred to the renal unit at Sydney Hospital. Before falling ill, Stanley Livingston had never taken a day off sick in his life. No AWLs there. Each day Evelyn made her way into the hospital, sat by Stanley's side, then caught the last bus back to Sans Souci. Evelyn and Stanley were never inclined to publicly show affection. They had no need to broadcast their love. Her quiet sacrifice and dedication said enough. It was six weeks before Stanley was well enough to return home, skeletal and weak, and one kidney short of a pair. Neither as a curious child nor as a self-indulgent adolescent did I ever pick up on the psychological humours of my parents, with the result that I failed to notice any hint of my father's post-operative depression. Unlike his battle with shell shock, this time he was fully certified nervous.

Stanley had apparently had one hell of a near-death experience. While never one for ghost stories, he became convinced he'd been to the other side and he didn't like what he saw. Hospital staff had to restrain him several times when periods of delirium had him convinced that he was in a POW camp and the nurses and doctors were the Japanese. He related that if he could have got hold of a knife he would have killed as many as he could get to, and he was planning how he might do so. Attending therapy sessions was not common practice among factory workers in the 1970s, but on the advice of his doctors, Stanley agreed to see a therapist, who came highly recommended. This eminent psychiatrist's name was Harry Bailey. Harry was about to become famous, for all the wrong reasons.

Harry ran a nice little private practice in Sydney. He took on all comers, from the schizophrenic to the pre-menstrual. No job too small. The problem for Harry was that not enough of them came back. On the first meeting you'd be given a handful of pills. Harry's cure for deep-seated anxiety was a deep-sleeping coma. While the authorities eventually woke up to the goings-on in Harry's practice at Chelmsford Private Hospital, up to eighty-five of his patients never did. Stanley woke up quick-smart. After two sessions he threw in the towel, declaring the doctor a bloody ratbag. Harry Bailey never saw gaol time. In 1985 he swallowed a few of his own pills and took a rather long nap himself. Toni Lamond also spent time under Dr Bailey's care. She describes herself as a survivor of 'that horror show called Chelmsford'. When pressed for further details Toni was for once speechless, as she has no recollection of the experience; in fact, the years 1972–74 remain a complete blank.

Stanley eventually regained his perk, but not his health. He was in constant pain, angina the worst of it. Still, he returned to work, getting up before dawn, packing his thirty pills before catching the 302 bus to Mascot from Sans Souci. Without fail he'd swing by the Tennyson on his way home before bussing back out. Stanley worked until they told him he couldn't anymore, when he turned sixty-five in 1983. After thirty-eight years in the trade he was given the cliché gold watch and a handshake and shown the door. No super. No bonus. No nothing. As he had in the war years, Stanley made lifelong friends on the factory floor. His mates got together and presented him with a gift: a miniature lathe lovingly crafted to scale on the machines that he set, chromed and polished like a trophy. He treasured it, and so do we.

He continued to see his army buddies once a year on Anzac Day. Stanley was never marching to glory. He was marching to the pub, as fast as he could, to join his mates for a quiet beer or nine. After his illness Stanley couldn't march anymore, but he never missed a post-march reunion. He wasn't unhappy in retirement. He had his cats and the dog. He was a magnet for any stray in the area—at one stage he had six tabbies in his care. He bawled his eyes out when one of them died.

•

While Stanley was resting in the care of Harry Bailey, I was having the joy of learning well and truly beaten out of me in a high school on the inskirts of Sydney that had its own policy for dealing with boys who refused to stick to the straight and narrow-minded. The cure for boys like myself and other underachieving miscreants was to force us into attending classes such as home economics, typing and art. Sharing a classroom with actual 'girls' was meant to somehow embarrass us into embracing more testosterone-fuelled subjects such as commerce, mathematics, woodwork, metalwork and science. But their attempts simply instilled in me a passionate desire to cook, paint and write. I clearly remember sitting at the back of a sewing class, sandwiched between two much larger, visibly and psychically agitated males, making no eye contact as we tried to ignore the sniggers of our female classmates. I recall the verve with which I wove with needle and cotton, in as masculine a hand as I could manage, the outline of a 1971 Valiant Charger into a sheet of brown hessian. I've still got it. When I arrived home with my school project Evelyn seemed genuinely proud. Stanley just went a bit quiet.

(To be fair, my own opinions of the schoolyard are not necessarily those of my peers. For example, my brother Brian sailed through with straight As, graduated from university and became a card-carrying member of Mensa. So just for the record, I do take some responsibility for my lack of responsibility.)

I spent my last year at high school AWL, with the result

that I failed every subject in the HSC. With no practical skills and no qualifications, where in this world was a working-class boy with a burgeoning interest in the arts to go? Stanley's advice for me was to get myself a trade. He had been setting tools for years, yet I still don't even own a hammer. So I made it my business to go AWL from a decent day's work. I conscientiously objected to the idea of working in a factory for the rest of my life. Eventually I went AWL from the family home. My parents immediately purchased a telephone so that I had something to call home to. From then on I was AWL from all of life's responsibilities: no job, no children, no car. At least Stanley and I had that last in common. As a young adult, my life could not have shifted further from that of my father. In my mid-twenties, an age when Stanley was hiding under well-aired blankets in the Middle East being strafed by Stukas, I was an art student living in a squat in Woolloomooloo. I used to pick up his pills for him down the road at Sydney Hospital. When the name Stanley Livingston was called out, I'd always get a laugh. On the days when he was up to travelling in to the city, we shared a beer and we talked. We continued our talks whenever I made it home to Sans Souci, sitting under that blanketed Hills Hoist in the backyard, always with a beer in front of us—we were just getting to know each other.

Gordon 'Storky' Oxman passed away in 1981 after being plagued by asthma all his life. The love of his life, Lilly, had died in 1978 at the age of fifty-eight, only months after the death of her sister Dorothy. Dorothy's husband Jimmy didn't make it past the sixties. Around the time of Lilly's death, Stanley was astonished and angered to learn from his surviving sisters that their father, Ernie, was not and never had been a Roman Catholic. Ernie was a Protestant, and had converted on his deathbed. Ernie's sisters-in-law insisted he convert or he wouldn't be buried with his wife, Bridget. Stanley's old man apparently chose not to throttle the priest as he was given the last rites.

Unlike stand-up comedians and cats, my father only managed to die twice. The last time I saw Stanley Livingston he looked frail, but then again, he'd looked frail for fifteen years, ever since he'd died outside the emergency room of the South Sydney Hospital. The last time I heard his voice was on the phone. He didn't sound too well—he had an aching pain in his neck and he quipped, 'You know you're crook when you can't even face a beer.' I said, 'You take care of yourself.' He then spoke the last words I'd ever hear him say: 'I'll put your mum on.' He booked himself into hospital the next day. He spent the night, and in the morning was given the all-clear. My brother was warming up the Holden to collect him when he received a call. Stanley was dead again. And he hasn't been back since.

On 20 October 1988, Stanley James Livingston went AWL from the planet. He was seventy. Stanley died with fifty dollars in his pocket. His coffin was draped in the Australian flag—a good thing too, we couldn't afford a decent box. Roy Lonsdale was one of the pallbearers.

Uncle Roy still had a few good years left; his turn didn't come until 1997. The other pallbearers I didn't recognise. They were all 2/17th boys and it wouldn't surprise me if by chance some have been mentioned somewhere along the way on these pages. I hope 'the Count' was there, and Sgt Littlewood, Pte Currie and little Alfie Drew. They each said a few words, then the Last Post was played. I can't remember what any of them said. I'd never been to a funeral before.

His timing couldn't have been worse. Within a year my recently adopted trade of stand-up comedian had taken me around the world. I'd even appeared on the telly. My brother had married and soon there would be two grand-children, both boys. I'd been determined to prise as many stories out of him as possible during those last months of his life. Enough maybe for a book. It's one thing to say they will not be forgotten; the question is, how will they be remembered? Ninety-nine per cent of my father's stories died with him, and after all my wanderings I'm still left with this sense of wondering. Could these attempts at rifling through the combined experiences of those closest to him really give me a hint as to the nature of the man? Have I misrepresented him completely? After all, a sure way to avoid creating a myth around someone would be to ease off on writing lengthy tomes about them.

What I am left with is a profound sense of the shared 'us-ness' of these men's experiences. The war was never about one man's deeds. Heroic individual exploits aside, whatever that show was, it had an ensemble cast, and as they say in my business, there are no small parts, only small actors.

I can't imagine what he would make of these ruminations. He'd probably be rolling in his rose bush. Why all the fuss? Stanley wasn't one for getting on the high horse. Low mules were more his style. And by the way, I never did find out where that photo was taken, so the question still remains: does that look like the fresh face of a young man enjoying his first overseas trip, a battle virgin? Or are we looking at a war-weary veteran of one of the most intense and bloody campaigns in military history? There's a definite spark in Stanley's eye. It's almost as if he's teasing me, this kid from suburban Zetland, in the middle of no-man's-land, with two of the boys, a wog, a donkey and himself.

# *Epilogue*

After we sprinkled Stanley on his rose bush, Evelyn held down the fort at Sans Souci for another fifteen years. She had the pleasure of watching her grandchildren grow, and her youngest son do whatever it was he was doing. She never quite understood what I was up to, and until her dying day she still wondered when I'd get a proper job. (Still working on that one, Eve.) She made it to a new century, and in the end she went quietly. I recall as an infant walking down Botany Road and reaching up to hold my mother's hand; on the other side my brother did the same. On a clear sunny day in 2003, Evelyn was resting peacefully, her two grandsons playing nearby. It had been eighty-one years since she'd breathed her first breath, and here she breathed her last with one hand clutching the hand of her eldest son and the other squeezing the hand of her youngest. I don't think a Mascot girl can ask for more than that.

Later that day I took a walk down Botany Road past the old shop. It looked even smaller than I remembered it to be. It was now a warehouse outlet for women's shoes. All that was left of the once bustling barber shop was a white cube full of shoeboxes. Feeling a little self-conscious after being caught staring by the bored sales attendant, I entered the store. Now doubly embarrassed, I pretended to look through assorted women's shoes as I took furtive glances around the cube, searching for any hint of the past. For some reason I felt like a giant. I looked to the corner where the tobacconist booth had stood, then to the closet under the now non-existent staircase where Jack Lonsdale had hidden, to the wooden bench where I'd watched my grandfather die and failed to recall his dying words, to where Squizzy Taylor and a thousand other larrikins and ratbags had trod. A million stories shared. How could such a small space hold so many stories? I smiled at the attendant, who frowned at me. I put down the mock-leopardskin pump I'd been fondling and picked up a larger sized beige peep toe. I swear I could smell hair burning. I would have liked to linger but I was running out of shoes. I thanked the woman sitting among a sea of new soles and said a quiet goodbye to all the old souls.

As I walked the rest of Botany Road past unfamiliar shops it struck me how ordinary Mascot had become, until I realised it had always been ordinary. The little shop wasn't a Tardis. The Tardis is my own head. I crossed the road and wandered into the bar of the Tennyson Hotel. I nodded towards the barman and said, 'It's my Wally Grout so get your Onkaparingas around a monkey's arse, pour me an Amos and Andy and I'll be Adrian Quist as a fairy dart in no Harry Lime.'*

He had no idea what I was talking about.

---

*Translation: It's my shout so get your fingers around a glass, pour me a shandy and I'll be pissed as a fart in no time.

# Acknowledgements

'Nobody wants to read other people's reflections on life and religion and politics, but the routine of their day, properly recorded, is always interesting.'

*Evelyn Waugh*

The backdrop and stage dressing for the front-line scenes was drawn primarily from two sources, *'What We Have . . . We Hold!' A history of the 2/17 Australian Infantry Battalion 1940–45* and Mark Johnson's *That Magnificent 9th: An illustrated history of the 9th Australian Division 1940–46.* The minutiae of daily military life was gleaned from the Australian War Memorial's Second World War official histories and war diaries. I am indebted to the staff of the reading rooms at the AWM and the National Archives of Australia for their help in gaining access to official records.

For setting the scene on the home front I combed through Daniel Connell's *The War at Home*, a collection of local recollections of life during World War II originally recorded for a 1986 ABC radio series.

Four personal memoirs provided the material to flesh out the main supporting cast: G.H. Fearnside's *Half to Remember*, Peter J. Jones' *The Reluctant Volunteer*, H.D. Wells' *'B' Company Second Seventeenth Infantry* and John Holmes' *Smiles of Fortune: A memoir of the war against Japan 1943–45*. Their generosity of spirit in sharing their candid revelations brought my father's footsteps closer to home.

I remain forever grateful to two special guest stars, participants in the original show who took me into their homes and into their memories: Eddie Emmerson, former Rat of Tobruk, and William Pye, former officer and still a gentleman.

Other firsthand insights from assorted friends, comrades and those who served near and far from my father were cast from personal records held in the National Archives of Australia.

A cameo appearance by Toni Lamond was greatly appreciated (it's handy having a national treasure for a neighbour). Key crew members who performed above and beyond the call of duty are Bernie Carr, Marlene Zwickler, Renate and David Mattiske, John Lethbridge, Michael Bates, Jennifer Warren, Sheila Livingston, James Livingston, Charles Livingston, the Buckley clan, Winifred Childs, John Maynard, Tony Melov, Melissa Lyne, Paul McDermott, Michael Petroni, the friendly staff of the Mitchell Library, Edwina Stuart, HLA Management Pty Ltd, Jane Palfreyman, Kathryn Knight, Sue Harvey, Clara Finlay, Isabella Penna, Jane Symmans and all at Allen & Unwin.

The germ of an idea for the entire production came when my brother, Brian Ernest Livingston, a habitual hoarder of family memorabilia, produced a faded copy of Stanley Livingston's court-martial record. Not only would Brian supply me with endless details of the family history, I was also delighted to receive a cache of secret tapes he had recorded of my mother and various uncles gasbagging in the family kitchen in the mid 1990s. Without this eldest son of a deserter's unflagging support, no pages would here appear.

I am beholden to uncles Roy and Gordon, the odd Jack, and Ernies too numerous to mention, and to the extended families of the Lonsdales, Livingstons and Oxmans, backstage and in the wings, and, I hope, cheering me on.

By far the highlight of the show for me has been the sharing of bounteous gossip with my aunty Dot around her kitchen table. Thanks for the laughs, Dottie, and the tea, the Scotch Finger biscuits and the perennial cream and jam sponge cake. Your memories animate these pages.

The final credits belong to the leading players, Evelyn and Stanley Livingston, for the breeding and the feeding, and a lifetime of memories.

# Notes

## TWO OF THE BOYS, A WOG, A DONKEY AND MYSELF

**p. 4**  **claims that Simpson was shot by an Australian**
Wilson, *Dust, Donkeys and Delusions*, p. 4

**p. 6**  **photography of which is prohibted**
Australian War Memorial, Second World War Diaries
AWM52 Item 8/3/17 (2/17 Infantry Battalion)

## 1    THREE MEN WALK INTO A BAR

**p. 7**  **before the bugler's lips were moist**
Barter, *Far Above Battle*, p. 15

**p. 8**  **the aim of destroying their capacity to wage war**
Phillips, *The Middle East Campaigns of World War II, 1940–1942*, p. 28

**p. 9**  **to keep and care for them in old age**
Stockings, *Anzac's Dirty Dozen*, p. 43

**p. 9**  ***All Quiet on the Western Front* in 1930**
Jones, *The Reluctant Volunteer*, p. viii

**p. 10**  **a way of overawing wishful thinking**
ibid., p. 208

**p. 10 and the requisite number of heads**

Fearnside, *Half to Remember*, p. 10

**p. 11 his predictions for the country's future did not go down well**

Reader's Digest, *Australia's Yesterdays*, pp. 342–3

**p. 12 the so-called Japanese menace to Australia is no bogey**

ibid.

**p. 12 Harry David Wells**

Wells, *'B' Company Second Seventeenth Infantry*, p. 9

**p. 14 recalls acting on an alcohol-induced impulse**

Fantina, *Desertion and the American Soldier 1776–2005*, p. 118

**p. 17 Australians would not be coming home**

Connell, *The War at Home*, pp. 17–18

## 2 ONE SMALL STEP FOR A ZETLAND BOY

**p. 19 to training camps in Palestine, just north of Gaza**

Jones, *The Reluctant Volunteer*, p. 19

**p. 21 error of feeling sorry for itself**

Fearnside, *Half to Remember*, p. 93

**p. 21 the first in and the last out**

Johnson, *That Magnificent 9th*, p. 61

**p. 22 illustrations of biblical scenes**

Jones, *The Reluctant Volunteer*, p. 26

**p. 23 avoid even looking at them**

Australian War Memorial, Second World War Diaries AWM52 Item 8/3/17 (2/17 Infantry Battalion); the routine orders from Hill 69 camp, and point 3 in 'Information to Assist Patrols'

**p. 24**   **an hour before morning roll call**
Jones, *The Reluctant Volunteer*, p. 93

**p. 24**   **What was the reality?**
Fearnside, *Half to Remember*, p. 116

**p. 25**   **a mistake to have attempted to recapture it**
ibid., p. 119

**p. 26**   **Abraham used to milk his cow**
ibid., p. 122

**p. 26**   **and remained that way into the twentieth**
ibid., p. 120

**p. 27**   **came to have its own brothel**
ibid., p. 123

**p. 27**   **not one case of venereal disease was reported in Latakia**
ibid., pp. 122–4

**p. 28**   **necessitating a change of direction by the plane**
Australian War Memorial, Second World War Diaries AWM52 Item 8/3/17 (2/17 Infantry Battalion)

**p. 29**   **'trumpets of Jericho', used essentially to unnerve those under attack**
AustralianFlying.com.au, 'Debunking Dive Bomber Myths', <www.australianflying.com.au/news/debunking-dive-bomber-myths>

**p. 33**   **the dog river north of Beirut**
Australian War Memorial, Item MSS1280; Title: Anonymous; Maker: Anonymous; Object type: Poem

p. 33 **Henrietta and her girls that afternoon**
Fearnside, *Half to Remember*, pp. 127–8

p. 34 **'Defeat is one thing,' he said, 'disgrace is another.'**
Phillips, *The Middle East Campaigns of World War II, 1940–1942: El Alamein*, p. 8

p. 35 **one of the best of the World War Two jokes**
2/17 Battalion History Committee (Australia), '*What We Have . . . We Hold!*', p. 394

p. 35 **893 packets of cigarette papers**
Australian War Memorial, Second World War Diaries AWM52 Item 8/3/17 (2/17 Infantry Battalion)

p. 36 **wives, mothers, fiancées, sweethearts, sisters, aunts and friends**
2/17 Battalion History Committee (Australia), '*What We Have . . . We Hold!*', p. 370

p. 36 **and six million hankies**
Connell, *The War at Home*, p. 82

p. 36 **produce camouflage netting**
ibid., p. 77

p. 36 **Post Traumatic & CSM Confusional State**
Australian War Memorial, Second World War Diaries AWM52 Item 8/3/17 (2/17 Infantry Battalion), May/July

pp. 37–8 Information in regard to 'digging in' sourced from Mark Johnson's comprehensive *At the Front Line*.

3    HOLE SWEET HOLE

p. 39 **I feel like I've grown a rabbit's soul**
This quote was taken from the diary of Signalman

Bob Anson for 23 October 1942 and included in 2/17 Battalion History Committee (Australia), 'What We Have . . . We Hold!', p. 159. He describes the day as hot and confined, and at night the men emerge from burrows like rabbits in the sand country of far west New South Wales. He then quotes the line from a poem called 'Rabbits' to two of his mates in the trench.

p. 39   **in this case a hole in the ground**
2/17 Battalion History Committee (Australia), 'What We Have . . . We Hold!', p. 449

p. 40   **forever digging holes**
Johnson, *That Magnificent 9th*, p. 95

p. 41   **and you can't find a hole**
Fearnside, *Half to Remember*, p. 135

p. 41   **was known as the Hill of Jesus**
Australian War Memorial, Second World War Diaries AWM52 Item 8/3/17 (2/17 Infantry Battalion)

p. 42   **you fat old bastard?**
Johnson, *That Magnificent 9th*, p. 97

p. 42   **The show, as they say, must go on**
Merrilyn's tale can be found in Johnson, *That Magnificent 9th*, p. 100

p. 44   **between themselves and the sandbagged dummies**
ibid., p. 104

p. 45   **worked the patrols**
Fearnside, *Half to Remember*, p. 144

p. 46   **the glamour of a film star**
Jones, *The Reluctant Volunteer*, p. 114

**p. 46**    **the myth of the Rommel invincibility**

Fearnside, *Half to Remember*, p. 141

**p. 46**    **with all supporting arms taking part**

Australian War Memorial, Second World War Diaries AWM52 Item 8/3/17 (2/17 Infantry Battalion)

**p. 47**    **the break-in, the guts-eating and the break-out**

Fearnside, *Half to Remember*, p. 149

**p. 47**    **a German division of 9000 men**

2/17 Battalion History Committee (Australia), 'What We Have . . . We Hold!', p. 139

**p. 48**    **bait for the trap**

Fearnside, *Half to Remember*, p. 148

**p. 48**    **diminish the effects of major injuries**

ibid., p. 150

**p. 48**    **following a path marked by shaded blue lights**

Jones, *The Reluctant Volunteer*, p. 116

**p. 49**    **and knew their parts well**

2/17 Battalion History Committee (Australia), 'What We Have . . . We Hold!', p. 139

**p. 53**    **they do not see well**

Fearnside, *Half to Remember*, p. 151

**p. 54**    **by a fury of frightening sound**

ibid., p. 154

**p. 55**    **bomb-happy pigeons**

2/17 Battalion History Committee (Australia), 'What We Have . . . We Hold!', p. 166

**p. 56**    **human endurance can survive**

Australian War Memorial, Second World War Diaries

AWM52 Item 8/3/17 (2/17 Infantry Battalion), Oct/
Nov/Dec 1942

**p. 57** **advanced past the Australian 9th Division**
Phillips, *The Middle East Campaigns of World War II,
1940–1942: El Alamein*, p. 25

**p. 57** **efforts as 'Homeric'**
Johnson, *That Magnificent 9th,* p. 135

**p. 57** **9.2 per cent killed, 28 per cent injured**
Australian War Memorial, Second World War Diaries
AWM52 Item 8/3/17 (2/17 Infantry Battalion), Oct/
Nov/Dec 1942

4    MAYHEM WAS ONLY A PART OF IT

**p. 58** **mayhem was only a part of it**
Jones, *The Reluctant Volunteer*, p. ix

**p. 58** **good hunting to you all**
Australian War Memorial, Second World War Diaries
AWM52 Item 8/3/17 (2/17 Infantry Battalion), Oct/
Nov/Dec 1942

**p. 58** **for these feelings to adjust**
2/17 Battalion History Committee (Australia), *'What
We Have . . . We Hold!'*, p. 178

**p. 60** **only that you must stand still**
ibid., p. 184

**p. 64** **Journalist Fred Smith's notes**
Lloyd and Hall, *Backroom Briefings*, p. 139

**p. 65** **then present for all time**
Wells, *'B' Company Second Seventeenth Infantry*, p. 143

**p. 67**  **strangely silent homecoming**
From an article in *The Sydney Morning Herald*, 24 March 1943

**p. 67**  **any mere German or Italian**
Johnson, *That Magnificent 9th*, p. 141

**p. 68**  **Was it a brawl in the street or something?**
Connell, *The War at Home*; this quote from Jim Flower of Kyogle is on, p. 57


5    THREE MEN AND A BARBER SHOP

**p. 84**  **spears and bush knives**
2/17 Battalion History Committee (Australia), '*What We Have . . . We Hold!*', p. 194

**p. 85**  **most soldiers were extra serious about it**
ibid., p. 195

**p. 88**  **acres of lantana, buddleia, flax and pines**
Barber, *Mascot 1888–1938*, p. 21

**p. 90**  **the driver still comfortably seated**
Gall, *From Bullocks to Boeings*, p. 21

**p. 92**  **do so at their own risk**
ibid., p. 31

**pp. 92–3**  **playing golf on the aerodrome**
ibid.


6    A NIP IN THE AIR

**p. 94**  **pre-Christmas attack on Pearl Harbor**
Reader's Digest, *Australia's Yesterdays*, pp. 344–5

**p. 95**  **ground troops would soon follow**
Connell, *The War at Home*, pp. 46–8

**p. 95**  **and even a sanitary cart**
Reader's Digest, *Australia's Yesterdays*, pp. 344–5

**p. 95**  **Adelaide River Stakes**
Connell, *The War at Home*, p. 46

**p. 95**  **emotional chaos remembered in tranquility**
James Thurber, originally quoted in the *New York Post*,
29 February 1960

**p. 95**  **drunkenness and looting**
Connell, *The War at Home*, p. 47

**p. 96**  **in the people of our stock**
ibid., p. 48

**p. 96**  **prisoner on home soil**
ibid., pp. 50–1

**p. 97**  **slightest bit of notice**
ibid., p. 63

**p. 97**  **setting off a massive explosion**
ibid., p. 62

**p. 98**  **now it was Sydney's turn**
ibid., pp. 63–6

**p. 98**  **refugee who had fled from Nazi Germany**
Reader's Digest, *Australia's Yesterdays*, p. 345

**p. 99**  **defend against just three mini subs**
Connell, *The War at Home*, p. 67

**p. 99**  **to invade Australia at that time**
Peter Stanley, 'Dramatic myth and dull truth: Invasion
by Japan in 1942', in Stockings (ed.), *Zombie Myths of
Australian Military History*, p. 144

**p. 99**  **at that time to penetrate further inland**
ibid.

**p. 100  they wanted more race meetings**
Lloyd and Hall, *Backroom Briefings*, p. 97

**p. 100  how dirty the yard is**
ibid., p. 122

**p. 100  Everybody seemed in a hurry to live**
Connell, *The War at Home*, p. 114

**pp. 100–1  kinship with the United Kingdom**
Reader's Digest, *Australia's Yesterdays*, pp. 346–7

**p. 101  I will handle the front**
ibid.

**p. 102  trousers around the knee, belts twirling**
Connell, *The War at Home*, p. 118

**p. 102  black troops be excluded from the club**
Reader's Digest, *Australia's Yesterdays*, p. 347

**p. 103  the greatest thing we have achieved**
National Communications Branch, Department of Immigration and Citizenship, Canberra, 'Abolition of the "White Australia" Policy', <www.immi.gov.au/media/fact-sheets/08abolition.htm>

**p. 103  equal-opportunity employer of indigenous Australians**
Gary Oakley, quoted in Elliot Brennan, 'Indigenous servicemen: their contribution', <www.australian geographic.com.au/journal/indigenous-australians-at-war.htm>, 25 April 2013

**p. 104  it was back to segregation, in pubs, schools and restaurants**
These issues are covered in detail in Glen Stasiuk's 2002 TV documentary *The Forgotten*.

**p. 104  Long Bay gaol**
Connell, *The War at Home*, pp. 20–1

**p. 104  Two thousand Austro–German Jewish refugees**
ibid., p. 30

**p. 105  secret messages intended for the Nazis**
ibid., p. 23

**p. 105  banned in Australia in 1941**
Reader's Digest, *Australia's Yesterdays*, p. 249

**p. 105  control over its citizens**
Connell, *The War at Home*, p. 87

**p. 105  715,000 men and women were in the armed forces**
ibid., p. 89

**p. 105  permission of the Manpower officials**
ibid., p. 90

**p. 105  Dedman alienated the majority**
ibid., p. 91

**p. 106  hotels forced to close even earlier**
Reader's Digest, *Australia's Yesterdays*, pp. 248–9

**p. 106  Manpower raids on hotels**
Connell, *The War at Home*, pp. 92–3

**p. 106  ban on the Communist Party was lifted**
ibid., p. 93

**p. 107  Citizen racketeering was rife**
Reader's Digest, *Australia's Yesterdays*, pp. 248–9

**p. 107  CSR suitcases**
Connell, *The War at Home*, p. 123

**p. 107  around four hundred dollars today**
Reader's Digest, *Australia's Yesterdays*, p. 248

**p. 107 employed soldiers who were AWL**

Connell, *The War at Home*, p. 91

**p. 108 one race-free Saturday every month**

ibid., p. 25


7    THE HOME-FRONT LINE

**p. 110 barbed wire on the beach**

Phillips, *The Home Front 1942–1945*, p. 6; quoted from
the unit history of the 17th AMF Battalion

**p. 110 not of calm but of imminence**

Connell, *The War at Home*, pp. 32–6

**p. 115 throw the enemy into headlong flight**

*The Sydney Morning Herald*, 24 March 1943, p. 6

**p. 117 Bob Dyer and The Crazy Builders**

*The Sydney Morning Herald*, 8 November 1943

**p. 117 scientifically cooled for your comfort**

*The Sydney Morning Herald*, 1 March 1943

**p. 117 donating their services**

Connell, *The War at Home*, p. 59

**p. 119 all the props were there**

Fearnside, *Half to Remember*, p. 168

**p. 120 under a deluge of caterpillars**

Wells, *'B' Company Second Seventeenth Infantry*,
pp. 146–7

**p. 120 Hairy curses tickle hairy arses**

Jones, *The Reluctant Volunteer*, p. 137

**p. 121 Protection on the move**
2/17 Battalion History Committee (Australia), '*What We Have . . . We Hold!*', p. 198

**p. 122 fell down a ravine during training**
ibid., p. 463

**p. 122 'Oily-Tongue' Larkins and 'Watering' Mellon**
ibid., pp. 425–6

**p. 122 the pipe-smoking general**
Johnson, *That Magnificent 9th*, p. 144

**p. 123 committal to trial by court martial**
Australian War Memorial, Second World War Diaries AWM52 Item 8/3/17 (2/17 Infantry Battalion), April/ May 1943

**p. 125 throwing masses of infantry against them**
Lloyd and Hall, *Backroom Briefings*, pp. 155–6

**8 EVELYN'S WAR**

**p. 127 voluntary recruitment had not met with demand**
Bolt, *Our Home Front 1939–45*, p. 164

**pp. 127–8 Change your job for him—won't you?**
*Australian Women's Weekly*, 17 April 1943, p. 2

**p. 128 nitrates in the manufacture of munitions**
Connell, *The War at Home*, pp. 96–102

**p. 129 'Deputy Premier alarmed at Moral Drift'**
Bolt, *Our Home Front 1939–45*, p. 168

**pp. 130–1 'A Disgrace to Sydney'**
*The Sydney Morning Herald*, 6 November 1943

**p. 133** **more than Australian men did**

Connell, *The War at Home*, p. 115

**p. 133** **home-made Australian maple syrup**

Murray, *A Home of My Own*, p. 15

**p. 133** **at half the retail price**

Reader's Digest, *Australia's Yesterdays*, p. 347

**p. 136** **A few adventurous women**

Gall, *From Bullocks to Boeings*, pp. 26–8; Eames, *Sydney Airport*, p. 48

9      RUN FOR YOUR DEATH

**p. 138** **shot for the offence**

Glenister, *Desertion Without Execution*

**p. 139** **AIF deserters should be put down**

Stanley, *Bad Characters*, p. 90

**p. 139** **swayed by our decision**

ibid.

**p. 139** **our very own 'No Death' clause**

Glenister, *Desertion Without Execution*

**p. 142** **Mrs Slovik was dead**

Fantina, *Desertion and the American Soldier*, p. 127

**pp. 142–3** **the individual is of small account**

Oram, *Military Executions During World War I*, p. 62

**pp. 143–4** **average man is to get out of the way**

ibid., p. 63

**p. 144** **Not Yet Diagnosed Nervous**

2/17 Battalion History Committee (Australia), '*What We Have . . . We Hold!*', p. 264

## 10    GAPS IN THE RANKS

**p. 146  supplement their income**

National Archives of Australia War Cabinet Agendum No. 417/1943, 'Payment of allotment and dependant's allowance in respect of members of the Australian Military Forces absent without leave', Series no. A2670, Control Symbol 417/1943, Item barcode 9019829

**pp. 147–8   obtaining labour through the National Service Office**

National Archives of Australia, 'Employment of Deserters and AWL Personnel', Series no. AWM60, Control symbol 362, Item barcode 519009

**p. 149  Stamp his papers deserter**

Klein, *They Stamped His Papers Deserter*, p. 31

**pp. 150–1   try and give them a hand**

Statement from the National Archives of Australia NX17773 Pte A. Harrison official court martial records, p. 6

**p. 153  How do we know that our complaints will be rectified?**

Statement from the National Archives of Australia NX18306 Pte J. Wilson official court martial records, 'Summary of evidence', p. 86

**pp. 155–6   but I got married instead**

Quoted from the National Archives of Australia M1455/114 Personal Papers of Prime Minister Chifley, correspondence relating to NX18306 Pte John Wilson (Grovely Mutiny), p. 99

p. 156 conduct an inquiry into the case
ibid., p. 98


11      ABSENT FRIENDS

p. 160 refusal to recognize the supremacy of a man's duty
to his family
Fantina, *Desertion and the American Soldier*, p. 127

p. 162 patients in a public hospital
From a transcript of The Hon. Patricia Forsythe
speaking in the Parliament of NSW in June 1996 on the
demise of the hospital, <www.parliament.nsw.gov.au/
prod/parlment/hansart.nsf/V3Key/LC19960626065>

p. 162 improve, but she didn't
Statement from the National Archives of Australia
NX54916 Pte S. Quillan official court martial records,
p. 10

pp. 155–6   when I went back to it
Statement from the National Archives of Australia
NX5836 Pte S. Glynn official court martial records,
p. 12

p. 166 was the same—very hysterical
Statement from the National Archives of Australia
NX52651 Pte J. Hamilton official court martial records,
p. 12

p. 167 is still very ill
Statement from the National Archives of Australia
NX19115 Pte P. Murrell official court martial records,
p. 16

**pp. 167–8  live with my wife alone**

Statement from the National Archives of Australia NX89527 Pte M. Pollard official court martial records, p. 11

**p. 168  I think death would be easier for me NX89527**

ibid., pp. 21–2

**p. 169  Lt Waterhouse: . . . No**

Statement from the National Archives of Australia NX32737 Pte A. Currie official court martial records, p. 25

**pp. 170–1  I just left**

Statement from the National Archives of Australia NX23799 Pte L. Campbell official court martial records, p. 11

**pp. 171–2  or words to that effect**

Statement from the National Archives of Australia NX40424 Pte A. Drew official court martial records, p. 12

**pp. 172–3  son and brother, Alf xxxxx**

ibid., pp. 18–20

**p. 174  'chocos', or chocolate soldiers**

Connell, *The War at Home*, p. 18

**pp. 176–7  Jack surrendered, and he was immediately charged with desertion**

National Archives of Australia, 'Harbouring and assistance of deserters and AWL [Absentees without Leave]', Series no. MP508/1, Control symbol 4/702/1012, Item barcode 3284045

## 12 FROM THE PIMPLE TO SCARLET BEACH VIA DEAD MAN'S GULLY

**p. 182 fully fit for front-line duty**
National Archives of Australia MP742/1, 85/1/39 'Discilinary [sic] action against personnel AWL (absent without leave) from operational areas', p. 5

**p. 182 returned to the mainland to serve those sentences**
ibid., p. 4

**pp. 182–3 as a fighting member**
ibid., p. 13

**p. 184 Most bets were on New Guinea**
Fearnside, *Half to Remember*, p. 179

**p. 184 some would be ground to flour**
Wells, *'B' Company Second Seventeenth Infantry*, p. 151

**p. 188 lost all their personal items**
Jones, *The Reluctant Volunteer*, p. 140

**p. 188 path through it with a machete**
Wells, *'B' Company Second Seventeenth Infantry*, p. 151

**p. 190 eventually got malaria almost to the man**
Jones, *The Reluctant Volunteer*, p. 141

**p. 190 hugging the coast of New Guinea**
Holmes, *Smiles of Fortune*, p. 21

**p. 191 who talked in low voices**
Wells, *'B' Company Second Seventeenth Infantry*, p. 152

**p. 191 the need to urinate**
Johnson, *At the Front Line*, p. 20

**p. 191 like prawns being shaken from nets**
Wells, *'B' Company Second Seventeenth Infantry*, p. 150

**p. 192 half of what they carried into El Alamein**
Johnson, *At the Front Line*, p. 7

**p. 192 squeeze the split-pins of our grenades**
Holmes, *Smiles of Fortune*, p. 23

**p. 193 cross of the German bombers**
2/17 Battalion History Committee (Australia), '*What We Have . . . We Hold!*', p. 405

**p. 193 dropping their eggs of death**
Wells, '*B' Company Second Seventeenth Infantry*, p. 152

**p. 195 'the Last Supper' as some called it**
2/17 Battalion History Committee (Australia), '*What We Have . . . We Hold!*', p. 433

**p. 195 away the landing force**
Wells, '*B' Company Second Seventeenth Infantry*, p. 156

**p. 196 too dark to see the shoreline**
Holmes, *Smiles of Fortune*, p. 33

**p. 196 firing directly at the landing barges**
Wells, '*B' Company Second Seventeenth Infanty*, p. 156

**p. 197 we had to move before lunch**
2/17 Battalion History Committee (Australia), '*What We Have . . . We Hold!*', p. 230


**13    DESTROY ALL MONSTERS**

**p. 201 but our stomachs did**
2/17 Battalion History Committee (Australia), '*What We Have . . . We Hold!*', p. 250

**p. 203 assault enemy positions**
Johnson, *That Magnificent 9th*, p. 166

**pp. 203–4   The jungle war lacked mutual respect**

Jones, *The Reluctant Volunteer*, p. 161

**p. 204   Creating demons is an old human habit**

Johnson, *At the Front Line*, pp. 36–40

**pp. 206–7   Jap bursting his grenade on you both**

Holmes, *Smiles of Fortune*, p. 36

**p. 207   soldiering in the jungle**

Fearnside, *Half to Remember*, p. 182

**p. 207   The uncontrollable prolapsing of the anus relented**

Holmes, *Smiles of Fortune*, p. 40

**pp. 207–8   darkness suddenly falling, and rain**

2/17 Battalion History Committee (Australia), 'What We Have . . . We Hold!', pp. 270–1

**p. 208   the history of the battalion**

ibid., p. 275

**p. 208   than any ten days at Tobruk or El Alamein**

Random House Australia, *Australia Through Time*, pp. 316–17

**p. 209   the assault as much mental as physical**

Johnson, *That Magnificent 9th*, p. 184

**p. 209   claustrophobic battle conditions**

Johnson, *At the Front Line*, pp. 34–6

**p. 209   'the hunting, hiding, listening part' of jungle warfare**

ibid., p. 35

**p. 210   movements of the jungle's non-human citizenry**

Jones, *The Reluctant Volunteer*, p. 192

**p. 210   before the art of self preservation takes over**

Wells, *'B' Company Second Seventeenth Infantry*, p. 155

**p. 210 their empty-eyed vacancy and unnatural quiet**
Jones, *The Reluctant Volunteer*, p. 147

**p. 210 which indeed he believed himself to be**
Fearnside, *Half to Remember*, p. 187

**p. 211 detect and bash back the neurotic; broadened channel leading to the way out**
Walker, *Australian War Memorial Second World War Official Histories: Australia in the War of 1939–1945*, Series 5: Medical, Volume I: *Clinical Problems of War* (1962 reprint), p. 705

**p. 212 region poorly designed for discomfort**
Jones, *The Reluctant Volunteer*, p. 147

**p. 213 even though it saw little action**
Johnson, *That Magnificent 9th*, p. 183

**p. 214 florally, arboreally, faunally, and aviarily**
Jones, *The Reluctant Volunteer*, p. 162

**p. 214 sixty-three fewer men than when it arrived**
2/17 Battalion History Committee (Australia), '*What We Have . . . We Hold!*', p. 283

**p. 214 skeletonic portrait of Joshua Smith**
Jones, *The Reluctant Volunteer*, p. 162

**p. 214 Or was I merely going 'troppo'?**
Jones, *The Reluctant Volunteer*, p. 159

**14    PRESENT AND ACCOUNTED FOR**

**p. 216 armies which are always in action tire as well**
Quoted in Barter, *Far Above Battle*, p. 252

**p. 218** **a fat, over-fed phrasemouthing parasite**
Johnson, *That Magnificent 9th*, p. 188

**p. 218** **galloping towards Japan**
Stockings, *Anzac's Dirty Dozen*, p. 138

**p. 219** **Allies had effectively won the war in Europe**
Connell, *The War at Home*, p. 129

**p. 220** **so frequent troops began to ignore them**
2/17 Battlion History Committee (Australia), 'What We Have . . . We Hold!', p. 286

**p. 221** **the mood was somewhat damper**
ibid., p. 194

**p. 221** **dodging bullets for years**
Johnson, *At the Front Line*, p. 25

**p. 222** **soldiers present seemed to be the most reserved**
*The Sydney Morning Herald*, 9 May 1945

**p. 222** **Pte Ralph Hopkins**
Jones, *The Reluctant Volunteer*, p. 181

**p. 223** **headed towards British New Borneo**
Johnson, *That Magnificent 9th*, p. 222

**pp. 223–4** **as they advanced towards Brunei Town**
2/17 Battalion History Committee (Australia), 'What We Have . . . We Hold!', p. 420

**p. 224** **fell dangerously close**
ibid., p. 300

**p. 225** **generally images of birds**
ibid., p. 435

**p. 226** **beheaded and set on fire**
ibid., p. 308

**pp. 226–7   and secure the valves**
Johnson, *That Magnificent 9th*, p. 227

**p. 229   saki was consumed**
2/17 Battalion History Committee (Australia),
*'What We Have . . . We Hold!'*, p. 420

**p. 229   Jack Littlewood and Stan Livingston were worried about the five-year plan**
ibid., p. 421

**p. 230   news from radio America**
ibid., p. 317

**p. 231   seemed anti climactic to me**
Jones, *The Reluctant Volunteer*, p. 205

**p. 231   I don't think he is right, really**
Holmes, *Smiles of Fortune*, p. 110

## 15   THE ORDINARY TRENCHES

**p. 232   as individuals we went home**
Holmes, *Smiles of Fortune*, p. 114

**p. 233   when there's a blue for us to go into**
Johnson, *That Magnificent 9th*, p. 242

**p. 236   a quarter of those who'd served in the division**
Johnson, *That Magnificent 9th*, p. 251

**p. 237   quieter, but no less happy**
*The Sydney Morning Herald*, 16 August 1945

**p. 237   'Delirious Joy in Australia'**
*The Sydney Morning Herald*, 16 August 1945

**p. 239   was mistaken for a drunk**
Connell, *The War at Home*, p. 139

**p. 239  in order to recover some composure**
Jones, *The Reluctant Volunteer*, p. 207

**p. 240  childhood would see him through**
Fearnside, *Half to Remember*, p. 198

**p. 240  the way you expected them to**
Connell, *The War at Home*, p. 137

**p. 240  should not be forgotten when we're gone**
ibid., p. 95

## 16    MEMOIRS OF A PACIFIST SMOKER

**p. 247  go to sleep, my little Buckaroo**
Lyrics from 'My Little Buckaroo', as performed by Dick Foran in *The Cherokee Strip*. Lyrics by Jake Scholl, music by M.K. Jerome.

## 17    DON'T GIVE AN OLD DIGGER THE GRIPES

**p. 262  A-riding in the last roundup**
Lyrics from 'The Last Roundup', recorded by Gene Autry in 1933, composed by Benny Hill

# Bibliography

## BOOKS

2/17 Battalion History Committee (Australia), 'What We Have...We Hold!': A history of the 2/17 Australian Infantry Battalion 1940–1945, Australian Military History Publications, Loftus, NSW, 1998

Barber, T. (ed.), Mascot 1888–1938: Fifty years of progress, Harbour Press, Sydney, 1938

Barter, Margaret, Far Above Battle: The experience and memory of Australian soldiers in war 1939–1945, Allen & Unwin, St Leonards, NSW, 1994

Bolt, Andrew (ed.), Our Home Front 1939–1945, Wilkinson Books, Melbourne, 1995

Coates, John Boyd (ed.), Internal Medicine in World War II: Volume 2, Infectious Diseases, Office of the Surgeon General, Department of the Army, Washington, D.C.

Connell, Daniel, The War at Home: Australia 1939–1949, ABC Enterprises for the Australian Broadcasting Corporation, Crows Nest, NSW, 1988

Connor, John, 'The "superior", all-volunteer AIF', in Craig Stockings (ed.), Anzac's Dirty Dozen: 12 myths of Australian *military history*, New South Publishing, Sydney, 2012, pp. 35–50

Eames, Jim, *Sydney Airport: 80 years as the gateway to Australia*, Focus Publishing, Edgecliff, NSW, 2000

Fantina, Robert, *Desertion and the American Soldier 1776–2005*, Algora Publishing, New York, 2006

Fearnside, G.H., *Half to Remember: Reminiscences of an Australian infantry soldier in World War II*, Haldane Publishing, Sydney, 1975 .

Gall, Jennifer, *From Bullocks to Boeings: An illustrated history of Sydney Airport*, Australian Government Publishing Service, Canberra, 1986

Glenister, Richard, *Desertion Without Execution: Decisions that saved Australian Imperial Force deserters from the firing squad in World War I*, La Trobe University, Bundoora, Vic., 1984

Griffiths-Marsh, Roland, *The Sixpenny Soldier*, Angus & Robertson, Sydney, 1990

Holmes, John, *Smiles of Fortune: A memoir of the war against Japan 1943–45*, Kangaroo Press, East Roseville, NSW, 2001

Johnson, Mark, *At the Front Line: Experiences of Australian soldiers in World War II*, Cambridge University Press, Port Melbourne, 1996

—— *That Magnificent 9th: An illustrated history of the 9th Australian Division 1940–46*, Allen & Unwin, Crows Nest, NSW, 2005

Jones, Peter J., *The Reluctant Volunteer*, Australian Military History Publications, Loftus, NSW, 1997

Klein, Tom, *They Stamped His Papers Deserter*, PennyRoyal Press, Parkes, NSW, 1995

Lloyd, Clem and Hall, Richard (eds), *Backroom Briefings: John Curtin's war*, National Library of Australia, Canberra, 1997

Murray, Mary (ed.), *A Home of My Own: Handy hints and images from domestic life in Australia in the 1940s and 1950s*, Mallon Publishing, Melbourne, 2001

Oram, Gerard, *Military Executions During World War I*, Palgrave Macmillan, Houndmills, Basingstoke, Hampshire; New York, 2003

Phillips, W.H.J., *The Home Front 1942–1945*, W.H.J. Phillips, Coffs Harbour, NSW, 2000

—— *The Middle East Campaigns of World War II, 1940–1942: El Alamein*, W.H.J. Phillips, Coffs Harbour, NSW, 2000

Random House Australia, *Australia Through Time*, Random House, Milsons Point, NSW, 2000

Reader's Digest Australia, *Australia's Yesterdays: The illustrated story of how we lived, worked and played*, Reader's Digest, Ultimo, NSW, 2008

Stanley, Peter, *Bad Characters: Sex, crime, mutiny, murder and the Australian Imperial Force*, Pier 9, Milsons Point, NSW, 2010

—— 'Dramatic myth and dull truth: Invasion by Japan in 1942', in Craig Stockings (ed.), *Zombie Myths of Australian Military History*, University of New South Wales Press, Sydney, 2010, pp. 140–60

Stockings, Craig (ed.), *Anzac's Dirty Dozen: 12 myths of Australian military history*, New South Publishing, Sydney, 2012

Thomas, Donald, *An Underworld at War: Spivs, deserters, racketeers and civilians in the Second World War*, John Murray, London, 2003

Wells, H.D., *'B' Company Second Seventeenth Infantry*, H.D. Wells, Toowoon Bay, NSW, 1984

Wilson, Graham, *Dust, Donkeys and Delusions: The myth of Simpson and his donkey exposed*, Big Sky Publishing, Newport, NSW, 2012

## OFFICIAL SOURCES
**National Archives of Australia personal records**
A471/8355969 Personal Record of NX32737
    Private Alfred Herbert Currie

A471/8329399 Personal Record of NX40424
    Private Alfred Frederick Clifton Drew

A471/8338606 Personal Record of NX55654
    Private James Arthur Andrew Ellicombe

B883/6229524 Personal Record of VX1607
    Edward Henry Emmerson

A471/8328064 Personal Record of NX17552
    Private Percy Field

A471/8829505 Personal Record of NX17063
    Private Leslie Milton Giles

A471/8320660 Personal Record of NX5836
Private Stanley James Glynn

A471/8320664 Personal Record of NX52651
Private James Gibb Hamilton

B883/4901034 Personal Record of NX17773
Private Alfred Henry Harrison

A471/8328232 Personal Record of NX39526
Private Lyndon Morris Harold Hurel

A471/8356029 Personal Record of NX20181
Private Stanley James Livingston

B883/5584196 Personal Record of NFX201096
Private Grace Florence Lonsdale

A471/7575928 Personal Record of NX56248
Gunner Jack Arthur Lonsdale

B883/4847385 Personal Record of NX20180
Private Roy Lonsdale

A471/8328834 Personal Record of NX19115
Private Patrick William Murrell

B883/4847388 Personal Record of NX20277
Private Gordon Grant Oxman

A471/8339795 Personal Record of NX89527
Private Mervyn Patrick Pollard

B883/4655012 Personal Record of NX76466
William Joseph Pye

A471/8338651 Personal Record of NX54916
Private Sydney Vivian Edward Quillan

A471/8370074 Personal Record of NX17246
Private Reginald Alexander Tait

B883/4901273 Personal Record of NX18306
Private John Wilson

**Australian War Memorial Second World War Diaries**

AWM52, Item 8/3/17

2/17 Infantry Battalion

<www.awm.gov.au/collection/records/awm52/diary.
asp?levelID=1056>

**Australian War Memorial Second World War
Official Histories**

Australia in the War of 1939–1945, various volumes

<www.awm.gov.au/histories/second_world_war>